175115

Global Nomads

D1609812

A uniquely 'nomadic ethnography,' *Global Nomads* is the first in-depth treatment of a counterculture flourishing in the global gulf stream of new electronic and spiritual developments. D'Andrea's is an insightful study of expressive individualism manifested in and through key cosmopolitan sites. This book is an invaluable contribution to the anthropology/sociology of contemporary culture, and presents required reading for students and scholars of new spiritualities, techno-dance culture and globalization.

> Graham St John, Research Fellow,
> School of American Research, New Mexico

D'Andrea breaks new ground in the scholarship on both globalization and the shaping of subjectivities. And he does so spectacularly, both through his focus on neomadic cultures and a novel theorization. This is a deeply erudite book and it is a lot of fun.

> Saskia Sassen, Ralph Lewis Professor of Sociology
> at the University of Chicago, and Centennial Visiting Professor
> at the London School of Economics.

Global Nomads is a unique introduction to the globalization of countercultures, a topic largely unknown in and outside academia. Anthony D'Andrea examines the social life of mobile expatriates who live within a global circuit of countercultural practice in paradoxical paradises.

Based on nomadic fieldwork across Spain and India, the study analyzes how and why these post-metropolitan subjects reject the homeland to shape an alternative lifestyle. They become artists, therapists, exotic traders and bohemian workers seeking to integrate labor, mobility and spirituality within a cosmopolitan culture of expressive individualism. These countercultural formations, however, unfold under neo-liberal regimes that appropriate utopian spaces, practices and imaginaries as commodities for tourism, entertainment and media consumption.

In order to understand the paradoxical globalization of countercultures, *Global Nomads* develops a dialogue between global and critical studies by introducing the concept of 'neo-nomadism' which seeks to overcome some of the shortcomings in studies of globalization.

This book is essential reading for undergraduate, postgraduate and research students of Sociology, Anthropology of Globalization, Cultural Studies and Tourism.

Anthony Albert Fischer D'Andrea has recently earned a PhD in Anthropology at the University of Chicago, where he is Research Associate at the Transnationalism Project.

Global Nomads

Techno and New Age as transnational countercultures in Ibiza and Goa

Anthony D'Andrea

Routledge
Taylor & Francis Group

LONDON AND NEW YORK

First published 2007
by Routledge
2 Park Square, Milton Park, Abingdon, Oxon, OX14 4RN

Simultaneously published in the USA and Canada
by Routledge
270 Madison Ave, New York, NY 10016

Routledge is an imprint of the Taylor & Francis Group, an informa business

Transferred to Digital Printing 2009

© 2007 Anthony D'Andrea

Typeset in Sabon by
Florence Production Ltd, Stoodleigh, Devon

British Library Cataloguing in Publication Data
A catalogue record for this book is available
from the British Library

Library of Congress Cataloging in Publication Data
A catalog record for this book has been requested

ISBN10: 0–415–42013–X (hbk)
ISBN10: 0–415–55367–9 (pbk)
ISBN10: 0–203–96265–6 (ebk)

ISBN13: 978–0–415–42013–6 (hbk)
ISBN13: 978–0–415–55367–4 (pbk)
ISBN13: 978–0–203–96265–7 (ebk)

Contents

Figures

Acknowledgments

This book is based on a doctoral research conducted over the course of several years, places and multidisciplinary incursions. I would like to thank Elizabeth Povinelli, Saskia Sassen, Joe Masco, Kesha Fikes, Tanya Luhrmann, Arnold Davidson and Arjun Appadurai for their advice at former and latter stages of my education at the Department of Anthropology at the University of Chicago.

From the field, I am grateful to Gary Blanford, Kirk Huffman, Ronnie Randall and Nora Belton for their contribution to the development of this project. I also thank Georgia Taglietti, William Crichton, Antonio Nogueira, Roberta Jurado, Peter Hankinson, Tirry and Toni for their generous support to my fieldwork in the club scene of Ibiza. In India, I wish to thank Swami Prasado and Boyan Artac, as well as Dilip Loundo and Alito Siqueira for interactions at Goa University.

I am also grateful to other friends and colleagues, in particular to Graham St John and Adam Leeds, who have read parts of my manuscript and made important comments. I also appreciate the kind permission of Ronnie and Stephen Randall, Ekki Gurlitt and Krishnananda Trobe to use photos and an extended quote. Finally, I thank John Urry for allowing that my work be available in book form.

This research was indirectly funded with a CAPES Foundation fellowship to conduct my doctoral studies at Chicago. I also thank the Center for Latin American and Iberian Studies and the Gay and Lesbian Studies Project, both at the University of Chicago, for sponsoring segments of my fieldwork with travel grants.

While grateful to the sedentary dwellers of Goa, Pune, Ibiza and Chicago, I wish to dedicate this book to global nomads – expressive expatriates, New Agers and Techno freaks – who enabled me to learn something about their lines of flight.

Anthony Fischer D'Andrea
Chicago, January 2007

1 Neo-nomadism

A theory of postidentitarian mobility in the global age[1]

'The nomad does not move.'
Deleuze and Guattari, *A Thousand Plateaus*

Global nomads: instance of cultural hypermobility

Ibiza island (Spanish Mediterranean), summer 1998 – We left *Café del Mar* in the busy touristy town of Sant Antoni, and drove north toward a secluded lighthouse where a 'Goa trance party' was scheduled to happen. 'Goa trance' is a potent subgenre of electronic dance music developed by Western neo-hippies ('freaks') on the beaches of Goa state (India) in the early 1990s. My companions that night were four UK and US expatriates who resided in Ibiza or visited the island regularly: two yoga teachers, a jewelry trader and a journalist, women in their thirties and forties, wearing light hippie, gypsy-like clothes and a crystal dot on the forehead. An Italian party promoter had told us about the event. The police busted his own party a week before, 'because of the vested interests of big business: club and bar owners.' In Ibiza, Goa and elsewhere, trance parties are usually illegal, being secretively announced through word-of-mouth across the alternative populace that, at various levels and degrees, embraces free open-air 'tribal parties' in secluded, natural settings.

In a confusing maze of precarious dirt roads, we joined a caravan of lost drivers and, having noticed several vehicles suspiciously parked amid dry vegetation, we decided to stop. The night was absolutely dark. Thin flashlights and the eerie stomping of techno music afar were our only leads as we blindly stumbled toward the venue. By the cliff edge, the lighthouse projected three solid light beams of mesmerizing beauty. Beside it, a camp formation with a few tents and banners was dimly lit in fluorescent purple. UV lights produced a phantasmagoric glow on colorful fractal drapes, white clothes, teeth and eyes. A delicate scent of incense pervaded the air, blending with the acrid smell of hashish smoking. A crowd danced in front of the DJ (disc jockey) tent located between thundering loudspeakers, while many others scattered around.

There were a few hundred people, mostly white young adults. Many wore hippie or military garments in a fashion resembling psychedelic guerillas. In their everyday life, they worked in 'hippie' (touristy) markets, nightclubs and bars, and in a variety of informal occupations in handicraft, music, wellness, therapy and spirituality. Outsiders readily labeled them hippies, punks, freaks, ravers or New Agers. However, refusing such labels, they rather represented themselves as 'alternative people': rebellious expatriates from European and American nations. By late autumn, many would have departed to India and their ambivalently rejected homelands, returning to Ibiza next spring.

Trance parties hybridize orientalist and cybernetic elements. Trance DJs are idiosyncratic men whose personalities well suit anthropological descriptions of witch doctors, now in digital edition. Psychedelic drapes displayed Hindu, Buddhist and fractal figures in fantastic shapes and colors. From potent speakers, Techno trance music pulsated in sonic gushes that reverberated pleasurably upon the skin. Its multilayered rhythms were extremely powerful and complex, yet monotonous and hypnotic. Topped by ethereal, often spooky arpeggios, the music pumped restlessly throughout the night. People danced individually, alone but in the crowd, and the predominant mood was joyous, albeit reverential.

As the morning came, the dancing crowd was seen covered in red dust, floating upward due to continuous feet stomping. Some young women, fashioned like barbarian warriors, screamed wildly whenever the music took an exciting shift, like the gears of an unstoppable machine. Some people danced with closed eyes, drawing gentle tai chi-like movements in the air. But, after long hours, the crowd was bouncing in a steady, remarkably dull fashion, indicating physical tiredness as well as various degrees of mind alteration. I spotted Shiva, an old blond German hippie, dancing in a seemingly trance state. Staring aloof into the sky, he jerked as if musical tweaks electrocuted his body. Recently returned from India, German Shiva now seemed to be on an 'intergalactic journey.' A hairy Frenchman in chef uniform was selling sandwiches over his rusty scooter, while a Brazilian drug trafficker observed the frenzy from his ostentatious Mercedes Benz parked nearby.

The Mediterranean now shined magnificently in bright golden and blue – a quasi-psychedelic experience in itself. But my friends were tired and wanted to leave. On the way out, we saw two skinny men dragging garbage bags, picking a few empty cans and cigarette butts, as usually done by ecologically minded promoters. Against the incoming flux of people, I overheard a variety of European languages and also Hebrew. Someone mentioned that the party would carry on for three days – as long as the crowd endured, and the police did not show up …

This anecdote depicts a rare density of multinational and expressive elements gathering at the margins of a tiny island. In it, Ibiza appears as a node of transnational flows of exoticized peoples, practices and imaginaries whose circulation and hybridization across remote locations suggests a globalized phenomenon. This story also indicates how digital and orientalist elements may congeal in a ritual assemblage that sustains alternative experiences of the self. In the convergence of the global and the expressive, mobility across spaces and within selves becomes a category that structures the social life of peoples claiming to embrace the global as a new home and reference.

By integrating mobility into economic strategies and expressive lifestyles, I refer to these subjects as *expressive expatriates*, and, more generally, as *global nomads*, notions employed to rethink and stimulate a debate on globalization and cultural change. The empirical dimension of this research was based on multi-site transnational fieldwork conducted in Spain and India from 1998 to 2003, and will be discussed in detail throughout the book. In this opening section, I will outline the general architecture of this investigation, summarizing its development in genealogical lines, and highlighting how its ethnographic horizon has posed specific methodological and conceptual challenges to current research and scholarship.

This is a book on cultural globalization, as an effort to understand how global processes of hypermobility, digitalization and reflexivity interrelate with new forms of subjectivity, identity and sociality. Considering the sheer scale, speed and intensity of transformations being brought about by globalization, this study is also, and by consequence, an inquiry into cultural change. In order to enable a clear and efficient strategy of analysis, I investigate cases of cultural change that appear as explicit, assertive, and even radical in the scope of contemporary possibilities. I thus selected the topic of countercultures, which can be tentatively defined as self-marginalized formations that, in various forms of experimentalism and contestation, seek to foster a critique that revises modernity within modernity. In this view, modern countercultures are at least 200 years old, referring back to Rousseau's nostalgic reflections on the malaises of civilization and reason.

In other words, this book investigates contemporary forms of counterculture that unfold under the impact of globalization. As I will later elaborate, Techno dance and New Age spiritual movements seem to provide lively instances of such a critique of modern institutional-ideological regimes, but not without their own problematic contradictions and blind spots, which are also scrutinized in this book.

Much will be said about the spatial and cultural sites of investigation, but an introductory note is important from the outset. In my preliminary explorations with Techno and New Age in a number of countries, a series of apparently serendipitous encounters and discoveries led me to the island of Ibiza located in the Spanish Mediterranean, a place which turned out to be as extremely rich as problematic for an empirical investigation of the interrelations between globalization and counterculture.

In Ibiza, I identified a unique populace of expatriate individuals who share some defining features, roughly summarized: (1) They reject their original homelands and seek to evade state–market–morality regimes. (2) They partake in a cosmopolitan culture of expressive individualism, manifested in multiple variations of New Age and Techno practice. (3) They seek to integrate labor, leisure and spirituality into a holistic lifestyle that romanticizes non-Western cultures, and particularly India. (4) They overlap with a cultural-artistic elite that establishes a symbiotic relation with political economies of tourism, entertainment, wellness and media sectors which appropriate alternative formations in commodity form. (5) These expatriates engage with practices of mobility that are pivotal in reproducing the other features.

The mobile feature of expatriate formations introduced a methodological challenge to my doctoral fieldwork. While following anthropological canons that prescribe a locally grounded fieldwork, I realized that Ibiza's expressive expatriates periodically depart to other countries where they stay for extended periods. Due to its material, cultural and temporal aspects, it became clear that this semi-deterritorialized phenomenon could not be properly grasped by conventional ethnographic methods alone. In order to obtain a more accurate picture, I would have to follow these subjects to places and along practices of mobility crucial to their material and symbolic reproduction. I had to follow and even travel with my natives to India. Yet, more than cruising the same pathways, the point was to foreground mobility as a practice and discourse of identity formation, considering that meanings and experiences of movement are better assessed within the movement itself.

Toward a methodology of hypermobile cultures, I sought to combine a nomadic sensibility for natives' routes, flows and rituals, with a macro-ethnography of translocal sites (Clifford 1997; Appadurai 1996). I qualify this macro-ethnography at three levels: (1) an ethnography of local formations and subjectivities in a locality or site; (2) the socio-economic contextualization of mobile formations in a place (thus corresponding to their vertical integration); and (3) a translocal ethnography that tracks flows, nodes, directions and periodicities (thus defining the horizontal integration across and beyond spaces). These tasks generate multi-layered datasets which enable the comparison between the vertical and horizontal integration, thus shedding light on the conditions of (im)mobility. More generally, the articulation between nomadic sensibility and macro-ethnography provides the grounds for a 'nomadic ethnography,' which embodies a transition from the Ptolemaic geocentrism of conventional anthropology to an Einsteinian perception of the relativity of placement and displacement in a globalizing world.

However, as this methodology allowed me to probe transnational countercultures as an empirical social phenomenon, the resulting picture introduced a new order of challenges, this time at a conceptual-theoretical level. As I located my study within the scholarship on globalization and critical theory, it became clear that none of these intellectual fields alone would suffice to address the cultural implications and possibilities of globalization, in particular those related to hypermobility pressures.

In anticipation of a discussion carried out later in this chapter, global studies currently stumble on two basic problems (Urry 2003; Povinelli and Chauncey 1999). Global studies have overemphasized the description of social forms (networks, flows, systems) at the expense of a conceptualization of cultural contents (subjectivities, experiences, desires) that unravel under the impact of global processes. In this connection, predominant concepts of network, diaspora and cosmopolitanism have been overused, precipitously crystallizing over the course of a decade in biases that preclude alternative ways of investigating and conceptualizing cultural globalization, such as its fluidic and metamorphic components.

In the scope of critical studies,[2] this book draws on Foucault, Deleuze and Guattari as seminal references whose thought empirically resonates with the expressive and mobile tropes of global countercultures. To begin with, in their social and ritual life, Ibiza expatriates fully instantiate Foucauldian notions of self-shaping/shattering and of aesthetics of existence. It is almost as if he had written a script that they decided to perform as their real lives. As will be discussed later, rather than dandyism, the aesthetics of existence must be understood as an ethics of the self that opposes dominant biopower regimes, and seeks to engender a holistic balance of life principles beyond modern fragmentation. However, while attempting to eschew the tentacles of nation-state regimes, expressive expatriates problematically replicate aspects of the logic of neoliberal capitalism. Yet, rather than dissolve the dialectic that permeates the book, I sought to keep it as a productive tension that is dynamically inscribed in global countercultures. I thus assessed them in relation to proximate contexts, rather than imposing some macro-sociological explanation that determines agency and consciousness, more or less arbitrarily defined by the intellectual according to their own theoretical affiliation. On the other hand, under conditions of globalization, it also became clear that the countercultural aporia vis-à-vis systemic co-optation cannot be addressed within the scope of critical studies alone. In face of the centrifugal drives that characterize expatriate countercultures in Ibiza, Foucauldian notions of aesthetic self-formation are not enough to address the fundamental issue of hypermobility that structures them.

A dialogue between global and critical studies is a necessary condition for understanding the cultural implications of globalization. An insight into this junction derives from the nomadology of Deleuze and Guattari. *A Thousand Plateaus: Capitalism and Schizophrenia* stands as a powerful even if intuitive entry into a semiosis of globalization as entailed upon issues of subjectivity and cultural change. In this connection, I have sought to integrate predominant tropes of global and critical studies into a conceptualization of 'neo-nomadism' which can be defined as an ideal-type that allows us to identify, describe and measure cultural patterns and effects of global hypermobility. In particular, neo-nomadism addresses new forms of identity that are based, not on sameness or fixity, but rather on a principle of metamorphosis (chromatic variation). In other words, neo-nomadic lifestyles, subjectivities and identities can be addressed as expressions and agents of the postidentitarian predicament of globalization. The point then becomes how we can operationalize this analytical device at the empirical level.

To this end, I turned to Techno and New Age multiple manifestations, yet focusing on those segments that produce these forms as a vanguard predicated on expressivity and mobility. In this book, I examine rave, therapy and travel as probable expressions of a countercultural regime, which also embodies and entails the impact of globalization upon self-identities and socialities. More specifically, Techno and New Age provide sites of experience, meaning and struggle, by which neo-nomadism manifests itself in two different ways: one as a stabilized form of self-cultivation (*nomadic spirituality*), the other as a temporary condition of acute self-derailment (*psychic deterritorialization*). In the former, this study verifies a cultural pattern of religious practice whose nature is multiple, ephemeral and contingent. It can be captured in the notion of nomadic spirituality, which operates as an empirical and analytical category that informs how flexible subjectivities navigate under the volatile conditions of flexible capitalism. Nomadic spirituality is empirically detected in most New Age forms of self-spirituality and other closely related practices of self-development, while more widely reflecting social processes of multiculturalism, reflexivity and consumerism. Conversely, in the latter, psychic deterritorialization stands at the intersection of schizoanalysis and the psychiatry of travel, and it refers to an acute condition of personal derailment by which the symbolic references of the self are radically uprooted, inferred from the dramatic alteration of behavioral, cognitive and affective modes of the subject in relation to its predominantly ordinary states. While varying in degree, intensity and duration, these cases are frequently reported during long-haul travel, meditation marathons and psychedelic experiences that mark 'contact zones' intersecting Romanticism, postcoloniality and globalism. Postidentitarian experiences seem more pronounced in spaces of symbolic power, usually locations embedded in Romantic imaginaries of exoticism and mystery.

Curiously, back at home the subject quickly regains his or her cognitive abilities to operate normally in daily life; however, assailed by existential dissatisfaction, the subject may no longer be willing to cope with conventional routines that structure urban life in advanced societies. Not by coincidence, most expressive expatriates that I interviewed in Ibiza and India reported that they experienced some sort of personal crisis around the liminal experience of travel, which consequently prompted them to take their chances in trying a new lifestyle in semi-peripheral locations. In their utopian narrative of crisis and conversion, traveling can be either symptomatic or etiological of processes of postidentitarian effect. Yet, in the case of expressive expatriates, spatial and identity mobility have combined as a neo-nomadic way of life.

Finally, even as cases of nomadic spirituality and psychic deterritorialization require a proper historical contextualization, I would rather argue that they index the possibility of metamorphic identities which, in turn, refer to the basic predicament of cultural globalization. They may or may not become more socially pervasive (although I would argue that such is the case, due to globalization processes in the rise). In any case, the research on cultural hypermobility sheds light on crucial aspects of contemporary life, particularly in sites extensively exposed to global influences.

It is within this general picture that this book seeks to make empirical, methodological and theoretical contributions. In addition to an empirical account on expressive expatriation, this study provides an analytical model that can be employed in the investigation of neo-nomadic formations and development processes in other paradoxical paradises (such as Bali, Bahia, Byron Bay, Ko Pangnan, etc.). Furthermore, this research speaks to a range of topics under the rubric of globalization and cultural change: expatriation, travel and tourism; countercultures, subcultures and lifestyles; alternative religiosities, youth and subjectivity formation, in addition to disciplinary interests in cultural studies and the sociology and anthropology of globalization. Finally, as mentioned, this research seeks to develop a conceptual bridge between global and critical studies, which may contribute to a re-evaluation of a model of identity and subjectivity formation under conditions of globalization.

As a necessary remark, although touching on a variety of geographical, topical and disciplinary scholarship strands, the main focus of this research lies on a populace of neo-nomadic expatriates that navigates those spatial and cultural sites, and within certain empirical and theoretical contexts. Within these parameters, I have sought to cover all the relevant studies about Ibiza, Goa, New Age, Techno, cultural globalization and critical studies (in addition to parallel incursions in studies on tourism, subcultures, dance and therapy, among others). I do not claim to have read all the available references, since this is not only unfeasible but also inefficient to a certain extent, insofar as the goal of investigating and understanding the relations between globalization and counterculture remains uncompromised.

The significance of expressive expatriation: circuits of mobility and marginalization

As a counterpoint in migration studies, the terms 'expressive' and 'expatriate' depart with the predominantly utilitarian and essentialized understanding of the mobile subject, whether in neoclassical, historical-structural or systemic-transnational strains (Castles and Miller 2003). Most studies have focused on material conditions that propel labor migrants, political exiles and wealthy expatriates to move geographically, usually against the restrictive conditions of the nation-state. The scholarship has thus tended to reify the macro, meso and micro factors that it detects empirically, thus reaffirming the determinacy of systemic and material conditions over agency.

Even relatively free-flowing subjects – such as businesspeople, 'expats' and other metropolitan subjects – stumble on economic and ethnocentric orientations that regiment them by systemic regimes. In a classic example, Aiwa Ong investigates highly mobile Chinese businessmen as agents of a global flexible capitalism enabling a modular type of citizenship. Within this logic, flexible citizenship is defined as 'the localizing strategies of subjects who, through a variety of familial and economic practices, seek to evade, deflect and take advantage of political and economic conditions in different parts of the world' (Ong 1999: 113). Their mobility is determined by economic interest and political negotiation, maximizing business opportunities on a transcontinental scale, as well as the basic parameter that defines their will to be 'cosmopolitan.' Cultural capital is thus accumulated in order to facilitate material gain in the arena of international opportunities. In the analysis of institutional regimes that enable displacement, Ong detects a type of agency which is propelled by the logic of flexible capitalism, resulting in a 'utilitarian post-national ethos' that combines economic instrumentalism with familial moralism (p. 130).

In contrast, although conditioned by political economies of postindustrial, post-welfare societies, global nomads embody a different type of agency, one that is informed by cultural motivations that defy strict economic rationale. Many have abandoned metropolitan centers where they enjoyed a favorable material situation (income, stability, prestige), whereas others no longer wanted to survive day by day under the exclusionary violence of neo-liberal economies. In either case, they have permanently or periodically migrated to semi-peripheral locations with a pleasant climate, in order to dedicate themselves to the shaping of an alternative lifestyle. They retain the cultural capital that would allow them to revert to previous life schemes if necessary, and, likewise, define new economic goals when entering alternative niches of art, wellness and entertainment. Nonetheless, they have accepted the instabilities and hardships that characterize alternative careers (parallel to those directly suffered in neo-liberal settings but not quite the same), insofar as they feel that they can actualize cherished values of autonomy, self-expression and experimentation. Ironically, these subjects seem to have reached the apex of Maslow's hierarchy of human needs by turning it upside down.

In considering the systemic conditions that constrain mobility, it is necessary to take into account the subject's profile (citizenship, class and race) in relation to *circuits of mobility* that include her. Certain nationalities (First

World), social class (upper strata), occupations (highly educated professionals) and ethnicities (white) greatly facilitate international travel. However, some destinations (tourist-dependent countries), exquisite occupations (artistic, therapeutic, expressive) and mobility trajectories (a copiously visa-stamped passport) may contribute to the movement of those who do not fit the ideal profile. In this regard, my study provides a contrast with migration studies which have emphasized conditions of immobility, and it also questions theoretical studies on cultural globalization that neglect an empirical fine-grained analysis of meanings and experiences that hypermobility entails.

Mobile peoples (migrants, expatriates, exiles, pastoral nomads, etc.) are internally differentiated in terms of motivations and life strategies. Most of them display parochial identities based on homeland nostalgias, reinforced by contexts of socio-ethnic exclusion (Appadurai 1996; Hannerz 1996): they are displaced peoples with localized minds. Conversely, expressive expatriates, such as those seen in Ibiza, reject their own homelands spatially and affectively, resituating national origins in terms of reversed ethnocentrism. They make critical assessments about compatriots, tourists and more conventional expatriates which they deem parochial and conformist: in effect, expressive expatriates are displaced peoples with *displaced* minds.

Important to say, this cosmopolitan expatriate type must be considered, not as an expression of any 'subculture,' but rather as an instance of an ideal-type relating to emerging forms of transnational practice, identity and subjectivity interrelated with global processes and conditions of hypermobility, digitalization and reflexivity. These subjects inhabit a shifting nebula of fluidic and blurred sub-styles that evade conventional codes defined by modern regimes of the nation-state, morality and market. In this connection, this book more specifically focuses on meanings that lie at the intersection of mobility and resistance, expressed as self-induced marginalization.

Despite the number of travelogues and autobiographies written by expressive expatriates (Odzer 1995; Stratton 1994), scholarly references remain scarce and elusive. Studies on bohemianism and cosmopolitanism make tangential comments about alternative subjects that, inhabiting the fringes of modernity, mysteriously overlap with artistic, cultural and economic elites of the metropole (Blanchard 1998; Watson 1995; Green 1986). Even the excellent study by Richard Lloyd on neo-bohemians takes place in the postindustrial city: Chicago (Lloyd 2006). In academic conferences and informal conversations, I observed that expressive expatriates have been sometimes compared with 'bohemian bourgeois' (Brooks 2000) and 'hub culture' (Stalnaker 2002), with whom they appear to share some basic features, such as the cultivation of expressive individualism, cosmopolitan tastes and travel experience in the form of leisure or self-discovery interests.

However, expressive expatriates sharply depart with metropolitan elites on crucial topics of consumerism, labor ethics and monadic individualism. Their critical stance has been more mildly articulated by mainstream authors, such as David Brooks and Stan Stalnaker. Brooks notes that the commodification of meaning fosters lack of solidarity, solipsism and even nihilism in post-suburban environments (Brooks 2000: 221–2). Similarly, Stalnaker – who writes from the perspective of a global marketing analyst – warns about the limits of unchecked consumerism: 'It is at this point, if you haven't somehow connected to something larger, past the material existence, that you find hate and despair' (Stalnaker 2002: 151). And he further suggests, 'In the near future, spiritualism will be a leading factor in the cultural conversation of the [urban] hubs' (p. 192).

By problematizing 'solidarity' and 'spirituality,' expressive expatriates hinge on crucial conditions of contemporary life, not only from the viewpoint of the elected periphery but also from the very center itself. While consumer societies, according to expatriates and marketing analysts alike, appear to be blindly marching toward the abyss of spiritual void, cultural dissent in the West often manifests itself in the will to escape toward marginal positions and locations. The margin seems to provide some favorable conditions for the experimentation of alternative lifestyles that attempt to integrate labor, leisure and spirituality in ways that are deemed more meaningful according to those who evade the center.

A curious paradox evinces the significance of alternative modernities. While attempting to eschew modern systemic regimes, expressive expatriates engender spaces, practices and imaginaries that are gradually captured by capitalist economies (tourism, entertainment, advertising) and regulated by the state. Places such as Ibiza, Goa, Bali, Ko Pangnan, Bahia, Byron Bay, San Francisco, Pune, Marrakesh, etc. have become attractive tourist and trendsetting centers *subsequent* to the arrival of bohemians, gays, beatniks, hippies, New Agers, ravers and clubbers (D'Andrea 2004; Ramón-Fajarnés 2000; Wilson 1997a; Odzer 1994). As it seems, despite being numerically small, expressive expatriates are disproportionably influential upon the cultural sphere of mainstream societies, particularly the youth and other dynamic segments of society. This process of evasion and capture reveals the ambivalent disposition of desire and confinement that mainstream (sedentary) societies displays toward countercultural (nomadic) formations.

Globalization: network, diaspora and cosmopolitanism

This section discusses the main concepts of globalization, noting that they do not account for the critical features of global nomadism. Globalization is, at once, an empirical reality, an umbrella term and an analytical paradigm. It refers to the growing importance of translocal connections in shaping social life, which becomes disembedded from the determinations of proximate spatiotemporal contexts. It derives from the intensification of multiple social, economic, political, technological and cultural processes that complexly interrelate in a manner that is unprecedented in nature, speed and scale. More empirically, globalization is characterized by:

- the worldwide integration of markets under flexible modes of production and volatile financial capital;
- the dissemination of new technologies of communication and transportation;
- the post-Cold War multi-polarity; the rise of transnational actors and new migration waves as well as the relative decline of the nation-state;
- the reconfiguration of city landscapes, within urban networks and hierarchies, alongside the rise of the transnationally linked 'global city';
- and the emergence of reflexive and fundamentalist forms of social organization and identity.

As this picture suggests, the highly disjunctive and hybridist nature of globalization results in new patterns, risks and opportunities that define the terms of a post-traditional order (Giddens 1994, 1991). In tandem, the interaction between local and translocal forces defines the spatiotemporality of a given social formation, meaning that an alteration in the composition of those forces is likely to reconfigure the levels of deterritorialization of the society. The difference between 'transnational' and 'global' is elucidative: the former refers to processes anchored across the borders of a few nation-states, whereas the latter refers to decentralized processes that develop away from the space of the national (Gille and Riain 2002: 273; Kearney 1995: 548). As such, global interaction means 'not the replication of uniformity but an organization of diversity, an increasing interconnectedness of varied local cultures, as well as a development of cultures without a clear anchorage in any one territory.' (Hannerz 1996: 102). Composites of local and translocal forces may occur at 'border zones,' shape 'contact zones' and constitute 'global ecumenes,' all of which can be understood as regions of persistent interaction and exchange, asymmetries and exploitation, resistance and hybridization (Clifford 1997: 195; Hannerz 1989: 66; Pratt 1992).

In globalization studies, the nature of agency and scale varies considerably, according to the object of study and the intellectual purview of the analyst. Studies that focus on systemic forces (capitalism, science, modernization) tend to consider actors and places as being subordinate to contexts of locality-making that lie beyond their control. Analyses of transnational connections consider actors with an ability to navigate sociospatial hierarchies. Diaspora studies, at last, investigate actors that are more actively engaged in the formation of imaginaries and public spaces (Gille and Riain 2002: 279).

However, over the course of a decade, these analytical strands have rapidly adjusted to issues of replication and normalization, without considering methodological or conceptual alternatives that could more efficiently and creatively address patterns and complexities of globalization that remain understudied (Urry 2003: 11–12). More specifically, notions of network, diaspora and cosmopolitanism have precipitously forged an understanding about mobile subjects that obstructs the perception of unknown features and possibilities.

The notion of 'network' is the conceptual device most widely employed in global studies. Comprising related notions, such as 'flow,' 'web' and 'circuit,' its prominence in social sciences reflects the impact of information technologies reconfiguring social life as a 'space of flows' rather than a 'space of places' (Castells 1996). Assuming different topologies (chain, hub, channel), a network is a system of interconnected nodes for maximizing information and energy output. Its potency is defined by the number of nodes, their interconnections and density, as well as by its relation to other environs. Networks may overextend insofar as new nodular lines remain possible. Nodes are not centers but switchers performing functions within a general system that operates through a rhizomatic rather than a command logic. Nodes vary in importance (depending on location, density and energy) but are interdependent and replaceable. Both in the physical and social realms, a network generates complex interconnections that survive its constitutive elements, extending across time and space (Urry 2003; Castells 1996).

However, the notion of network has been overused in global studies, constraining the perception and sidestepping issues of power, meaning and change. 'The term "network" is expected to do too much theoretical work in the argument, glossing over very different networked phenomena ... [It] does not bring out the enormously complex notion of power implicated in diverse mobilities of global capitalism ...' (Urry 2003: 11–12). John Urry also notes that the scholarship has relied on a model of 'globally integrated networks' (GINs), complex and enduring structures characterized by predictable connections that nullify time-space constraints. Transnational corporations and supranational organizations are examples of GINs. These structures tend to be inertial, rigid and dependent on the stability of macro systems (international markets, contracts and media/rumor systems).

Yet, there are networked-like formations that cannot be understood through the notion of GIN. Urry proposes the notion of 'global fluids,' characterized as highly mobile and viscous formations whose shapes are uneven, contingent and unpredictable. 'Fluids create over time their own context of action rather than seeing as "caused"' (p. 59). Traveling peoples, oceans, the internet and epidemics are variegated examples of global fluids. However, Urry does not provide further evidence for advancing his claim that global fluids constitute 'a crucial category of analysis in the globalizing social world' (p. 60).

Neither concept of network (GIN or fluid) can address the meanings and temporalities of the entities they seek to explain. As an alternative, the notion of 'diaspora' has been largely employed in anthropological studies of ethnic dispersion. Differing from linear migration and structured networks, a diaspora includes a full cross-section of community members spread across diverse regions, while retaining a myth of uniqueness, usually linked to an idea of homeland, real or imagined (Kearney 1995: 559). A descriptive definition of diaspora includes 'a history of dispersal, myths and memories of the homeland, alienation in the host country, desire for eventual return, ongoing support of the homeland, and a collective identity defined by this relationship' (Clifford 1994: 306). Upon the tension between local assimilation and translocal allegiances, a diaspora is diacritically shaped by means of political struggles with state normativities and indigenous majorities (Axel 2002; Clifford 1994: 307–8).

Nonetheless, the relation between diaspora and locality is further fractured by the socio-spatiotemporal disjuncture of globalization, engendering 'degrees of diasporic alienation' (Clifford: 315). Under global conditions, the space and identity of such ethnic dispersions must be reconsidered in terms of a 'diasporic imaginary.' Diaspora is conventionally understood as being founded on a locus of origin that defines a people as diaspora. However, '[r]ather than conceiving of the homeland as something that creates the diaspora, it may be productive to consider the diaspora as something that creates the homeland' (Axel 2002: 426). As Brian Axel proposes, 'My conceptualization of the diasporic imaginary not only repositions the homeland as a temporalizing and affective aspect of subjectification; it also draws the homeland in relation with other kinds of images and processes.' (p. 426).

By breaking the social-spatiotemporal link that constitutes identity, globalization enables a new form of diasporic imaginary, one whose nature is post-essentialist. Under these circumstances, diaspora becomes, in the words of Kobena Mercer, a 'site of multiple displacements and rearticulations of identity, without privilege of race, cultural tradition, class, gender or sexuality. Diaspora consciousness is entirely a product of cultures and histories in collision and dialogue' (Mercer 1994: 319; see also Clifford 1994). Rather than origin, it values the critical voice in history, established by means of power relations and cultural encounters. Although some historians may note the risk of premature pluralism in this argument, there is a distinction between historical and essentialist accounts of diaspora, for globalization introduces conditions of possibility for the emergence of postidentitarian formations.

In this light, global nomads constitute a *negative diaspora*, as they see themselves as part of a trans-ethnic dispersion of peoples that despise home-centered identities. Their identity as a diasporic formation is not based on ethnic or national nostalgias, but rather on a fellowship of counter-hegemonic practice and lifestyle. For consciously rejecting predominant ethno-national apparatuses, their centrifugal moves do not configure diasporic alienation; quite the contrary, although perhaps heralding the ideal of an alternative homeland, their utopian drives are propelled by a pragmatic individualism, often predicated on reflexive modes of subjectivity formation (Lash 1994; Foucault 1984c, 1984f). Other than making one's soul the Promised Land, expressive individualism opposes diaspora as a basis of personal identity. Therefore, diaspora does not suffice for addressing hypermobile formations that nest a type of sensibility that, in the lines of Mercer, tends to reject exclusionary modes of identity formation based on gender, race, class and religion.

Negative diaspora thus reflects the reconfiguration of self-identity under the impact of global processes and structures. Media, urban and techno-scientific apparatuses generate an unprecedented volume of images, signals and information that gradually undermines the fixity of social roles, identities and cognitive frames. These have to be renegotiated, as subjects are forced to make uneasy decisions about their lives: 'we have no choice but to make choices' (Giddens 1994: 187). This condition has been identified as 'the problem of inculturation in a period of rapid culture change [. . .], as the transgenerational stability of knowledge [. . .] can no longer be assumed' (Appadurai 1996: 43). Frederic Jameson notes that the emergence of colossal global systems has derailed the human capacity of social perception and cognition, thus engendering disorientation (Jameson 1991: 45). On the other hand, Anthony Giddens and Scott Lasch are more optimistic in assessing such semiotic excess as, in part, reflecting reflexive demands which arise from the fabric of social life (Beck *et al.* 1994). In this case, the problematization of locality-making becomes a resource rather than a barrier in the production of meaning, inasmuch as the aesthetic reflexivity that is entailed by modern reflexivity remains capable of recalibrating notions of time, space and belonging at the local level (Appadurai 1996; Lash 1994).

The question then becomes how reflexive subjectivities are constituted under the deterritorializing conditions of globalization. However, although dependent of specific objects and scales of analysis, the development of new methodologies capable of addressing issues of deterritorialization has been limited, since global studies have privileged the analysis of social forms over cultural contents:

> A troubling aspect of the literature on globalization is its tendency to read social life off external social forms – flows, circuits, circulations of people, capital and culture – without any model of subjective mediation. In other words, globalization studies often proceed as if tracking and mapping the facticity of the economic, population, and population flows, circuits, and linkages were sufficient to account for current

cultural forms and subjective interiorities, or as if an accurate map of the space and time of post-Fordist accumulation could provide an accurate map of the subject and her embodiment and desires.

(Povinelli and Chauncey 1999: 7)

Within current scholarship, one possible way of overcoming this lacuna involves the deployment of the concept of cosmopolitanism, retooled as a mediation that translates aesthetic reflexivity into a social disposition that is malleable to global environments. Cosmopolitanism has been described as a 'perspective' or a 'mode of managing meaning' that entails 'greater involvement with a plurality of contrasting cultures, to some degree on their own terms' (Hannerz 1996: 103). Large cities have been celebrated as spaces of multiculturalism, but long-haul traveling prevails as the manner by which one is dramatically exposed to and potentially transformed by the contact with alterity. According to Ulf Hannerz, 'genuine cosmopolitanism is first of all an orientation, a willingness to engage with the Other. It entails an intellectual and aesthetic openness toward divergent cultural experiences, a search for contrasts rather than uniformity' (p. 103). However, this openness usually presupposes material and educational privileges that are restricted to a few. Most tourists, migrants, exiles and expatriates are not cosmopolitans due to a lack of interest or competence in participating or translating difference: 'locals and cosmopolitans can spot tourists a mile away' (p. 105).

Openness to plurality is not an altruistic gesture, for the main goal of the cosmopolitan is to understand her own structures of meaning. 'Cosmopolitans can be dilettantes as well as connoisseurs, and are often both, at different times. But the willingness to become involved with the Other, and the concern in achieving competence in [alien] cultures relate to considerations of self as well' (p. 103). In a psychoanalytical vein, cosmopolitanism exposes an element of narcissism in the development of the self that is carried out through cultural mirroring (p. 103). In this connection, it can be understood as a 'therapeutic exploration of strangeness within and outside the self' by which 'detachment from provincial identities' alters personal references of self and alterity (Anderson 1998: 285).

However, proponents of a more localized and nativist form of cosmopolitanism have criticized the predominantly universalist approach as being tainted with elitism and aestheticism (Robbins 1998: 254; Clifford 1994: 324). These 'discrepant cosmopolitanisms' propose a different density of allegiances that values local worldviews and affirms cultural and historical specificity. In it, hybridity overcomes translation by subverting colonial dichotomies and hierarchies. Intellectuals have, in fact, been idealized as cosmopolitans par excellence (Hannerz 1996; Braidotti 1994), even if their competence is, more often than not, restricted to sophisticated rationalizations about the Other. To wit, although noting the performatic dimension of the intercultural encounter, Ulf Hannerz and Rosi Braidotti claim that cosmopolitanism is, above all, a process of management of meaning and translation. This conception virtually ignores the impact of affective and visceral engagements with radical alterity in reshaping personhood. Such a view reduces cosmopolitanism to little more than detached aestheticism, as more popularly illustrated in bobos and hub influentials' safe consumerism of exotic commodities (Stalnaker 2002; Brooks 2000).

Nonetheless, both nativist and universalist schools of cosmopolitanism neglect three critical issues. First, there is a substantial difference between aesthetics and aestheticism that debates have overlooked. As will be discussed in this chapter, aestheticism refers to a form of detached appreciation as outlined above, whereas aesthetics relates to an ethical orientation that potentially confronts the fixity of biopower domination while rebalancing life-values. Second, current debates reduce cosmopolitanism either as a cognitive or as a behavioral capacity, respectively incarnated in sophisticated intellectuals or skillful migrants as iconic examples. Instead, cosmopolitanism must be understood as a holistic disposition or attitude (in social psychology terms), which comprises cognitive, affective and behavioral components altogether. Third, debates on cosmopolitanism are often anchored on speculative and idealistic assumptions, neglecting empirical research and validation, particularly by means of cross-cultural analysis.

Among different types of mobile subjects, it seems that the ethical, attitudinal and empirical dimensions of cosmopolitanism tend to overlap in the figure of the 'expatriate.' Hannerz's observations resonate with the expressive expatriates foregrounded in this book:

> The concept of the expatriate may be that we will most readily associate with cosmopolitanism. Expatriates (or ex-expatriates) are people who have chosen to live abroad for some period [. . .]. Not all expatriates are living models of cosmopolitanism; colonialists were also expatriates, and mostly they abhorred 'going native.' But these are people who can afford to experiment, who do not stand to lose a treasured but threatened, uprooted sense of self. We often think of them as people of independent (even if modest) means, for whom openness to new experiences is a vocation, or people who can take along their work more or less where it pleases them; writers and painters in Paris between the wars are perhaps the archetypes.
>
> (Hannerz 1996: 106)

As a writer in Paris between the wars, Walter Benjamin twice fled to Ibiza in 1932 and 1933. As a forerunner of expatriate life on the island, Benjamin stayed at a friend's house in the fisherman parish of Sant Antoni.[3] 'There were only a few foreigners there,' according to French art historian Jean Selz, 'a number of Germans and also some Americans. The foreigners were often together, so I got to know him. Benjamin was 40, and I was

28' (Scheurmann and Scheurman 1993: 68). In a letter, Benjamin wrote that Ibiza allowed him to 'live under tolerable circumstances in a beautiful landscape for no more than 80 marks per month.' (Witte 1991: 33). Because Ibiza was so isolated, his attempts to develop editorial contacts in Paris proved unsuccessful. Nevertheless, he enjoyed the beauties of *La Isla Blanca* amid a lively community of expatriates. Benjamin spotted bohemians in bars and restaurants, toured with Gaugin's grandson, and flirted with a Dutch painter whom he said to have almost included in his 'angelology' (Witte 1991). In Ibiza, Benjamin also experimented with opium and hashish in the context of his interests in surrealism as a countercultural, liberation movement (Thompson 1997).

In the early 2000s, connectivity would not have been such a problem for Benjamin. With email and low-airfare jets, he would perhaps have stayed longer in Ibiza, although intense urbanization and price inflation have become main complaints among residents more recently. Nevertheless, throughout the century, Ibiza has been imagined as a utopian paradise, hosting successive waves of marginal subjects fleeing the metropole: artists, bohemians, beatniks, hippies, gays, freaks and clubbers. For such a density of cultural experimentation in a setting of intense modernization as that island has suffered, French sociologist Danielle Rozenberg has claimed that, 'Ibiza is paradigmatic to those who interrogate the development of contemporary societies' (Rozenberg 1990: 3). These expressive expatriates have inadvertently contributed to Ibiza being imagined as an icon of pleasure and freedom amid large segments of the Western youth, an icon that is now rampantly exploited by leisure capitalism, with contradictory effects. But, while globalization conceals the forces of history, neo-nomadism embodies a much longer diachrony that can be traced back to the 1960s counterculture and even further back to nineteenth-century Romanticism.

Aesthetics of the self: post-sexualities in a digital age

The subjects discussed in this book ascribe to a cosmopolitan culture of expressive individualism. Any practice that allows for the exploration of personal capabilities in creative, pleasurable and transcendent ways are of potential interest for expressive expatriates. As such, after fleeing the homeland, they become personally and/or professionally involved with therapy, art and spirituality, and their experimentations with hedonism and sexuality often reflect conscious decisions about transforming their self-identity modes. These dispositions and their wider circumstances resonate with philosophical discussions about an aesthetics of existence which, according to Foucault, refers to the possibility of an ethics of the self that is capable of confronting the axiological challenges of modernity. Self-aesthetics, as a practical lifestyle or philosophical speculation, is predicated on a fundamental question: how does, can and must one conduct one's own life under conditions of moral freedom?

In this context, self-aesthetics must be considered in its crucial interrelations with ethics and politics, schematically considered at three different levels: (1) aesthetics as an emphasis on *forms* of coexistence that results from a world of polytheism of values; (2) aesthetics as a site of *resistance* against power-knowledge (biopower) regimes forged by the state and science; and (3) aesthetics as a *lifestyle* that sustains alternative experiences of the self and sociality.

The axiological crisis of modernity is marked by the acute fragmentation of life-spheres (religion, economy, politics, science, pleasure, intimacy, etc.) and their gradual colonization by technical reason. The overwhelming expansion of objective culture undermines the subject's ability to develop autonomously (Simmel 1971). To this challenge, Romantic thinkers have proposed the aesthetic as a realm of self-cultivation (*Bildungsideal*) by which a holistic personality can be cultivated against the corrosive effects of modern specialization. Yet, in face of the imperatives of modernity, such a view resulted in a withdrawal from the world of action, fostering a narcissistic style of excessive refinement, formalism and detachment, also characteristic of cosmopolitan aestheticism.

Within this intellectual context, Max Weber rebuked the Romantic view, seeing it as a powerless response to the meat-grinding effects of modern rationalization. In order to tame the 'iron cage' of modernity and the everlasting specters of demagogy and tradition, Weber proposed an ethics of personhood that integrates vocational specialization with an acute political awareness. The self must adhere to a secular ideal of vocation (*Beruf*), which presupposes an 'irrational' choice for compliance with one life-sphere and its core regulatory principle. Nonetheless, Weber soon realized that the vocational stance is better actualized by means of a political aesthetics that strives to balance such ends-oriented ethics (embodied in the principle of conviction, as in science or religion) with a means-oriented ethics (regulated by the principle of responsibility, as in politics) (Weber 1918). He thus hoped that the cultivated subject would be able to regain its ability to intervene in reality, while retaining some degree of autonomous development.[4]

Presenting remarkable similarities with the iron cage diagnosis, Foucault uncovered how science and state coalesce in *biopower* regimes, a complex institutional-ideological apparatus geared toward the administration of individual and collective bodies. It correlates with the more socially diffused apparatus of 'sexuality' which forges the modern subject of discipline and interiority.[5] In this light, the subordination of the self to a scientific vocation, as proposed by Weber, would reaffirm relations of domination entailed by biopower. In other words, by recurring to science and natural law as sources of legitimacy, liberation gestures, practices and movements remain entrapped in the epistemic vectors that they ultimately seek to transcend.

Conversely, power-knowledge regimes entail a multiplicity of forces that escape and resist them. As Foucault noted, mechanisms of subjectification inadvertently enable tactical resistance, for power is better understood as modes of relation that are both repressive *and* productive (Foucault 1976). The exclusionary logic of the normal-pathologic thus contributes to proliferate abnormalities that unfold both as representation and effect.

Furthermore, the historical decline of moral orthodoxies requires an ethical response that, in highly reflexive sites, has revolved around the problematization of the self in relation to itself. As such, once repression is lifted, the problem becomes how to define and exercise one's own freedom in relation to others and to one's own experience. In the scope of sexuality, the subject thus becomes a battleground between moralities of bourgeois interest and of bohemian expression:

> A morality of 'interest' was proposed and imposed upon the bourgeois class – in opposition to other arts of the self that can be found within artistic and critical circles. The 'artistic' path [...] constitutes an aesthetics of existence that opposes self-techniques prevalent within bourgeois culture.
>
> (Foucault 1984a: 629)

This is where latter Foucault meets post-Ascona Weber. The aesthetics of existence substantially differs from aestheticism. As an ethics of the self, it has effects of power with a potential for breaking away from regimes of subjectification that constrain experiences of the self and reality. It is in this sense that Foucault envisages the aesthetics of the self as a life politics. '"Couldn't everyone's life become a work of art?" This was not some vapid plea for aestheticism, but a suggestion for separating our ethics, our lives, from our science, our knowledge' (Hacking 1986: 239). Liberation movements would not only be aligned with values, methods, orientations and dispositions that define an ethics of self-mastery (Giddens 1994; Foucault and Lotringer 1989; Foucault 1984a). A post-sexuality age would also require 'new forms of community, co-existence and pleasure' capable of nurturing subjective and social modes that redefine terms of control, discipline and interiority.

How to scrutinize this conceptual horizon empirically is a critical question. In this book, I investigate the possibility of a post-sexuality apparatus being engendered in specific sites of Techno and New Age counterculture and sustained by expressive expatriates. Yet, a bibliographic search on the topic is disappointing. Besides a few sociological studies dedicated to a taxonomy of sectarian subcultures, most accounts have focused on historical outlooks about the 1960s 'radicalism,' the 1970s 'decline' and the 1980s 'co-optation' (Brooks 2000; Frank 1997; McKay 1996; Roszak 1995; Zicklin 1983; Bellah 1979). The presumed disappearance of countercultures conceals the fragmentation of 'the sixties' into a variety of single-issue movements, in turn, paralleled by a host of academic studies: queer, ecological, feminist; subcultural, new religions, popular studies, etc. (Clifford 1998). Within a wider socio-historical perspective, nonetheless, all of these empirico-conceptual formations manifest a basic dissatisfaction with the promises and rewards of modern civilization.

A note on the notions of 'subculture,' 'counterculture' and 'alternative culture' is pertinent. These have derived and been questioned from diverse academic purviews, notably those inspired by functionalism and popular resistance (Bennett and Kahn-Harris 2004; Muggleton and Weinzierl 2003; Bennett 1999; Redhead 1997; McKay 1996; Roszak 1995). But, in the scope of this book, I propose a pragmatic deployment of such definitions. The notion of 'subculture' refers to shared values, symbols and practices of a group whose members also adhere to or function (more or less normally) within a larger society. The adjective 'alternative' denotes subcultures that seek some level of autonomy from or replacement of major social schemes. It connects with the notion of 'counterculture,' which differs, nonetheless, in intensity and amplitude: a counterculture is characterized by more acute degrees of dissatisfaction, a critical stance and refusal of major institutions, norms and values, in addition to the cultivation of transgressive practices, identities and lifestyles that more consciously seek to confront dominant culture. A counterculture is thus a type of radicalized subculture, operating as a potent ideological referent in times of crisis. In the scope of this study, I am interested in alternative formations that uphold countercultural drives that can at least partially be traced back to the 1960s cultural upheaval and, further back, to nineteenth-century Romanticism. Contemporarily, scholarly studies and some empirical evidence suggest that Techno and New Age potentially embody powerful sites of problematization of modern life, questioning modernity *within* modernity.

As a hybrid of art, technology and proto-religion, Techno is ritualized in multimedia dance events known as 'raves' or 'underground nightclubs' in urban 'wild zones' (Stanley 1997) and as 'trance parties' in secluded rural areas. These gatherings constitute temporary spaces of ecstatic experience induced by technological devices with the implicit aim of shattering and reshaping self-identities (Hutson 2000; Corsten 1998b; Hemment 1998; Reynolds 1998; Saunders 1995). 'Rave is more than music plus drugs, it is a matrix of lifestyle, ritualized behavior and beliefs. To the participant, it feels like a religion; to the mainstream observer, it looks more like a sinister cult' (Reynolds 1998: 5). Studies have debated on Techno's cultural and political meaning, notably its emphasis on hedonistic hyper-stimulation and communitarian effervescence under digital paraphernalia (St John 2004; Gibson 2001; Borneman and Senders 2000; Gaillot 1999; Gilbert and Pearson 1999; Ingham *et al.* 1999). Nevertheless, Techno seems to develop through a cyclic pattern of popularization and decline (Best 1997; Grossberg 1997; Thornton 1995), which conceals its origins amid marginal subcultures

in global cities and secluded paradises during the 1980s, as classically typi-
fied: ethnic gays in Chicago and New York (giving rise to house and garage
music), blacks in Detroit and London (techno and jungle music), and hip-
pies/freaks in Ibiza and Goa (trance music) (Silcott 1999; Reynolds 1998;
Collin 1997). New digital technologies of music, drugs and media have
become constitutive of these cultures of resistance which sought to oppose
the neo-liberal order of Thatcher and Reagan. Since then, these counter-
hegemonic formations have been disseminating through transnational flows
of music, fashion and people, assuming new forms and meanings as they
localize and are appropriated by larger segments of the youth and entertainment sectors.

In this book, Techno is an umbrella term that comprises the whole range
of electronic music genres (house, techno, jungle, trance, ambient, etc.), its
ritual sites (rave, nightclub and trance parties) and subcultural components
(fashion, music, drugs, lifestyle), all of which are associated with the rise
and popularization of digital technologies of art production, diffusion and
consumption, notably music and iconography. Techno, in sum, signifies
the emergence of aesthetic–political–technological forms regimented within
a global counterculture that has to interact locally with multiple national
cultures and institutional apparatuses in a variety of places globally.

New Age refers to hybridizations of religion, art and science supporting
individualistic spiritualities. It can be seen as a cultural process that transforms the religious sphere, as well as a rhizomatic 'network of networks'
interlinking a heteroclite universe of practices and ideas (D'Andrea
2000; Heelas 1996; York 1995). Underlying its multifarious labels, the
New Age's basic premise lies on the cultivation of the self (*Bildung*),
rendered as a precondition for a new secular and spiritual age. Deriving
from the early 1970s counterculture, its ethno-ecological, parascientific
and psychospiritual syncretisms reflect the social diffusion of a *reflexive
mysticism* formerly confined within erudite circles of Romanticism
(Luckmann 1991; Bellah 1985). Manifested in casual statements such as
'I don't have any religion but my own spirituality,' growing interest in
Zen, Yoga, Sufi, Cabala, Alchemy, Wicca, etc. indicates the psycholo-
gization of world religions and native traditions, resituated as instruments
for the reflexive and expressive cultivation of the self. Its basic artifacts
– music, meditation, body therapies, encounter groups, diets, drugs, etc.
– are conceived of as special techniques for the attainment of special
subjective moods. Yet, at a deeper level, the New Age also embodies a
contradiction between a logic of 'love-wisdom' and 'power-control,'
reflecting either historical trends toward expressive individualism, or neo-
liberal ideologies of consumerism and competition (Bellah 1985). Inter-
facing religion and individualism, the New Age refers to the globalization
of a meta-spirituality that indexes multiple references and terminologies
about the cultivation of the self.

Critical outlooks on Techno and New Age often reduce them to functions or expressions of larger socio-economic processes. Their practices,
artifacts and imaginaries can be reformulated as charismatic commodities,
consumed by dynamic segments of the middle class to satisfy pseudo-
cosmopolitan consumerism (Carrete and King 2005). Techno and New
Age also operate as ideological icons that legitimate the rise of a new
global middle class (Stalnaker 2002; Mehta 1990). And, finally, by means
of leisure, self-effacing spaces, they provide compensatory escape-valves
for the (real or imagined) hardships of modern life. While not disagreeing
with the economic, ideological and functional aspects of such a critique
of Techno and New Age, it is necessary to reconsider the pertinence of
such claims for contributing to the understanding of further developments
and meanings of cultural phenomena that remain largely ignored, particularly in their interrelations with recent processes of globalization.

Although studies on New Age and Techno do not usually interface
(except St John 2004), a careful comparison reveals a very tangible
common horizon, as this book will explore in detail. Initially, they unfold
through dynamic tensions that simultaneously entail social diffusion and
distinction, cultural transgression and co-optation, economic singularity
and commodification, reflexivity and fundamentalism, utopia and dystopia.
They similarly embody cultural projects that strive for a lifestyle that
integrates expressive labor, leisure and spirituality, coupled with critical
discourses about regimes of state, market and morality. Their ritual and
discursive practices very similarly dramatize the impact of globalization
upon selves, identities and socialities. While praising local traditions and
celebrities, both movements celebrate global ecumenisms, sustained by
means of transnational exchanges that engender spaces of cosmopolitanism, expression and mysticism. At the turn of the twenty-first century,
Techno and New Age seem to coalesce into a single, globalizing *digital
art-religion*.

However, because transnational flows of Techno and New Age necessarily reterritorialize in local sites of struggle and signification, a basic
dimension of analysis must consider the social and physical spatiality that
nest such formations. Due to their historical, geographical and cultural
features, Ibiza (Spain) and Goa (India) have been central nodes and iconic
references for these globalizing countercultures. Not only are these places
charged with 'charisma' and 'movement,' they are also linked through the
circulation of such alternative peoples, their practices, artifacts and imaginaries. In addition, both locations exhibit a similar picture: among the
wealthiest places in India and Spain respectively, Goa and Ibiza economies
are led by leisure industries that recast charisma as leisure commodity.
Global countercultures have to negotiate with localized national societies,
implying that expressive expatriates have to navigate turbulent environments of flexible capitalism at the global and local levels, while establishing
fluidic networks of support.

In sum, as the iron cage of modernity becomes the *silicon cage* of global capitalism, the 'spiritless specialists' (that Weber alludes to) reduce the human into a *carbon cage*, a map of commodified genes and rights colonized by high-tech engineering and legal intervention. In this dystopian scenario, Techno and New Age provide ambivalent sites of resistance to biopower. They defy the centralizing logic of legal administration of bodies and spaces, by conducting nomadic practices and rituals. They appropriate techno-scientific knowledge, by transgressing their disciplinary boundaries and original usages. They amoralize desires, by indulging in degenitalized pleasures; and they criticize modern economic rationality, by pointing out its ecological irrationality. Yet, the question to be asked is to what extent such erotic-aesthetic moves constitute an overcoming of biopower and sexuality. Through playful moves of micro-transgression, Techno and New Age may be engendering either exercises of emancipation, or innocuous narcissistic escapes, or, echoing Weber and Foucault, something other we don't know yet what it is. Curiously, some of the iconic characters of critical philosophy – the mad, the criminal, the artist and the vagabond – are metonymically condensed on the 'global nomad,' a figuration that leads us to the next section.

Neo-nomadism: postidentitarian mobility

As this book will detail, for global nomads, mobility is more than spatial displacement. It is also a component of their economic strategies, as well as of their own modes of self-identity and subjectivity formation. In this case, practices of spatial displacement are entwined with experiences of auto-metamorphosis. Since studies on counterculture and consumerism have shown that alternative practices tend to diffuse later into the social, economic and corporate mainstream, it can be assumed that the global countercultural experiences here investigated may provide invaluable insights into new patterns of cultural globalization recoding contemporary societies.

As previously discussed, prevalent notions of global studies – network, diaspora, cosmopolitanism – are insufficient for addressing the nature of global nomadism and what it may more widely indicate about globalization. An alternative conceptualization takes on the perception that hypermobility tends to be more explicitly embodied in formations that combine mobility and marginality. This combination is not unique to expressive expatriates, but has been historically found among pastoral nomads as well. At the level of the imaginary, nomads have long fascinated the West, either as a contemptuous case of pre-civilizational barbarism or as a romanticized figure of holistic freedom. Perhaps, it is not by chance that socio-material forms of nomadism have contemporarily reappeared in sites of hypermobility, such as motorized subcultures, alternative markets, itinerant art, transnational lifestyles, computer hacking and science fiction, to name a few. However, traditional nomadism cannot account for the meanings and forces that enmesh such hypermobile formations in contexts of globalization.

Considering the incommensurable differences, it would be misleading merely to transpose an analytical model of pastoral nomadism upon contemporary hypermobile formations. On the other hand, a series of symmetries should not be so readily discarded, since a series of insights may be gained by means of a limited comparison between traditional and post-traditional nomads. As noted by George Marcus, while requiring an embedment in proximate contexts of analysis, high theories – such as Deleuze and Guattari's nomadology – 'often anticipate many of the contemporary social and cultural conditions with which ethnographers and other scholars are trying to come to terms with' (Marcus 1998: 86–7).

Keeping these remarks in mind, a dialogue between the anthropology of nomadism and philosophy of nomadology provides conceptual foundations for addressing cultural hypermobility as a rising global condition that reshapes identity and subjectivity forms. This genealogy of nomadology seeks to produce a theory of *neo-nomadism* as an *ideal-type of postidentitarian mobility*. The recourse to the Weberian device not only alleviates the aporia of representation that is raised in the anthropological critique to nomadology (Miller 1993), but it also moderates nomothetic excesses that tend to erase historical difference. Neo-nomadism must be seen as a heuristic construct for describing, measuring and interpreting subcategories of cultural hypermobility: displacement, marginality, deterritorialization and metamorphosis.

Nonetheless, there has been no interaction among studies of nomadism, nomadology and globalization. Global and critical studies neglect evidence on nomadism, whereas (mis)representations about the nomad freely circulate in cultural studies, literature and pop culture (Cresswell 1997; Miller 1993). In its turn, the scholarship on pastoralism is not immune to its own bias:

> anthropologists have often perpetuated a stereotype by deliberately seeking out the most conservative of the nomads for study. Rather than representing the norm, such ideal 'pure nomads' are exceptional [. . .] [N]omadic pastoralism is made to appear far more isolated than it actually is.
>
> (Barfield 1993: 214)

In face of such scholarly disjunctures, an assessment of these diverging perspectives on mobility may contribute to identify significant correlations between cultural and mobile processes toward a conceptualization of cultural hypermobility.

Nomadology refers to a style of critical thinking that seeks to expose and overcome the sedentary logic of state, science and civilization (Braidotti

1994; Deleuze and Guattari 1980). It denounces a categorical binary of civilization whereby the dweller is positively assessed over the wanderer, seen as menace, distortion and problem (Clifford 1997; Malkki 1992). Migration studies have inadvertently embodied the imperial bias: 'The point is obviously not to deny that displacement can be a shattering experience. It is rather this: our sedentarist assumptions about attachment to place leads us to define displacement not as a fact about sociopolitical context, but rather as an inner, pathological condition of the displaced' (Malkki 1992: 33). The privilege of fixity over mobility – of roots over routes – hinges on the issue of conventional modes of subjectivity: a dialectic of identification/alterity sustains a model of identity that constrains the self within rigid and exclusionary boundaries.[6]

While denouncing the moral premise of arboreal science, nomadology is also the theoretical counterpart of radical experiments that seek to undermine sedentary identity (see introductory anecdote, Pini 1997; Reynolds 1998). In neo-nomadic sites of experience, identity is ritually questioned as an apparatus of colonial domination whereby the self is encoded by references imposed from the outside. The imprisoning model of identity is denounced as totalitarian – hence, the provocative rhyme 'identitarian' (Braidotti 1994; Miller 1993; Deleuze and Guattari 1980; Foucault 1976). Foucault's valuation of transformation as a productive category of self-formation illustrates the nomadologic gesture to avert the closure of identity: 'Don't ask me who I am, or tell me to stay the same: that is the bureaucratic morality which keeps our papers in order' (Foucault 1972: 17; see also Foucault 1978). To note, the bureaucrat is the icon and agent of the sedentary State. Nomadology thus rethinks identity as 'always mobile and processual, partly self-construction, partly categorization by others, partly a condition, a status, a label, a weapon, a shield, a fund of memories, etc. It is a creolized aggregate composed through bricolage' (Malkki 1992: 37). Within this conception, nomadologic modes of representation replace the exclusionary binary 'either-or' with a logic of additive possibilities that 'synthesizes a multiplicity of elements without effacing their heterogeneity or hindering their potential for future rearranging (to the contrary)' (Masummi's preface to Deleuze 1980: xiii).

Both nomads and neo-nomads have deployed mobility as a tactic of evasion from dominant sedentary apparatuses. As such, while globalization tends to favor countercultures by undermining the biopower of the nation-state, neo-nomads emulate old patterns of pastoral nomadism. The discussion below unbundles some of these affinities, elaborating on how nomadism unfolds into nomadology. As an important remark, most studies on pastoral nomadism adopted in this chapter were chosen for their cross-cultural and generalist approach, yet some ethnographies and localized studies were also employed as control readings. My account on nomadism is not merely a work of plain description, but a rereading driven by current concerns with hypermobility and identity in a global age.

Traditional nomadism can be defined as mobile household communities that carry their means of production within a single ecological niche (Cribb 1991: 20; Khazanov 1984). By seasonally moving animals into better pastures, nomads can accumulate a larger livestock, resulting in more food, trading luxuries and prestige (Barfield 1993: 12). Likewise, neo-nomads (such as hippie traders, handcrafters, DJs, alternative therapists and smugglers) exercise their skills along the way, and traveling becomes a source of learning and charisma convertible into professional advantage (D'Andrea 2004; McKay 1996; Rao 1987). Displacement does not define nomadism if economic activities lie ahead or behind those on the move (such as in the case of labor migrants and businesspeople). Nomadic movement is defined by both economic goals and cultural motivations: 'In no case do nomads "wander." They know where they are going and why' (Barfield 1993: 12). Nomads value the ownership of goods and tools. Insofar as they remain able to move and use free spaces, they have little interest in owning or remaining attached to land (Barfield 1993: 193). Their deterritorialized relation with space is a central feature of nomadic culture and mentality, one that reinforces their will to move.

However, political structures of central government have historically curbed autonomous movement. Intermittent repression of Turkic tribes by Central Asian states until the 1980s, state subsidies for the sedentarization of Bedouins in Egypt and Israel during the 1960s, and difficulties imposed by neo-liberal Britain upon gypsies and 'New Age travelers' since the 1970s illustrate the coercive drives of nation-states to control nomadic populations (McKay 1996; Cribb 1991). As a generalization, nomads face more difficulties whenever central states concentrate power. Less mobile pastoralists (due to livestock composition) are more vulnerable to state control. These experiences thus indicate a positive correlation between mobility and autonomy.

Nomadic modes of production are oscillatory and dependent on larger societies (Barfield 1993; Rao 1987; Khazanov 1984). Nomadism's relation to 'the outside world,' as Anatoly Khazanov puts it, is pivotal for understanding that it has arisen from both ecological and politico-economic pressures (Abu-Lughod 1999: 42; Khazanov 1984: xxvii, 95). Archaeological evidence suggests that nomadism probably emerged as a specialization that stemmed from complex sedentary societies (Barfield 1993: 4; Cribb 1991: 10; Khazanov 1984: 85). In this sense, agriculture and urbanism anteceded pastoral nomadism, as flexible capitalism and gentrification anteceded neo-nomadism. In this context, relations between nomads and dwellers are asymmetrical. While constituting the core of armies and extortive bands, 'nomads need cities for necessities of life, whereas sedentary populations need them for convenience and luxuries' (Khazanov 1984: 82). Western neo-nomads, likewise, adhere to 'luxury' fields (art, fashion, wellness and spirituality), which have, nonetheless, gained prominence in high-modern societies.

Neo-nomadic formations have emerged under varying historical conditions. For example, whereas the 1960s countercultural exodus resulted from affluent technocratic societies against which it rebelled (Roszak 1995), the late 1980s rave diaspora sprang from the economic depression and police repression of neo-liberal agendas (Reynolds 1998; McKay 1996). 'In the 1960s the young dropped out, in the 1980s they are dropped out' (McKay 1996: 52). Despite its dependent nature, nomadism, in both traditional and post-traditional forms, has been highly malleable in adapting to turbulent conditions and economic uncertainties, such as those that are now characteristic of globalization:

> Nomadism with its flexible multi-resource economic strategy is ideally suited to the unpredictable environment [. . .]. External factors such as trade routes, governments or states are grist to the mill; they are the necessary substrate. [Nomads] change because the economic and political climate changes, and nomadism is still the best method of adapting and surviving.
>
> (Lancaster and Lancaster 1998: 32)

Nomads likely are the most ancient 'global fluid' (to use Urry's term) on the planet. Old and new stories that integrate mobility and marginality provide valuable insights into an understanding of globalization predicaments. Nomads are not the desert hermits that sedentary imaginaries have romanticized. Their conduct is informed by strict codes of reciprocity and belonging that nest them in social networks indispensable for survival (Barfield 1993: 205). Yet, more than in most traditional sedentary societies, there has been considerable room for agency and decision-making among nomads. In fact, the central feature of nomadism is the 'maximization of unit autonomy' (Abu-Lughod 1999: 79):

> Each household is responsible for managing its own resources. [. . .] The ability to move away from people with whom you are not getting along [. . .] is one of the great psychological advantages of being a nomad. It also highlights the common belief that once a household establishes its autonomy, its success or failure is individual. [. . .] And the price of failure is not only economic ruin, but in many cases the loss of tribal identity itself.
>
> (Barfield 1993: 104)

A feeling of pride emerges from such representations of freedom, which is far more important than land property and other riches. Despite their dependence on economic exchanges with sedentary societies, nomads do believe in the superiority of their way of life: 'In the eyes of nomads, an agriculturalist is a slave because he is tied to one place and is enslaved by his own arduous labor, unable to resist them in any proper way'

(Khazanov 1984: 160). Bedouins have been admired for 'taking orders from no one' (Barfield 1993: 64). The nomad's 'supreme value is autonomy, [. . .] the standard by which status is measured and social hierarchy determined' (Abu-Lughod 1999: 78–9). Such pride has even motivated Arab statesmen to claim nomadic ancestry, a populist gesture facilitated by 'genealogical amnesia,' which is an ancient mechanism for forging alliances (Ginat and Khazanov 1998; Khazanov 1984: 143). Contrary to the belief of state and development officials, nomads avoid being sedentarized, and much less so assimilated, even when economic gain is promised: 'Sedentarization means that stereotypes of thinking, behavior, a traditional system of values and a traditional way of life are broken. [. . .] [It] tears the nomad from a traditional system of social ties and deprives him of important lines of defence' (Khazanov 1984: 199; see also Abu-Lughod 1999: 43–4).

Nomadic women are also self-represented as being more autonomous and virtuous than sedentary ones (Davis-Kimball 2003; Abu-Lughod 1999: 46; Barfield 1993). As tight controls would hinder the economic efficiency of mobile households, nomadic women live by values of modesty and autonomy. In the Bedouin case, despite being theoretically subordinate to men, 'some women can achieve more honor than some men,' as 'the system [of veiling] is flexible, leaving room for women to make judgments about relative status and even to negotiate status' (Abu-Lughod 1999: 118, 163). In contrast with female dwellers, 'they are never utterly dependent of their husbands, and, having alternative paths to support and respect, they rely less on a strategy [. . .] for security than do women in other patricentered systems, such as the Chinese' (p. 149). Because of that, the sedentarization of nomadic societies often results in the deterioration of the socio-economic status of women (Abu-Lughod 1999: 73; Curling and Llewelyn-Davies 1974). Nonetheless, in any measure, 'the status of women in pastoral societies was generally higher than their sedentary sisters' (Barfield 1993: 15).

Nomadic women – both pastoral and postmodern – often embody warrior-like values and dispositions of honor, superiority, and disinterest in romantic matters (Abu-Lughod 1999: 46, 153; Barfield 1993: 146). In a mythological vein, they have been feared as brave warriors, as Hippocrates and Herodotus narrate about Sarmatian women who participated in mounted raids and could only marry after killing a man in battle (Barfield 1993: 146; Davis-Kimball 2003). In contexts of postmodernist subcultures and predatory neo-liberal capitalism, Techno women cultivate wildness, toughness and dexterity as impressive personality traits. Wearing combat garments and dark sunglasses, they ride potent motorcycles down dangerous roads in India, thus incarnating a motorized version of the Amazon.

While sedentary societies generally fear nomads as untrustworthy and irrational, more ambivalent segments of urban dwellers imagine such mobile beings as veritable embodiments of a holistic self and wholesome community. The impersonalizing and fragmenting character of modern life has motivated discontented intellectuals, from Romantics to post-modernists, to praise the nomad for mastering a variety of social roles: a shepherd and warrior, a worker and storyteller: 'nomads already in some measure exemplify that multiplicity of roles, that overcoming of the division of labour, that multi-faceted human personality, which Marx in the *German Ideology* predicted only for the liberated man of the future' (Gellner 1984: xxi). Contemporarily, nomadism stands as an emblem for oppositional segments of the urban youth in search of charisma, meaning and togetherness (St John 2004; Comaroff and Comaroff 2000).

Paradoxically, the holistic shaping of the self is often accompanied by experiments of self-shattering effect. In Western countercultural sites, the modern identitarian self must be undermined before the holistic self-shaping may take place. This is usually carried out by means of 'intoxicating elements of orgiastic sensuality' (Weber 1913): music, drugs, dance, sex – devices that exacerbate the senses and overtake reason. Deleuze and Guattari noted that, 'architecture and cooking have an apparent affinity with the State, whereas music and drugs have differen-tial traits that place them on the side of the nomadic machine' (Deleuze and Guattari 1980: 402). *Psychic deterritorialization* is thus unleashed as 'spiritual journeys effected without relative movement but in intensity, in one place: these are part of nomadism' (p. 381). In collective rituals led by cathartic therapists, New Age healers or Techno trance DJs, frames of memory, cognition and self-identity are shattered in the realm of the trau-matic/sublime, wherein the self is exposed and imploded as a heteronomic prison, in part social violence, in part biographic illusion (Braidotti on Foucault, 1994: 12; Foucault 1978).

It is in the context of these postidentitarian exercises that 'becoming minoritarian' – a pivotal aspect of counter-hegemonic subjectivities – must be understood. By emphasizing the macro-social dimension of violence, Rosi Braidotti ignores the actual target of nomadic violence (Braidotti 1994: 26). Likewise, Christopher Miller misses the point when he criticizes Deleuze and Guattari for overlooking the physical violence perpetrated by Western African nomads during totemic rituals of 'becoming leopard' (Miller 1993: 30). Considering the force and target of countercultural experiments (cathartic therapies, queer sexualities, radical sports, collective psychedelia, mystical spiritualities, etc.), Miller's argument must be re-deployed: neo-nomads channel the destructive power of 'becoming animal' against the subject itself. By unleashing visceral forces against the cog-nitive-affective-behavioral structure of the subject, the identitarian fortress of the self is pounded and undermined, and recoded under the principle of multiplicity (chromatic variation). But metamorphosis is never a guar-antee of subjective or ethical freedom, as the lines of flight that open up the realm of creativity are also the ones that may degrade in lines of

death, which reterritorialize in fixity, alienation or self-destruction (Deleuze
and Guattari 1980: 513).

The derailment of subjectivities may interfere with institutional apparatuses, as nomadologic practice de-signifies the legitimacy of state control
over bodies and populations (biopower). However, as the absolute erad-
ication of transgression is impossible, these experiments are deflected and
marginalized, while exclusionary codes are reinforced through the very
process of suppression. The ritual exploration of the postidentitarian self
is then confined to secret societies, to whom orgiastic devices remain as
catalysts of problematization and transcendence of the fixed subject. Both
as tactical move and systemic effect, the postidentitarian self more likely
reemerges from a position of marginality, whereby metamorphosis may
operate more intensely. According to Deleuze and Guattari:

> Minorities are objectively definable states, states of language, ethnicity,
> or sex with their own ghetto territorialities, but they must also be
> thought of as seeds, crystals of becoming whose value is to trigger
> uncontrollable movements and deterritorializations of the mean of
> majority. [. . .] The figure to which we are referring is continuous vari-
> ation, as an amplitude that continually oversteps the representative
> threshold of the majoritarian standard, by excess or default. In erecting
> the figure of a universal minoritarian consciousness, one addresses
> powers of becoming that belong to a different realm from that of
> Power and Domination. [. . .] Becoming-minoritarian as the universal
> figure of consciousness is called autonomy. It is certainly not by using
> a minor language as a dialect, by regionalizing or ghettoizing, that
> one becomes revolutionary; rather, by using a number of minority
> elements, by connecting, conjugating them, one invents a specific,
> unforeseen, autonomous becoming.
>
> (Deleuze and Guattari 1980: 106)

Autonomous becoming is the principle of the war machine, a political
figuration that must be considered in anthropological and nomadologic
terms. According to pastoralist studies, nomads congregate in tribal con-
federations as a response to external pressures. The Zulu expansion during
the nineteenth century was motivated by the Dutch–British colonization of
Southern Africa (Barfield 1993: 47). Yet, it is the thirteenth-century Mongol
empire that epitomizes the war machine. How do peaceful herdsmen
become terrifying warriors? How did a tiny population of pastoralists con-
quer both China and Russia? Main historical conditions include the relative prosperity of the Chinese empire as well as the unification of Mongol
tribes under Temujin's leadership; nonetheless, it was the rational milita-
rization of the mounted archer that secured Mongol supremacy over Asia
for over four centuries (Turnbull 2003; Torday 1997; Barfield 1993).
According to Deleuze and Guattari, the mounted archer is a paradigmatic

example of a machinic assemblage: inertial elements – animal, man, tool – come together under certain circumstances resulting in extraordinary effects: the continental conquest. At the realm of neo-nomadism, 'raving' also functions as a machinic assemblage (of music-body-drugs-dance) that emerges under certain conditions (of digitalization, hypermobility, reflexivity, neo-liberalism), resulting in the undermining of the identitarian self (D'Andrea 2004). Resonating with globalization as an eschatology that derails cognitive abilities (Jameson 1991), Techno is the first counterculture to have emerged under the direct impact of global processes.

In sum, the neo-nomad instantiates the action of the postidentitarian predicament upon the self, its identity and subjectivity, recoded under conditions of globalization (Braidotti 1994: 1). Interpreting this action, at the level of molecular aggregations, neo-nomadism develops as a war machine that opposes the state, unleashing forces of chromatic variation that breaks down molar formations, deterritorializing identities into the smooth space of multiplicity. The tracing of a line of flight opens up the possibility of new experiences of the self and sociality, usually arising from self-marginalized sites of modernity, yet developing from its center toward the periphery and then back in an oscillatory pattern. The war machine is not war but uncontrollable mobility that creates a smooth space of creativity, beyond rather than against the state.

> The war machine was the invention of the nomad, because it is in its essence the constitutive element of smooth space, the occupation of this space, displacement within this space, and the corresponding composition of people: this is its sole and veritable positive object (*nomos*). Make the desert, the steppe, grow; do not depopulate it, quite the contrary. If war necessarily results, it is because the war machine collides with States and cities, as forces (of striation) opposing its positive object [. . .]. It is at this point that the war machine becomes war: annihilate the forces of the State, destroy the State-form.
>
> (Deleuze and Guattari 1980: 417)

Nomadic ethnography: methodological challenges

The empirical horizon of this research derived from a multi-sited mobile fieldwork which, assuming Ibiza and Goa as its analytical nodes, has focused on the social and ritual life of expressive expatriates that live and travel within global circuits of countercultural practice, contemporarily embodied in Techno and New Age formations, and paradoxically enmeshed in local politico-economical apparatuses of state and tourism. I have conceptualized these people through the notion of expressive expatriation, in order to avoid essentialist notions of migrant community or youth subculture (as bounded fixed entities), and to enable a direct assessment of cultural patterns of globalization and counterculture, as outlined in previous sections. The research orientation is thus both idiographic and nomothetic, examining specific empirical phenomena, in order to illuminate and understand wider processes of cultural globalization.

As its basic hypothesis, this research proposes the existence of a globalized counterculture: mobile formations constituted by transnational flows of subjects, practices and imaginaries self-identified as cosmopolitan yet critical of regimes of the nation-state, market and morality. More specifically, Techno and New Age formations have been analyzed as ritual sites of experience and meaning that dramatize how globalization processes affect subjectivity forms, which tend to become more fluidic, metamorphic and cosmopolitan.

The basic methodological question is, therefore, how the postidentitarian effects of cultural hypermobility can be empirically identified, analyzed, measured, interpreted and generalized. Due to the disembedded nature of social life under conditions of globalization, such transnational fluidic formations cannot be properly captured within the highly localized strategies of conventional ethnography (Appadurai 1996: 52). Arjun Appadurai has proposed the need of a 'macro-ethnography of translocal sites' in order to address the new role of social imagination, which partially overlaps with a mapping of transnational formations dubbed 'scapes' (p. 33). Yet, despite the insightfulness of global metaphors (cyborg, scape, nomad, rhizome, etc.), 'there have been no guides for designing research that would exemplify and fulfill such visions. This requires a more literal discussion of methodological issues, such as how to construct the multi-sited space through which the ethnographer traverses' (Marcus 1998: 89).

Some specific methodological issues must be considered in the ethnography of hypermobile formations. First, taking on my critique of global notions outlined above, global studies still need to integrate meaning and scale into a model that is capable of addressing the topic of subjective interiorities under conditions of globalization (Povinelli and Chauncey 1999). Second, global nomadism must be understood less for its multi-sitedness and more for its fluidic and deterritorialized nature. As such, a strategy of analysis must integrate displacement and deterritorialization as main processes in the production of subjectivities and localities. Yet, third, a research on cultural hypermobility is also challenged at the levels of data collection and representation, since academic requirements of systematization often contradict the intrinsically fluidic, contingent and metamorphic nature of neo-nomadic patterns. The activity of data collection must become, accordingly, more flexible, informal and context-dependent, partly mimicking mobile phenomena in their own suppleness:

> The key to doing research in complex transnational spaces devolves less from methods, multidisciplinary teams, or theoretical frameworks – although these are, of course, important – than from the suppleness of imagination. Transnational migrants are exceedingly creative in

finding regulatory loopholes, resolving daunting financial problems, or more globally, making their way through tough transnational spaces that require imaginative and decisive solutions to ongoing economic, political, social, and legal problems. If we can appropriate some of that epistemological suppleness, we will understand a method that will change the way we do anthropology.

(Stoller 1999: 92)

Having these issues in mind, I have sought to develop a methodology that tries to integrate a nomadic sensibility toward routes and rituals of mobility, with a notion of macro-ethnography that deploys methods of multi-sitedness and translocality in context (Marcus 1998; Clifford 1997; Appadurai 1996). The result is a nomadic ethnography that tends to undermine the excessively localized yet disengaged strategies that characterize conventional fieldwork: 'These [new] techniques might be understood as practices of construction through (preplanned or opportunistic) movement and of tracing within different settings [. . .] given an initial conceptual identity that turns out to be contingent and malleable as one traces it' (Marcus 1998: 90).

Using the fast car race as a metaphor, the ethnographer must expand her perception of movement by going beyond the spectator gallery. By engaging as a pilot, the analyst will richly perceive and experience the trembling of slowly moving entities running at high speed through blurred surroundings. By engaging *movement within the movement*, this analytics of hypermobility displaces the geocentric (Ptolemaic) paradigm of mainstream anthropology in favor of a relativist (Einsteinian) perception of spatiality. This investigative disposition requires more than applying the formula of 'following the people' (Marcus, p. 90). Nomadic ethnography includes multi-site comparison, not as serial units of analysis, but as 'a function of the fractured, discontinuous plane of movement and discovery among sites' (p. 86). In simpler words of pragmatic effect and conceptual repercussion, in addition to traveling toward the native, the analyst needs to travel with and like the native, sharing positions, perspectives and sites while on the move and throughout the uncontrollable and shifting circumstances of hypermobile field research.

Even though each research project is tailored according to more specific questions, some general procedures are likely to recur in nomadic ethnography, more so during initial stages of fieldwork. Agreeing with George Marcus, this type of research 'is designed around chains, paths, threads, conjunctions, or juxtapositions of location in which the ethnographer establishes some form of literal, physical presence with an explicit logic of association or connection among sites that in fact defines the argument of the ethnography' (Marcus 1998: 90). The researcher must thus consider the *links* among places, peoples and experiences, considered as heuristic resources that may lead to a disclosure of underlying patterns, motivations and intervenient conditions that constitute mobile formations. Spatial and cultural sites can be thus visualized as centrifugal vortexes ('powerful and fluid currents') by which local and translocal intertwinements can be more easily detected. Although seemingly complicated at first, this approach compensates the initial effort by facilitating the scope of choices and inferences in a second plateau of investigation.

As a general orientation, the analysis must assess political economies and socio-cultural processes that envelop the hypermobile phenomena under consideration. At the political–economic level, it is necessary to investigate what is the role of material contexts in enabling and reproducing neo-nomadic formations; how these formations participate in such contexts; how different actors under variegated interests appropriate space; and how translocal (global and national) forces enable and constrain proximate contexts. At the cultural level, it must be asked what is the nature of motivations and meanings that regiment subjects in hypermobile formations in given locales and circuits; how specific sites of experience and meaning sustain their everyday life; and how their ritual practices entail forms of subjectivity, intimacy and sociability enmeshed with mobility and other global processes. In order to answer these questions, a host of sites, scales and links must be considered in the design arrangement and the implementation of the methodology, which will be structured at three ethnographic levels:

1 *Ethnography of mobile subjectivities, lifestyles and identities*: in each geographic site, the fieldworker must identify and translate sub-scenes, practices and imaginaries that constitute hypermobile formations locally. Through analysis of ritual and social interactions, the goal is to identify forms of subjectivity and sociality as well as the categories that frame experience and interpretation.

2 *Socio-economic contextualization of mobile scenes, subjects and communities*: in each geographic site, the fieldworker must locate neo-nomadic formations in socio-economic, political and environmental contexts, both at local and translocal levels. It is necessary to understand how economies (e.g. tourism, leisure, media), major moralities and state surveillance affect trajectories and strategies of mobile subjects and deterritorialized communities. This picture defines the vertical integration of neo-nomadism in a given locale.

3 *Translocal ethnography*: the goal here is to identify the fluidic and connective nature of hypermobile formations across different spaces (two, at most three, geographic locations), in order to verify their horizontal integration beyond given locales. The fieldworker must identify which and how translocal flows, circuits and webs sustain hypermobile subjects and communities. The degree of overlap or disjuncture between the vertical and horizontal pictures discloses how neo-nomadic formations are integrated locally and globally.

In this book, methods of data collection were geared toward generating knowledge about the biographic, subcultural and contextual dimensions of transnational countercultures, as an empirical phenomenon and a conceptual instance of cultural globalization. These datasets therefore seek to provide empirical elements whose analysis may illuminate the nature of related agencies, meanings and structures. The methods mostly employed in this research can be qualified as follows.

Archival search

Archival search of primary, press and scholarly sources were carried out to inform other fieldwork procedures, and was particularly useful before and after the fieldwork. Ibicencan and Goan newspapers, Techno and New Age magazines and audio-visual materials, scholarly articles and technical reports were systematically clipped and indexed into a bibliographic management software. Although open to novelties, three basic topics remained central to this inquiry: (1) narratives about expressive expatriation (trajectories, lifestyles and imaginaries); (2) relations between alternative formations and political-economic institutions defining contexts of constraint and deterritorialization; and (3) transnational circuits through which alternative elements circulate, thus seeking to identify patterns of mobility and fixity.

Interview methods

According to field observations and other studies, formal interviewing methods may actually hinder data collection, depending on the topic of analysis and circumstances surrounding the ethnographer-informant rapport (Saldanha 1999; Stoller 1999). In order to secure good inflows of information, I conducted mostly unstructured and informal interviews, which were often resumed along random encounters, and always transcribed as soon as possible. I sought to detect spatiotemporal itineraries, economic strategies and life orientations that constitute countercultural and expatriate formations. Information was consolidated in order to evince patterns of social network and native categories. In this connection, I frequently interrogated their opinions about visual and audio artifacts, both countercultural and popular ones, as a way of identifying the native's point of view.

Ritual analysis

Participant observation in Techno and New Age rituals was a main method of data collection in order to examine the multi-layered interrelations among subjectivity, counterculture and globalization, in terms of social structure and experience. Conceptualized as dramatic sites of cultural analysis, I attended holistic centers, nightclubs, Techno parties (raves) and hippie markets, seeking to identify spatiotemporal narratives, performance and interactivity. In specific rituals, I observed how key characters (therapists and DJs) interacted with the audiences seeking to identify relations of power and knowledge, as well as corporeality, affection and identity. These datasets contributed to address the nature of subjectivity and sociality forms prevailing within transnational countercultures.

Network analysis

By envisioning Ibiza and Goa as strategic lenses into global countercultures, I sought to map the spatiotemporal flows of subjects, practices, objects and imaginaries outlining the shape and identity of global circuits. I located their trajectories by means of interviews, follow-up (mostly email) correspondence and by traveling with them. The goal was to identify nodes, timings and periodicities that they adopt for moving and resting, in addition to underlying motivations and strategies. By tracking a series of individual trajectories (via first or third person reports), I was able to detect recurrences which probabilistically outline a global map of alternative sites and cycles. I paid particular attention to how mobile subjects manage economic budgets (at daily, seasonal, yearly, and life cycles) and participate in local and translocal environments and networks. These datasets contributed to assess the possibilities and conditions that enable molecular trajectories of mobility within the molar blocks and cracks of sedentary society in a global age.

Book overview

Perhaps it is not surprising that an ethnography of hypermobility would combine thick description with travelogue as its main narrative genre. Although any research enterprise comprises a retrospective construction which coadunates a priori objectives of inquiry with an a posteriori review of empirical results, specific events in the empirical and methodological horizons may confer a distinct shape to ethnographic representation. In this book, rather than reclustering datasets according to discrete topics of analysis, the multiple encounters between ethnographer and subjects, places and situations are presented in a way that mostly reflects the actual chronology of field engagements in space and time. Each chapter is thus based on a geographical location (Ibiza, Pune or Goa) where sub-sites (Techno and New Age) and themes (biographies, scenes, contexts and ideologies) are examined.

This genealogy of field discoveries is very useful in devising an adequate methodology for scrutinizing hypermobile formations. As such, it is necessary to foreground field engagements and the micro-decisions implied, as they actually occurred, in order to evince how they impact on the ongoing assessment of research strategies, thus corresponding to a logic of investigation that is simultaneously rational and improvisational. In other words, the genealogical thread induces an archaeology of cultural patterns related to the effects of globalization upon self-identity and sociality forms, as verified and anticipated in the transnational countercultures of expressive expatriates.

At a very basic level, the book seeks to provide an unmediated account of global countercultures and their proximate contexts. For a simple reason, this move is necessary because, despite their influential interrelations with mainstream societies, neo-nomadic formations remain largely unknown in and outside academia. In this connection, this geneological-archeological travelogue seems to be the narrative genre that best reflects the need of a proximate interpretive account about hypermobile formations as a veritable 'total social fact,' to paraphrase Marcel Mauss. This representational strategy seeks to enable an organic perception of the spatiotemporality as restructured by cultural hypermobility, while reflecting the rhizomatic and fluidic nature of globalized formations. In addition, it provides an ontology of countercultural subjectivity by which a sedentary subject becomes a neo-nomad: minoritarian and metamorphic.

Besides this introductory chapter, the book comprises four ethnographic chapters and a conclusion. The current Chapter 1 is titled 'Neo-Nomadism: a Theory of Postidentitarian Mobility in the Global Age,' which, as it was seen, develops a theoretical discussion on how hypermobility engenders new forms of subjectivity and identity predicated on a pattern of chromatic variation. As notions of network, diaspora and cosmopolitanism preclude a better understanding of emerging forms of cultural hypermobility, I propose that tropes of fluidity, rootlessness and aesthetic sensibility must be reassessed through the prism of nomadism, enabling an alternative way of understanding global mobility as a trend and predicament. To that end, the chapter is developed upon a dialogue between the anthropology of pastoral nomadism and the philosophy of nomadology, suggesting neo-nomadism as an *ideal-type of postidentitarian mobility*, a heuristic device that describes and measures the interrelations of spatial displacement, psychosocial deterritorialization and cosmopolitanism. The nomothetic assessment of how such categories behave then seeks to shed light on how deterritorialized phenomena imbricates with the plane of locality and toward limited generalization. The term 'neo-nomad,' in sum, designates a social type and a concept that refers to the loose institutionalization of hypermobile strategies and post-identities in sites of intensified globalization. The need of empirical engagement with such conceptual framework leads us to the following ethnographic chapter.

Chapter 2 is titled 'Expressive Expatriates in Ibiza: Hypermobility as Countercultural Practice and Identity.' It focuses on Euro Latin-American expatriates who migrated to Ibiza island in order to shape an alternative lifestyle. The chapter identifies their economic strategies, biographic trajectories and social practices, all of which coalesce in a cosmopolitan culture of expressive individualism. By examining an economy of representations about expatriate life, the island and mainstream life, this mostly descriptive chapter provides the first stepping stone into the world of global countercultures, and introduces the main empirical argument of research: expressive expatriates embody hypermobility and expressivity as pivotal counter-hegemonic practices of subjectivity and sociality formation in tune with the effects of globalization. A contradiction, however, complicates this picture: their presence on the island is a magnet that attracts a much larger number of sedentary peoples, such as tourists and migrants, interrelating with the development of socio-economic and state apparatuses that, at a second moment, threaten the sustainability of alternative sites, practices and imaginaries – a phenomenon that leads to the next chapter.

Chapter 3 is titled 'The Hippie and Club Scenes in Ibiza's Tourism Industry.' By focusing on the political economies of entertainment that structure the island's socio-economic life, this chapter elaborates on the paradox of the commodification of countercultures. To that end, a structural analysis of hippie markets and nightclubs is provided within the contexts of mass tourism and modernization. In addition, critical evidence is provided about the transnational character of these alternative scenes, both locally and abroad. Expressive expatriates regularly travel to exotic locations and their ambivalently valued homelands in a nomadic-like triangulation. In particular, they value India highly, both in terms of the exotic commodities that are brought to Ibiza's boutiques and hippie markets, as well as in terms of symbolic references to spiritual and body practices, as instances of a reflexive aesthetics of existence. Considering the material and symbolic significance of romanticized (non-Western) cultures within expressive expatriate formations, I was compelled to take my fieldwork to India.

Chapter 4 is titled '*Osho International Meditation Resort*: Subjectivity, Counterculture and Spiritual Tourism in Pune,' based on ethnographic fieldwork about a quasi-religious organization, fashioned as a 'meditation resort,' located in Pune (India). Ibiza expatriates have been attending the place, in a frequency that defies statistical chance. There they engage with meditation and therapy practices centered on the radical cultivation of the self, as elements of what can be termed more generally as countercultural spiritualities. The resort is inspired by the teachings of Osho, formerly known as Bhagwan Rajneesh, who died in 1990. After an outline of the organizational structure, typical groups and biographies, the chapter analyzes main ritual practices that disclose core tensions in the formation of Western subjectivities. Upon evidence, I examine two contradictions: first, how the organization simultaneously promotes and controls expressive behavior, and, second, how countercultural therapies fail to intervene in non-Western subjects. These conundrums are considered within the context of a gentrified commodification of Osho resort (an 'ashram' turned into a 'commune' and then into a posh 'resort'). However, dissenting voices have broken apart from this official orientation and seasonally gather in 'underground' sites of transgression and illegality located in northern Goa, leading to the subject of the next chapter.

Chapter 5 is titled 'Techno Trance Tribalism in Goa: The Elementary Forms of Nomadic Spirituality.' It identifies the main economic, social, biographic and cultural elements that constitute the 'Goa trance scene' in Goa, known as the global capital of Techno trance counterculture, attracting thousands of 'trance freaks' from all over the world each winter season. The chapter examines the extent to which such formations instantiate and illuminate issues of mobility and marginality in relation to contexts of globalization: the contact zone and global countercultures. The chapter thus analyzes how expatriates have to negotiate with local actors and forces in order to territorialize the trance scene in Goa, and consequently to enable the ritualization of alternative subjectivities, identities and socialities. More specifically, I argue that a trance party is a ritual practice whose patina of sacredness dangerously problematizes the modern self by means of a *nomadic spirituality*, basic category that sustains meanings and practices of a postidentitarian lifestyle. Finally, the chapter opens up for a discussion about the interrelations between spatial and subjective deterritorialization, by assessing field evidence with seminal studies on the psychiatry of travel, and under the light of Deleuzian schizoanalysis.

This study is located within global and critical studies, which I attempt to integrate by means of an empirical and conceptual investigation of countercultural expatriation. As such, in the context of globalization, Techno and New Age formations, particularly those of expressive expatriates, are assessed as globalized phenomena that express and entail the socio-spatiotemporal disjuncture of globalization: mobility, digitalism, multiculturalism and reflexivity. In specific, the investigation of the fluid cosmopolitan features of expressive expatriates requires the development of new methodologies of translocality and network mapping which I have sought to outline in this chapter.

In the context of modernity, these countercultural formations are examined as sites of experience, meaning and struggle that contradictorily resist and reflect modern regimes of subjectivity formation (see discussion on biopower and aesthetics above). The hypothesis is that Techno and New Age coalesce in a counter-apparatus whose practices foster metamorphic and post-national forms of subjectivity, identity and sociality, as instantiated in semi-peripheral sites of aesthetic-erotic experimentation, such as the cosmopolitan pockets of Ibiza and Goa. This counter-hegemonic apparatus seeks to depart from the modern regimes of the market, state and morality that forge the modern subject of sexuality (desire, discipline and consumption), heralding the possibility of alternative experiential–institutional–ideological formations, here termed 'post-sexuality.' In sum, I attempt to examine how the hypermobile and expressive practices of neo-nomadism refer to a field of possibilities, contradictions and agencies that is in tune with the rise of complex globalization.

2 Expressive expatriates in Ibiza

Hypermobility as countercultural practice and identity

'*Si vols ser algú, acudeix a Eivissa.*'
'If you want to be somebody, go to Ibiza.'
                    El Temps magazine, 2000

Introduction: 'fluidity of experiences' in Ibiza

Summer 1998, Barcelona – my pre-fieldwork explorations on transnational networks of alternative spirituality in Spain were coming to a standstill. Just as in any other big city, New Age practices, artifacts and symbols have become innocuous commodities for a gentrified middle class, losing its original drive to re-form subjectivities beyond religious dogma and modern fragmentation. However, while I reassessed my field engagements, I also noticed a rising culture of electronic dance music which excited segments of the urban youth in dynamic cities such as Barcelona, Paris and Chicago. As these enthusiasts claimed, Techno culture heralds the possibility of self-emancipation by means of the new technologies of digital art, manifested in multimedia dance events characterized by their effervescent nature and the digitalization of spiritual tropes. Upon these pieces of evidence, I questioned to what extent Techno and New Age would share the same cultural space dedicated to issues of self-formation in a globalized world. In terms of research operationalization, I was told that Ibiza would be the best place in Spain for conducting this type of investigation.

A few days later, I attended a yoga teleconference in uptown Barcelona, and, by chance, met Nora, a yoga teacher and American expatriate who, by sheer coincidence, lived in Ibiza. As I mentioned my interests in developing a field study on the island, she agreed with my ideas, and noted that there was a 'guest room' in her apartment whose informal reservation had been canceled. I thus extended my pre-fieldwork into Ibiza, and found an extremely rich site for investigating the interrelations between countercultures and globalization.

Ibiza is a small island in the Spanish Mediterranean, long imagined as a 'utopian paradise.' The 1969 cult film *More* (with soundtrack by the

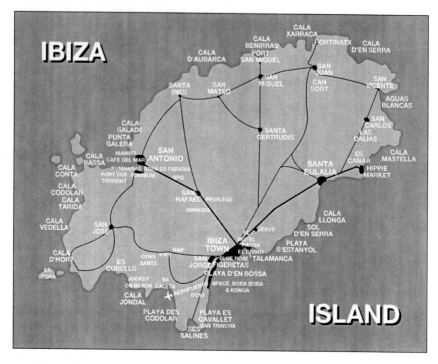

Figure 2.1 Ibiza map – the main road from Eivissa to Sant Antoni extends for 14 km.

Source: Courtesy of Ronnie and Stephen Randall.

band Pink Floyd) depicts Ibiza as an atemporal garden where young bodies explore hedonistic pleasures in unimaginable freedom. In addition, Ibiza is 'the clubbing capital of the world,' featuring the largest and the best nightclubs on the planet (Dancestar 2004; Guinness 2003). With a population of 108,000 inhabitants, Ibiza socio-economic life is largely dependent on tourism, which brings about 1.7 million visitors each year (Govern de les Illes Balears – Conselleria de Turisme 2006, 2003; Govern de les Illes Balears – IBAE 2004). In anticipation of the detailed statistical data provided below, it must be noted that, along with many social indicators, Ibiza features one of the highest per-capita income rates of Spain. On the other hand, mass tourism resulted in intense urbanization and ecological degradation of its resources and landscape. As a result, the international press has come to benchmark Ibiza ambivalently, either as an exciting paradise or as a saturated tourist trap. This begs the question of why, among so many tour destinations, has Ibiza become an index of (a threatened) paradise on earth.

Ibiza's demographic profile is revealing. About half the island's population is non-Ibicencan, mostly working-class people from mainland Spain,

Latin America and Africa. As they emphasize, economic advantage is their basic motivation for migrating to the island, where they mostly work in the construction and hospitality sectors. A segment of wealthy European citizens, mostly Germans and British, purchase their 'second homes' in Ibiza, while isolating themselves in ethnocentric enclaves, criticized by the Spanish press for their limited interest in local culture. For many of them, Spain merely provides good real-estate opportunities coupled with the notion of 'home-plus-sun.'

However, another segment of foreign residents do not fit any of these migrant or expatriate types. They came neither for better wages nor for reproducing their nation in sunny lands. Quite the contrary, they left their homelands in order to shape a singular lifestyle, by which they attempt to integrate labor, leisure and spirituality in a cosmopolitan and expressive fashion. In fact, many have abandoned favorable material conditions (income, career, prestige) in their homelands and accepted a new order of instabilities that characterize alternative careers in semi-peripheral locations, as long as they feel that they can actualize cherished values of autonomy, experimentation and expression. These 'expressive expatriates' become hippie traders, handcrafters, musicians, DJs, party promoters, body therapists, yoga teachers, gardeners, food artisans, spiritual healers, drug dealers, tour guides, alternative entrepreneurs, etc. Most are drawn from educated, middle or upper social strata in advanced societies, often well connected to artistic, cultural and economic elites both locally and abroad.

In their biographies, experiences of mobility are significant and usually related with some cosmopolitan interest. As a result, nationalities are fading references in the increasingly hyphenated mosaic of mixing citizenships. Many expressive expatriates are born of bohemian or artistic parents of differing nationalities, hold dual or multiple citizenships, and speak various languages fluently. Their cosmopolitan taste often verges on naive xenophilia, as they report intense experiences with traveling, propelled not by strict business interest but rather by a personal quest frequently referred to as 'spiritual' or 'existential.' Many have lived in three or more countries, including long stays in South Asia or Latin America. India in particular stands as a very important symbolic, and even material reference. Mobility thus seems to lie at the core of how expressive expatriates cultivate self-identities and lifestyles.

Quantitatively, they comprise a smaller share of the 12 per cent of non-Spanish inhabitants who are officially recognized as residing on the island (Govern de les Illes Balears – IBAE 1996). Nevertheless, the following observation requires our attention:

> Demographic data do not reflect the fluidity of experiences taking place in Ibiza. The island has seen a quantity of foreigners that is much higher than what a census can register. [. . .] Many travelers

stop by Ibiza and Formentera for undetermined periods, while many others voluntarily have chosen the islands to enjoy a different lifestyle.
(Rozenberg 1990: 117)

In this chapter, I examine this 'fluidity of experiences' as a result of transnational mobility and aesthetic reflexivity which are constitutive features of neo-nomadic lifestyles. As such, I seek to demonstrate that mobility is more than spatial displacement for expressive expatriates: it also corresponds to reflexive forms of subjectivity formation that seek to eschew dominant apparatuses of the nation-state, market and society (biopower – see theoretical discussion in Chapter 1, pp. 17–23). In addition, I propose that Ibiza's problematic modernization in part derives from the entwinement between globalization and countercultural formations on the island. In other words, Ibiza's utopian imaginary has arisen from the continuous presence of these *self-marginalized* subjects who inadvertently occupy the *center* of its creative life, an expatriate populace that crafts much of the seductive charm of the island. As such, 'the social study of Ibiza is paradigmatic for those who interrogate the development of contemporary societies' (Rozenberg 1990: 3).

This chapter is divided into four main sections. First, socio-economic data about Ibiza is provided as an outline of the general contexts that embed expatriate formations locally. Second, I identify typical biographic trajectories as well as media representations of expressive expatriation, as evidence that indicates how mobility practices are interrelated with utopian imaginaries, particularly in privileged locations. Third, I examine 'international schools' as an instance of the tense institutionalization of expatriate ideals vis-à-vis main legal and moral apparatuses. These are small privately run organizations that, originally founded by expatriate teachers under the countercultural influences of the 1970s, currently embody a heteroclite, often contradictory host of parochial, nationalist and cosmopolitan orientations, which sheds light on issues of education, citizenship and cosmopolitanism in a global age. Fourth, the chapter further elaborates on the cultural dimension of expressive lifestyles, by examining spiritual and bohemian practices, as well as by detecting the limits of such expatriate cosmopolitanism, as the concern with the self often stumbles in narcissistic discourses about the exotic Other. In sum, this chapter unravels a pattern of religious individualism that I call 'nomadic spirituality,' a notion that accounts for the multiple experimentation with practices and discourses of self-development that seek to attain certain states of behavior, desire and interiority.

Ibiza contexts: entering the field

I usually took the overnight ferryboat from Barcelona to Ibiza in my field trips from 1998 to 2003. The ship was modest in size and comfort, but large enough to accommodate several dozen vehicles inside. From the rear deck, teenagers watched the harbor shrinking in size, as the boat slowly dragged itself out of the maze of industrial docks, and then firmly heading south. Speakers amplified the bored voice making announcements in Spanish, English and Catalan. As the night grew damper and colder, only a few youngsters remained outside, drinking beer and smoking hashish. A solitary female 'hippie' wearing a poncho stared at the dark horizon, while a dreadlocked 'freak' couple held an ethnic drum. The atmosphere indoors was quite different. In noisy halls, serious women wearing vintage dresses looked after their boxes of sweets and other gifts. Daring tourists tried the restaurant, with its food of dubious quality and rude staff, while others chatted loudly in smoke-clouded bars. Later in the night, the monotonous humming of boat engines resonated with the snoring of passengers here and there. In the large passenger room, someone passing by would invariably wake me up. I got up and walked over the legs of those sleeping across the passageway. Speakers then announced that breakfast was being served, and arrival was due in a couple of hours.

Out in the open, a beautiful sunrise and a cold morning breeze stood in contrast. Alongside the east coast of Ibiza island, the boat passed Tagomago rock, and the white-dotted town of Santa Eulária. Groggy passengers came out in the wind, juggling with jacket buttons, cigarettes and cameras. The boat finally turned right into the bay of 'Ibiza town' (known as Eivissa by natives). On the left side, the imposing medieval fortress overhangs uptown. On the right side, people danced by the flashing lights of a marina terrace, the elegant nightclub *El Divino*. Down in the harbor a dozen people waved at acquaintances on the boat side decks. Tour guides yawned, holding logo plaques and mobile phones, ready for their workday.

I usually chose the ferry trip over the forty-minute flight, mostly for ethnographic reasons. Despite being somewhat tiresome, the spatio-temporal insulation of the maritime journey seemed to remit passengers and crew into a space of hopes and stereotypes that in part reflects social life in Ibiza. The boat trip could in a sense be seen as a ritual, performed in quasi-ceremonial timings, spatializations and behavioral patterns. More personally, it somehow facilitated my tuning in with the island, literally making me feel 'the entrance in the field.'

Geographically, Ibiza is located in the Western Mediterranean sea, about 92 km east of the city of Valencia in the peninsula, and in an imaginary line that vertically links Barcelona to the Algerian coast.[1] Being the third largest of the Balearic Islands (Mallorca, Menorca, Ibiza and Formentera), it extends 41 km by 19 km, comprising a total area of 541 sq km. Due to its smallness and isolation, Ibiza displays a high level of insularity both in geographical and psychological terms (Maurel 1988). The topography consists of elevations of about 400 m high, smooth tops, irregular shapes and open valleys. The coast is characterized by steep cliff formations and only a few sand strips. The climate is Mediterranean with sub-tropical influence: mostly warm and dry, with an average temperature of 17°C rising to 25°C during the summer. Moderate rain falls during early autumn, while the winter is fresh and humid. Vegetation and fauna are poor, restricted to small pine and olive trees, seabirds and salamanders (Maurel 1998).

Tourism is responsible for 80 per cent of Ibiza's wealth (Govern de les Illes Balears – IBAE 2004; Maurel 1988). With a 108,000 population, this tiny island hosted over 1.7 million tourists each year during the early 2000s, generating annual revenues of US$1.5 billion[2] (Govern de les Illes Balears – IBAE 2004; Govern de les Illes Ballears – Conselleria de Turisme 2003; Govern de les Illes Ballears – Conselleria d'Economia 2002). Seven mega-nightclubs are a pivotal attraction. It has been estimated that about 11 per cent of visitors fall into the 'club tourism' category (El Temps 2000). Official figures indicate that Ibiza's clubs and disco-pubs amass annual revenues of about US$110 million (Govern de les Illes Ballears – Conselleria de Turisme 2002). In this connection, tabloid press and tourism campaigns in Europe capitalize on the idea of 'sun, fun and sex galore,' attracting a carefree youthful clientele, as an important segment of the tourist activity. In general, most tourists are drawn from the British and German working class (40 and 20 per cent of the total, respectively), followed by the Spanish and Italian middle class (15 per cent each) (Govern de les Illes Ballears – Conselleria de Turisme 2006: 23). As economic fluctuations in Britain and Germany have a direct impact on local tourism, Ibiza has been seeking to diversify its clientele by recurring to Spanish and other national markets.

Overall, local governments have been trying to moderate the intense urbanization and hotel concentration which followed the airport's opening to international flights in 1966 (Ramón-Fajarnés 2000; Joan I Mari 1997). But high seasonality remains as a problematic feature of Ibiza's tourism, since 70 per cent of visits are concentrated in the period between June and September. This creates environmental pressures on water and energy, in addition to problems with pollution, traffic jams and social stress. In correspondence, seasonal unemployment affects the population during winter, even though the state provides welfare benefits. By all means, after centuries of poverty and isolation, *La Isla Blanca* often tops Spanish and even European rankings for economic growth and per-capita income, as well as social indexes for inflation, consumption, divorce and drug abuse (Govern de les Illes Ballears – Conselleria d'Economia 2002; Joan I Mari 1997; Rozenberg 1990). While gaining a reputation for such rampant massification and hedonistic debauchery, Ibiza has dazzled as a charismatic icon of freedom and pleasure among segments of Western youth.

Politico-administratively, the island's capital Eivissa has a population of 35,000. Among expatriates and tourists, it is known as 'Ibiza town.' The island has four district towns (Sant Antoni, Santa Eulária, Sant Josep and San Joan) and various small parish villages.[3] An Insular Council located in Eivissa is democratically elected to govern the islands of Ibiza and Formentera (smaller portion in the south with 4,000 inhabitants – both islands are known as Pitiusas). The council reports to a larger inter-insular organization located on Palma de Mallorca, the largest of the Balearic Islands. Likewise, Catalan is the language adopted in bureaucratic and educational systems, as Balearic populations speak both Spanish and local dialects of Catalan (Ibicenco, Mallorquín and Menorquín). In the electoral arena, after decades of conservative rule in Ibiza, a coalition of the Socialist and Green parties was elected to power in 1999, reflecting general concerns with environmental and urban issues. However, backed by the mighty hotel and tourist sectors, the right-wing Popular party regained power in 2003, and actively sought to cancel the chief Socialist deliberations: the 'construction ban' that had revoked most building licenses in the countryside, and the '*ecotasa*,' a tourist tax charged on hotel guests for funding environmental projects.

Demographically, Ibiza displays a very peculiar configuration, as census agencies diverge on exact figures. According to the 2001 national census, Ibiza had 93,000 inhabitants (against 76,000 in 1991, 64,000 in 1981, 45,000 in 1971 and 38,000 in 1961). However, two years later, this figure jumped to 108,000 (Govern de les Illes Balears – IBAE 2004). This discrepancy stems from the amnesty which incorporated a number of unregistered foreign migrants. In private correspondence, a state technician explained to me, 'Considering that the Pitiusas have witnessed strong immigration in recent years, it has become difficult to know their exact population at any specific moment.' In terms of origin, about 55 per cent of island residents were born in Ibiza, 35 per cent are immigrants from mainland Spain (mostly working-class families from Andalusia, and the remainder from Catalonia, Valencia and Castilla), and the remaining 10 to 15 per cent are foreign, dual and multinational citizens of the EU and abroad (Govern de les Illes Balears – IBAE 1996). In decreasing order, foreigners are Germans, British, Latin Americans, Moroccans, French, Italians, Dutch, in addition to a myriad of other nationalities. This mosaic reflects the fluidity of foreigners living and moving across the island, in ways that render impossible to quantify precisely the expatriate population (Rozenberg 1990).

Spatial and inner mobility: traveling and nomadic spirituality

Upon disembarkation, I took a bus to Sant Antoni on the West coast of the island. Nora lived near 'The Egg,' a Columbus monument located beside the marina sidewalk. It was 9:00 and street commerce was just about opening. Only a few people were on the streets. Rowdy groups of white kids were apparently returning from a night out, as they looked untidy and drunk, stumbling and speaking English with a sharp British working-class accent.

Figure 2.2 Expatriate children at a hippie party.

Nora rented the top (third) floor of an empty building located at the end of a sunny alley. She divided the apartment into two areas. The 'working area' comprised two rooms. The largest was reserved for yoga classes, with wide curtains hiding the veranda, and pictures of body *chakras* (centers of energy), Hindu gods and the Indian guru Gurumayi were on the wall. The smaller room was reserved for massage therapy, and contained a massage table, sets of colorful crystals, a CD player and a map of the human feet (for reflexology massage). The 'more intimate' area, in Nora's words, comprised three bedrooms, for herself, her daughter and summer guests, besides a bathroom. A light curtain separated both areas by the kitchen, where clients, friends and acquaintances usually gathered before or after sessions.

The apartment location reflected the juxtaposition of rural and urban sceneries characteristic of Ibiza. The front area faced a ten-story hotel which catered for expansive British kids in 'party mode' during the summer. In contrast, the three bedrooms enjoyed a bucolic view of the countryside with a few hotels dotting in white an olive-green hill at the horizon. Nobody lived on the two floors below. The building belonged to a hard-working native family. Two years later, an English DJ and I rented the smaller ground-level apartment during the season. Toward the end of my doctoral fieldwork, Nora moved out, as the family had plans to revamp the building, renting out rooms for foreign seasonal workers and young tourists.

Nora's daughter Adina was 12 years old when I first met her in 1998. A few years later she initiated a career in modeling. Her multinational background was typical of expressive expatriates. Adina spoke fluent Spanish, English, German, Catalan and French. Born in Ibiza, she held rights for three citizenships. Her father was a musician and judo teacher, a German expatriate (separated from Nora when she was four). Adina defined her national identity in complex ways, assessing her sentimental and rational preferences over different affiliations, settings and labor possibilities. Nora commented: 'Adina should follow her heart and her mind when making decisions.' She believed that Adina's terms of allegiance should be defined not in relation to nationalist ties but to her own personal aspirations.

This multinational profile embarrassed Adina in the predominantly parochial environments of Sant Antoni, a town mostly populated by working-class residents and tourists. At school, she stood out from other Spanish kids due to the expressive occupations of her parents (yoga teacher and musician), a Germanic-like semblance, multiple language skills and travel experiences. Nevertheless, Adina remarked to have friends 'like me,' she said: multinational, multilingual, often multiethnic, children of expatriate parents. Stevie was her best friend, a Dutch-Spanish citizen, also a polyglot at age 11. Her mother was a Dutch handcrafter who had lived in India and become a 'sannyasin' (a disciple of Osho/Rajneesh). During vacation months, Stevie traveled with her family to Madrid, Holland or Argentina. Such patterns of cosmopolitan mobility were recurrently verified among most expatriate children.

Nora's biography and motivations well illustrate those of most expressive expatriates, as will become clear throughout the book. Daughter of trade unionists in California, Nora studied dance, French and psychology as an undergraduate at Iowa and Berkeley. In the late 1970s, she moved to Paris in order to develop language and dance skills, but she felt that she was stagnating after a few years, because her career did not develop as she had wished. Dissatisfied, it was suggested that she take a break in Ibiza. She fell in love with the island and decided to move there. In order to make a living, Nora began teaching yoga classes, a system that she had learned from her mother during childhood. Nora also worked as a musician at hotels with her German partner. After separation, Nora went to India and stayed in an ashram, and had plans to live there. In the ashram, she worked as a translator in various meditation workshops. However, a disagreement with the management led her to return to Ibiza, where she developed a small business with a Colombian expatriate, producing and selling tofu (soy cheese) at 'hippie' (touristy) markets. This brief summary of Nora's biographic trajectory reveals a significant level of travel and residence in different countries (the US, France, Spain, India), which begs the questions of why Nora decided to return to and stay in Ibiza for so many years (since 1984). She explained:

> Ibiza is a very powerful place like nowhere else. But if I didn't have Adina I would have traveled more, maybe coming to Ibiza and staying here for a while from time to time. I decided to stay here because Spain is a good place to raise a child. After separation, I could have come

back to America, but that country is just too paranoid, they see a child, and say "don't touch, don't touch!" while, here, people are more relaxed, they are warmer. They may hold your child, say marvels, and everything is all right. Adina would not be as happy in America, and she knows it, although she loves to visit her grandparents in California. Later, when she grows up, she can decide where she wants to live and what to do. And maybe I will move again.

In this passage, Nora rejects the homeland for cultural traits that she renders negative. Her basic concern was in raising a child, a situation that made her less mobile than a childless adult. She also claims that Spain is 'healthier' than the US for raising a child – a comparison between a less and a more 'developed' country, which more deeply indexes the Romantic dismay with excessive civilization. Yet, Nora also notes that Ibiza is more interesting than the rest of Spain, and emphasizes that the island is unique in allowing her 'to be [herself]' and 'to learn how to grow':

In Ibiza you do whatever you want, and nobody will judge you. You can wear anything you want. Unlike other parts of Spain, you can do anything here, and just be yourself, and this is very important to me. The island has a group of very interesting people from all over the world. Everybody who came here has some 'issues' with the places they come from, and this is why they came. In Ibiza I learn a lot about myself, and it has really helped me to grow.

As I recurrently heard from many other expatriates, Ibiza was ascribed a key-role in enabling them to cultivate an expressive lifestyle. They appreciated Ibiza in a way that was unseen among natives. In fact, various non-governmental organizations with cultural or environmental ends on the island were founded by these expatriates. Nora was just one case of cosmopolitan expatriates who dearly cared about topics of holistic wellness, travel and self-development. As this and next chapters will evince, these subjects play a pivotal role in shaping the island's 'scenes' of clubbers, gays, bohemians, hippies and New Agers, all of which index tropes of art, leisure, hedonism and spirituality.

Nora basically worked as a massage therapist and yoga teacher. During the summer, her workday was flexible yet quite intense. She would get up around 9:00, depending on her schedule, and practice yoga for one hour. Her breakfast was usually macrobiotic, with herbal tea, porridge with spices, organic bread – no dairy products. She would then place a massage table in the car, a Renault 4L ('*cuatro latas,*' a hippie pun meaning 'four pieces of tin,' in reference to the rustic model popular among alternatives – years later Nora bought a more modern car), and drive to attend wealthy clients around the island.

A typical summer day for Nora is described next. She had an appointment for massage therapy at 11:00 in Ibiza town. While driving, Nora jocosely taught me about a typology of tourists, according to islanders and alternative expatriates. German tourists are dubbed *'cap quadrats'* (squared heads, in Ibicencan dialect), an expression denoting the allegedly mechanic ways, narrow-mindedness and body clumsiness of mainstream Germans. English tourists are pejoratively known as 'lager louts,' due to the excessive alcohol consumption and their expansive behavior that regularly distressed Sant Antoni inhabitants.

In Ibiza town we parked at D'Alt Villa, historical uphill sector of ancient houses in a maze of alleys surrounded by thick fortress walls. Nora's client was a German businesswoman who suffered back pains. Nora bemoaned, 'Like many people, they don't want to change their lifestyle. All they want is a temporary fix.' We met an hour later, and she seemed a bit upset about the dismissive manner by which her client handed her the money. Nora charged Ptas 10,000 (pesetas) (about US$66) for a domiciliary session.[4]

With some free time available before the next appointment, Nora suggested a quick dive in a beach nearby. Although within the urban perimeter of Eivissa, it was a highly secluded area, down a vertical cliff. It consisted of a small patch of sand surrounded by large rocky cliffs. There were a few couples – all men and all naked. Nora informed me that it was a gay area. She also stripped off, and plunged into the sea. Afterward, she exclaimed, 'Ah, wonderful! I feel so energized! I need it . . . '

We headed toward the hotel on the outskirts of Sant Antoni. It was a large resort hosting mostly Austrian families. Nora entered the massage room located near a swimming pool, and attended two tourists in a row. The hotel management telephoned her to arrange appointments. They paid Ptas 4,000 (US$27) for a fifty-minute massage. Despite the smaller remuneration, Nora considered it to be a good deal since it provided extra income, which compensated for the scarcity of work during wintertime.

We had to rush, as another massage was scheduled at 18:00 in her home. We arrived just in time. Nora gave some house instructions to Adina who was playing the piano, and went for a quick shower. Nora entered the massage room for a few moments of silence, by relaxing New Age music, as she later explains. Adina opened the door to a foreign lady who then waited in the kitchen. She was a Dutch expatriate who worked in public relations. Nora charged Ptas 8,000 (US$53) for a one-hour session at her home, but many clients tipped her an extra, totaling 10,000.

Among the island residents Nora was better known as a yoga teacher, her first and long-term professional activity since her arrival in Ibiza. Taught by her mother, yoga had been part of her life since childhood. The need to work compelled Nora to teach it. Nevertheless, she also felt the need of an official certification.[5] During a stay in London, she therefore attended a training course at a Shivananda Center, but it only served to confirm within herself that she was already capable of teaching yoga. In fact, the director invited Nora to teach yoga at a retreat for British tourists in Egypt, and they have been friends since then.

Nora taught four yoga classes per week. Charging a Ptas 500 fee per person and seven participants on average per class, Nora earned Ptas 3,500 (US$23) each time. Yoga thus corresponded to a minor share of her income. Nonetheless, she maintained the classes as she considered them rewarding to herself and her students on both an emotional and spiritual level. She claimed to gain 'energy' and to be able to 'focus [her] mind,' attributes that she deemed to be necessary during the hectic summer days. She was also pleased that her students benefited from yoga. In a survey for a radio interview, they reported that they experienced body aware-ness, physical health and emotional balance due to their yoga practice.

In addition to yoga, Nora hosted several alternative practices at her home, for she was avidly interested in learning other body and spiritual techniques (such as macrobiotics, Bach flower remedies, chromotherapy, chiropractice and Biodance). She rented out the large yoga room to other colleagues and often joined their sessions. A couple of Brazilian therapists imparted group sessions of a body-movement practice called Biodance (to be examined later). A Spanish expatriate[6] physician led an active medi-tation practice called 'Osho Dynamic Meditation.' Like Stevie's mother, they were coincidentally followers of Osho, and attended his communes in Pune (India) and Oregon (US). Chapter 4 focuses on the Osho move-ment, but suffice it to say at this point that Osho was a polemical spiritual leader, renowned for his heterodox meditation and therapy techniques coupled with a radical critique of religion and society. Known as 'neo-sannyasins,' his disciples sought to live a liberating lifestyle that affirms both mundane and spiritual experiences.

In between sessions, people informally gathered at the kitchen or main room, and desultorily shared comments about an exercise, arranged meet-ings or social outings, and paid fees. These relations extended beyond strict professional-monetary relations that characterize therapeutic settings in big urban centers. Instead, they were part of webs of warm sociability that included a larger number of acquaintances and practitioners of the alter-native world. These relations also ramified into other social and economic spaces, such as hippie markets, nude beaches, sunset bars, nightclubs, trance parties, etc. To be further explored in this chapter, they prioritized ideals of self-exploration, integrating expression, pleasure and intuitive insight within a cosmopolitan community of like-minded individuals.

Because of the multiplicity of national backgrounds, expressive expatri-ates developed singular linguistic abilities. Besides Spanish and English, they could swiftly shift into a third, often a fourth language or dialect, back and forth dexterously. German and Dutch expatriates tended to speak more languages, whereas British and Mediterranean ones were usually more limited in their linguistic skills. Ibicencans spoke Spanish and Catalan fluently, but fared poorly in English, even in the British-dominated Sant Antoni. In my case, I noticed that in Ibiza I employed English and Spanish almost equally, in addition to some Portuguese and improvised pidgins of Romanic languages. These multiple linguistic exchanges are characteristic of a 'contact zone' that concentrates a diversity of natives, migrants, expatriates and tourists. This notion will be particularly important and resumed in Chapter 5.

It was in this context of multicultural encounters that Nora introduced me to Rochelle, a US expatriate whom I would recurrently meet by chance in other alternative spaces of Ibiza, and even on a flight from New York to Barcelona. As a methodological note, Nora's home was a holistic center from which I established various contacts with other peoples and scenes of Ibiza and abroad. Considering that virtually everybody in the expatriate community knew each other or a third who did, snowballing was a sufficient method of recruitment by which I could access the types of people that my research required.

Rochelle divided her time across Ibiza, India and the US.[7] She arrived in Ibiza by May or early June to seasonally reopen her beach boutique with exotic artisan clothes imported from places such as Bali, Bahia, Thailand, Nepal, etc. She then stayed on the island until November, after the tourist season was over.

She lived in a house magnificently located on a coastal plateau facing Es Vedra,[8] the giant sea rock whose shape and luminosity fueled fantastic stories about UFOs, prophecies, hermits, suicides and 'energies.' Throughout the years, Rochelle transformed the rustic hut into an exquisite bungalow integrating hippie and peasant elements. Her life in Ibiza was featured in a book by a US diplomat who resided on the island during the 1980s (Stratton 1994). According to Stratton:

> The beauty of Ibiza's expatriate women lay not so much in their physical attributes as in their intense feelings and the insecurity with which they lived, which gave a wildness, an edge to everything.
>
> (Stratton 1994: 195)

Nature, women and peasants were trivially romanticized in expressive imaginaries, as their 'essence' has not been contaminated by the malaises of civilization, incarnated in the city, men and urban dwellers. Throughout the twentieth century, expressive expatriates fled the metropole in order to shape a simpler life near nature (Ramón-Fajarnés 2000; Scheurmann and Scheurman 1993; Green 1986). With gusto they engaged in manual and bucolic activities, such as gardening, carpentry, artisan farming, recycling, 'natural' diets and expressive therapies, while upgrading derelict houses purchased from amazed peasants. Nevertheless, these expatriates did not absorb folk elements in the void, but revamped them within modern frames of usage and meaning. They installed electricity and sanitation, and transformed their *fincas* into modestly elegant residences decorated in chic cosmopolitan fashion.

In this post-traditional scenario, Rochelle organized special parties, inviting friends and relatives. In the dry vegetation, the area around her house was specially decorated with exotic gypsy-like silks, cushions, torches and tents. Fire acrobats, belly dancers, Moroccan drummers and Flamenco guitarists were hired to deliver magic performances. Rochelle nostalgically told me that these gatherings reminded her of her hippie years back in the early 1970s. She actively participated in the peace movement, and lived in hippie communes in the US and UK. In London, she bought an old postal van which her children renamed 'Amazing Grace,' and they hit the roads traveling across Europe. In 1973 she went to Morocco, and cultivated plans to stay but could not find a school for her children. 'Around that time,' she recalls, 'everybody was talking about Ibiza.' They went to Ibiza in that same year, enjoyed the place, and found an international school for her kids.[9] The children later returned to their father in the US, but Rochelle remained on the island, traveling regularly to India, Nepal and Indonesia (Bali). By the mid-1980s, an American couple left Ibiza for good, and offered their beach boutique to her, and she has been running it ever since. With reliable suppliers in India and the advent of internet communication, Rochelle dispensed with traveling to India, as she reached the age of sixty.

In conclusion, Rochelle's extensive experience with travel and multicultural environments honed her skills in trading exotic products from Asia to the West. She was thus able to develop economic strategies that combined her desire for mobility with an alternative lifestyle centered on aesthetic values. More widely, her trajectory demonstrates how countercultural agency is forged within singular historical and transnational contexts, notably: the hippie countercultural movement and emerging globalization (*New York Times* 2004).

Barbara is another example of expressive expatriation whose identity is also marked by mobility across spaces and interests. Originally from Germany, Barbara moved to Ibiza in 1993. Working as a language teacher, she lived in a countryside house shared with a Spanish 'expatriate' couple. We met in the context of a body therapy session (Biodance),[10] and frequently came across each other in other alternative venues regularly frequented by expressive expatriates: sunset bars, hippie markets, alternative parties, nude beaches, etc.

At the preamble of a Biodance session, Barbara announced her decision to stop attending the group. She said that, even though Biodance had helped to improve important aspects of her personality, it was time for a break because her inner experiences with Biodance had been gradually stagnating. About ten people listened to her, including the therapist and me. The group was slightly sorry, but understanding and supportive anyway. Validating her decision, the Brazilian therapist (and Osho sannyasin) said that 'in life, there were periods of growth' (as her hands moved outward), 'followed by periods of introspection' (moving her hands inward), and that 'both deserve equal attention.' There was no commotion about Barbara's announcement, because everyone took for granted that, as it usually turned out to be the case, they would keep interacting in other alternative spaces.

In New Age circles, people share a strong interest in self-cultivation, developed through the participation in multiple practices, systems or pedagogies, in sequence or often simultaneously. For example, Barbara could teach tai chi which she learned in Barcelona, and, following her experience with Biodance, pursued studies in Maya Astrology and became a professional apprentice in a body education system titled *Grinberg Method* (to be discussed later). Barbara was also very interested in Osho and closely interacted with sannyasins. Not only did she own over 25 books by Osho (mostly given to her) and eventually participated in Osho meditation sessions, Barbara also had plans to attend the 'Osho Commune International' in Pune. In fact, many expatriates thought that Barbara was a sannyasin because of her highly 'independent' and 'genuine' personality. These representations were recurrently employed to characterize expatriate women (see Stratton quote on p. 53), particularly sannyasin ones, as Osho's teachings explicitly empowered women (Palmer 1994). Such representations about the expatriate women of Ibiza, real or imagined, resonate with the myth of nomadic women (Chapter 1) as being assertive, independent and dexterous, and, by all means, freer than sedentary women.

Likewise, Barbara's trajectory reproduces New Age patterns of self-spirituality, characterized as post-traditional hybrids of therapeutic, pedagogic and divinatory practices. As soon as the subject believes that a specific practice no longer provides the expected returns in terms of insight or behavioral change, this will likely be interpreted as a moment to move on, according to one's assessments over one's one life circumstances and intuition. New Age affiliations are thus better understood as being adverbially temporal: '*Yesterday* I was into ..., *today* I am into ..., and *tomorrow* I may want to try ...' Therefore, it makes sense to name such a cultural pattern of flexible and metamorphic cultivation of the self as *nomadic spirituality*.

At the material level, nomadic spirituality usually correlates with travel practice and flexible, often informal labor conditions, such as Nora's, Rochelle's and Barbara's cases illustrate. Having grown up near the Dutch border, Barbara moved to Hamburg where she worked in movie production, while socializing with vanguard artists, such as the band *Kraftwerk*, 1970s precursors of techno music (Sicko 1999; Reynolds 1998). Barbara spent a few months backpacking across Indonesia and Brazil, an experience that motivated her to leave Germany definitely. She lived in Barcelona for several years, where she worked in movie production. However, she felt that urban life was increasingly stressful for her. A holiday in Ibiza in 1992 prompted her to move to the island, where she met other expatriates with similar trajectories and interests: individuals fed up with conventional urban routine, with a desire for developing a more meaningful way of life, near nature and with 'time for yourself,' as she put it.

Barbara, Marta and Miguel resided in a traditional Ibicencan house in the southern countryside. Originally from northern Spain, Marta and Miguel cultivated a tranquil lifestyle revolving around ecological values. Miguel worked as a gardener, and Marta did massages and had a part-time job in a naturalist shop in Sant Antoni. The couple traded recycled clothes and appliances in the weekly 'flea market' of San Jordi, and sold organic cheese and vegetables in the weekly 'ecologic market' of Can Sort farm (to be described later). Miguel got up at 6:00 and drove to tend gardens in the region (usually at 'second residences' of wealthy expatriates), while Marta practiced yoga and read books on Spanish literature and spirituality. Around 10:00, she left for the organic shop or a massage appointment. Miguel returned to cook lunch, always healthy vegetarian dishes. They had lunch and then slept a typical *siesta*, getting up about 15:00 to resume work. They watched the TV news and eventually drove into town to socialize with friends. A few years into my fieldwork, they bought an old caravan and left for a long journey around mainland Spain.

Barbara taught language classes as her main income source and occupation. She taught German and Spanish at home, or drove her car (a Renault 4L, '*cuatro latas*') to towns nearby. She charged Ptas 2,000 per class (later adjusted to €15). In teaching about twenty classes per week, her monthly income was about Ptas 360,000 or €1,200 (US$1,100). However, her income was slashed by about 40 per cent during wintertime, because she or her students traveled or just wanted to do other things and rest from the laborious summer. Barbara eventually did other jobs, such as translation, gardening or tai chi classes, depending on personal desire and income needs. In one summer, for example, she was hired by a firm to sell jewelry around a circuit of hotels – most of her colleagues were German women with polyglot skills.

Consumption patterns among expressive expatriates were parsimonious and reflected their concerns with health and the environment. They are critical about consumerism, assessed as ecologically pernicious and psychologically symptomatic of inner malaises (neediness, unhappiness, conformism). Considering that public transportation in rural areas is almost nonexistent, they own rustic vehicles. Accordingly, liabilities (home utilities, insurance, school tuition, etc.) correspond to a smaller share of expenses, when not virtually inexistent.

Conversely, certain items weighed more heavily in their budgets. First, participation in alternative therapies and spiritual practices could cost monthly from Ptas 10,000 to Ptas 40,000 (US$60–240). These figures can be multiplied tenfold in the case of a professionalizing apprenticeship. Second, special foods and diets are an object of concern among expatriates. They favor 'organic' groceries as well as special foods with almost medicinal properties often imported from remote locations (Japan, Africa, the Amazon, etc). Alternatively, younger alternatives may consume drugs, a costly item, particularly among those who attend trance parties or enjoy clubbing marathons. Finally, international airfares comprise a hefty expense, as expatriates leave the island each year, annually spending from US$500 to US$1,500 or more.

The informal and seasonal nature of labor in Ibiza creates difficulties to expressive expatriates. Income drops dramatically during the tourist off-season (winter), creating massive unemployment on the island. Hardships in cases of accident and illness, let alone retirement, are concerns among expatriates, particularly ageing ones. But whereas Spanish citizens are safely protected by the welfare system, the reality is quite different for non-European expatriates, living irregularly on the island, and hoping for a migration amnesty that would allow them to 'get the papers.' Furthermore, the acute modernization and high inflation in Ibiza (after the euro was introduced in 2002) has forced expatriates to engage in tighter labor and expense regimes. (The monthly rent of Barbara's house, for example, jumped from US$360 to US$640 – a 78 per cent increment.) During my fieldwork years, I noticed a change of attitude on the part of expatriates who complained about physical tiredness due to excessive work, or about the unprotected nature of labor. As they aged, they started to patiently file into state apparatuses, less reluctant to face the hurdles imposed by the Spanish bureaucracy in line with new EU standards: to extend labor, social and civic rights to all European citizens living in Spanish territory, in addition to regularizing the situation of non-European immigrants.

Despite such structural hindrances, and considering their travel proclivities, expressive expatriates preferred to stay on the island notwithstanding. Like other migrants, they claimed that Ibiza provided good work and wages, enabled by a prosperous tourist economy and wealthy residents. Yet, they also added that the island allowed them to integrate rural and urban life interestingly, living in the countryside while having easy access to a quite dynamic social life ideal to the tastes of expressive expatriates. As importantly, they praised the possibility of sharing their interests in aesthetic, erotic and spiritual forms with other many similarly minded individuals.

It is important to note that the decision of expatriatates to remain on the island did not contradict their will to travel. Quite the contrary, the economic and climatic seasonality of the island propelled them to be mobile. While Ibiza hibernates during the winter, the tourist season in South Asia and Latin America begins, thus providing the conditions of possibility for a global circuit by which these expatriates can economically sustain their expressive lifestyle by means of mobility practice.

Expatriate media: 'people from Ibiza'

Expatriates are always featured in the press and TV shows about Ibiza. Such exposure provides an analytical window into the utopian imaginary and social questions that envelop their lives, and we will notice again the recurrence of mobility and expressivity as marks of their way of life. *Ibiza Now* is a small but renowned newspaper produced and consumed by expatriates since 1984. In monthly editions in English and German, it seeks to integrate foreign residents with the island's social life, promoting their economic, cultural and artistic ties locally and beyond. The publication also includes a summary of local news which reflects some of their main interests: tourism industry, environment, urbanization, cultural life, international integration and local politics. Also noticeable are a number of small pieces covering Ibicencan history, folklore and dialect, suggesting an interest of some informed expatriates to understand the intricacies of their chosen home.

In each monthly issue throughout the 1980s and 1990s, *Ibiza Now* interviewed an expatriate in a one-page session, curiously titled 'People from Ibiza.' The same set of questions was applied across all issues, a feature that facilitated some likely inferences about this community and their relation to Ibiza. I collected thirty-one profiles picked at random from issues published between 1994 and 1998. Despite primarily catering to the British community (half of the interviews featured British citizens), it can be assumed that *Ibiza Now* reflected interests and sentiments of the international middle-class populace residing on the island. At the core of these representations, Ibiza is recurrently depicted as a place that transforms subjectivities, often dramatically.

In terms of national origin, fifteen of the interviewees were British, five Spanish (only three Ibicencans), five Germans, three Americans, one Danish, one Australian and one New Zealander. There were sixteen women and fifteen men, with ages mostly ranging from forties to fifties. In terms of occupation, two main groups could be identified: half were hoteliers, restaurateurs or official retirees. The other half was involved in expressive, creative and alternative careers: artists, writers, New Age therapists and leaders of alternative organizations (international school, eco-cooperative, folklore preservation, expatriate bookstore and an artsy internet café).

The profile included information about their parental background, travel experience, motivations for coming to Ibiza and a general assessment of the island. Several respondents recalled that their expatriate trajectories began with a traveling father on military or diplomatic duty. Other parental backgrounds included artists, shopkeepers, teachers, natural therapists and liberal professionals. The three Ibicencans in the poll were hotel businessmen, drawn from families of limited means. They represented themselves as self-made men forged by the hardships of life, work and family values. They seemed to show off, apparently a little forcefully, their knowledge about tour destinations and classical music (in a way that Bourdieu would have identified as self-defeating).

Expatriates (including two peninsular Spaniards) were concerned with existential issues and aspirations. Some of them, such as a retired actress and a gypsy dancer, claimed that their personalities were too 'untamable' and 'passionate' for a sedentary life. A third of respondents came to Ibiza right after quitting a relatively successful career in the homeland. Despite favorable material conditions, they claimed that their lives were too boring. They opted to take the risky leap into the unknown, and moved to Ibiza where they rapidly delved into new careers that often sprang from former hobbies and suppressed interests. Travel and occupation were no longer merely means for economic gain, but became intrinsic components of an exciting lifestyle. Extended trips to Asia were seen as a way to 'break up with a Christian upbringing.' Just as in the cases of Nora and Barbara, Ibiza was often discovered in the context of a tour: a fortuitous vacation or a business opportunity on the island triggered a thirst for self-transformation. As some hippies would put it, the 'Ibiza bug' had bitten them.

About Ibiza itself, many interviewees noted that the place suits lifestyles driven by 'passion,' 'fun' and 'bohemianism.' Others praised the variety of social types that coexisted there. New Agers pointed out the 'spiritual' and 'energetic' qualities of the island, considered a center for 'spiritual learning and healing.' Opinions about the general situation were prompted under the caption 'the best and the worst in Ibiza.' Two typical answers referred to the negative side. Alternative expatriates regretted that mass tourism led to environmental degradation, consumerism, selfishness and undesired work rhythms. Businesspeople, however, readily criticized the bureaucracy as the main hindrance to the economic development of the island. Yet, they all agreed that the worst of Ibiza lies in Sant Antoni, a town with low-quality tourism for rowdy 'lager louts' hosted in cheap two-star hostels. On the other hand, there was unanimity about the best in Ibiza: the natural beauties and the countryside, which exerted a mesmerizing effect upon expatriates.

They represented Ibiza as a space that enables self-development, expression and self-actualization. It is 'a community of expression,' according to an American masseur; 'a place for self-realization,' as noted by a German environmentalist and a German art director; a 'relative paradise' according to an English sculptor; a 'place of beauty and non-conformism' for an Australian dancer. Others defined the island in simpler terms: a 'nice place' for a British bar owner; a 'unique place' according to a German internet businessman; 'the nicest place' for a British singer; and, still, a 'place I fell in love with' according to a German ecologist. The news publication did not register any negative comments about Ibiza, other than those about Sant Antoni, bureaucracy and the massification of tourism.

The final question in 'People from Ibiza' required a decisive answer, consolidating the respondent disposition toward the island, with the question, 'stay or go?' From this pool of thirty-one mostly expatriate people, only four revealed plans to leave. A cultural producer from Germany felt stagnated after years managing an upbeat bookstore. She wished to 'transform [her] life again.' Two English bar owners felt that their lives became too attached to their businesses. The fourth respondent was Linda, a globally traveled hippie trader turned into a spiritual healer. Originally from New Zealand, after residing in Ibiza for nineteen years, she decided that it was about time to move again.

Linda used to sell self-made clothes in the 'hippie market' of Es Canar. Since her arrival in 1976, she enjoyed a simple life in the countryside. Previously, Linda was a social worker in Australia and then in England, respectively assisting Aboriginal mothers and troubled adolescents. She noted that the trip from Australia to England was done mostly overland. After a few years in the UK, Linda traveled around Europe and the Middle East, settling down in Greece for three years. She produced batik and leather clothes. It is in this context of long-haul traveling that her wish to leave Ibiza must be understood. Staying nineteen years in Ibiza was, in her case, exceptional.

Her decision to move, this time, stemmed from her development as a spiritual healer. Linda began to manifest psychic powers during therapy workshops. People claimed that she was able to diagnose the psychological state, past and traumas of anyone who sat in front of her. Linda has been traveling since 1995. About every two years, she returns to Ibiza, where she stays for a month or two, meeting friends, attending clients and recomposing her 'energies.'

Linda's case demonstrates how hypermobility may penetrate the core of self-identity and social practice. She transposed her proclivities to aid people from a secular level (as social worker) to a spiritual one (as psychic healer). It may be suggested that her later spiritual development relates to her wish to travel again. Moreover, the economic strategies that she deploys to make a living have usually allowed her to travel, which, in turn, has contributed to enhance her charisma and cultural capital. In sum, her trajectory embodies Romantic predispositions, which include a deep appreciation of the exotic Other (notably Ibicencan peasants and Australian Aborigines), a refined withdrawal from mundane engagements and a cosmopolitan suppleness to navigate various cultural universes. Underlying all of these features lies the ideal of self-cultivation, operating as a main category that orients Linda's life, interests and worldview.

Whether staying or leaving, Ibiza expatriates regularly traveled to Europe, South Asia or South America. Those who left the island for good, sought to return for short periods, then staying with friends. In their new homes elsewhere, they sought to recreate similar conditions, usually in places with similar utopian-like qualities: sunny, semi-peripheral, inexpensive, relaxed, pleasurable, experimental and cosmopolitan. As Deleuze and Guattari note, 'nomads do not move': they try to keep the smooth space of desire and experimentation (Deleuze and Guattari 1980). Even for those expatriates who did not travel as regularly, mobility remained as a spiritual disposition – a drive for self-discovery and potential metamorphosis.

Expatriate education: 'international schools'

Despite the relatively high levels of education and reading interests, expressive expatriates tend to despise intellectualism. For them, 'Reason' crippled the subject from its vital energy, and, instead, they emphasize forms of knowledge centered on the body and legitimated via experience. On the other hand, they welcome grand cosmological explanations, insofar as they can be sustained with rational-empirical explanations in a para-scientific fashion. Overall, embodying Romantic dispositions, they are rather skeptical about the promises and prescriptions of modern civilization. This session summarizes trajectories of well-educated expatriates, and briefly examines special 'international schools' founded by expatriate teachers in the early 1970s.

Nora introduced me to Kirk, an anthropologist who lived across Ibiza, Australia and Vanuatu. His former (deceased) wife and Nora shared a small business producing and selling tofu (soy cheese) in hippie markets. Kirk was a British-American expatriate, off the Western 'so-called civilization,' as he often put. From 1966 to 1977 he studied at Oxford and Cambridge (UK). He did fieldwork in northern Africa and Colombia, but devoted most of his lifetime to Vanuatu, an archipelago state in the South Pacific, where he contiguously lived from 1978 to 1990. There he founded the National Museum, a salvage institution with organic connections with local communities. Kirk moved to Ibiza in 1990 when he and his wife inherited a house located in the countryside of Sant Antoni (a traditional peasant house: large, with enormously thick walls and impressively tiny windows, multi-layered rooms and low arch passageways). In addition to studying Ibicencan peasant folklore, Kirk decisively contributed to the foundation of Ibiza's Ethnological Museum in 1994. He often criticized the negative effects of mass tourism, and particularly the high levels of drug abuse among young tourists. He often lectured in international museums, but refused most academic positions offered to him until the early 2000s, when he remarried and moved to Australia. In fact, as he explained, Kirk was too free-spirited to care about the formalities involved in obtaining a doctoral degree, even though he is a reputed world-class professional in his area of expertise. His personality is indeed singular: a captivating storyteller, Kirk developed amicable relationships with peoples from all walks of life, in and outside academia.[11]

Ignasi provides another example of a countercultural anti-intellectual. Barbara introduced us during a body-technique workshop that he imparted at the German 'international school.' His wife Charlotte was a German expatriate, teacher and principal of the school, and also participated in the workshop. He was an instructor of the *Grinberg Method*, as he described, a pedagogy of self-development based on the conscious work upon the body. He refused to be labeled as a 'therapist' (due to the notions of hierarchy and illness that it evokes). In individual or group sessions, the method involves exercises with unusual body movements, localized pressure, induced pain (for emotional release) and rhythmic breathing, all of which are carried out with or without music. These exercises are geared toward engendering a mindful awareness about the self, particularly attentive to how social conventions constrain the body and, consequently, its cognitive-affective patterns. He invited Barbara and me for a dinner at their house, near the German school. Our conversation was in Spanish. I mentioned my research, and asked Ignasi and Charlotte how and why they came to the island.

Ignasi initiated by disclosing his past as a Catholic priest. In the mid-1960s he left Barcelona to study at a Jesuit seminary in Paris. Out of the sphere of Franco's censorship, Ignasi could study matters of Marxism and existentialism, which captivated his generation. The second half of the seminary took place in Barcelona, and Ignasi became renowned for his unique personality. Priest superiors found him 'too mystical,' referring to Ignasi's intense engagements with prayer and meditation practices (in detriment of pastoral tasks, deemed priorities in the context of growing opposition to Franco). His main concern during his time at the seminary, Ignasi says, was in searching within himself. However, his situation in the seminary deteriorated dramatically when his superiors discovered that he was enjoying the nightlife in Barcelona. He remarked that mysticism and bohemianism were not a contradiction in itself, and added that he wanted to experiment with life independently of any moral shackles. Although no parish was willing to accept Ignasi as a new priest, a bishop offered him a small church in a remote corner of Spain – Ibiza – and Ignasi arrived there in 1972.

However, he soon decided to abandon the priesthood. In addition to being reprehended for secretly supporting socialist meetings in the church, Ignasi had an affective relationship with a parishioner. The couple moved to Barcelona where he got an office job, but returned to Ibiza two years later. In the meanwhile, Ignasi had become interested in countercultural lifestyles and developed a semi-communal relationship with his partner until they separated. In 1998 Ignasi published a book with strong existentialist undertones relating Zen and Tarot, titled *Llegar a Ser* ('Come to Be'). He became a *Grinberg Method* practitioner, and later met Charlotte.

Similar to many expressive expatriates, Charlotte was dissatisfied with her life in Germany. During the 1980s, she worked as a public education officer in a town near Düsseldorf. A friend vacationing in Ibiza told her about a teaching position in a primary school that catered for German families on the island. Charlotte applied and was accepted. Her initial plan was to stay for only one year, but the experience was so enjoyable that she extended it for another year, and then permanently. She later became the school principal, assuming teaching and administrative activities.

Among expatriate parents, education is not only an ideal of holistic self-development, but also a practical issue of providing a school for their children. Since conventional schools are seen as extensions of national ideologies, several 'international schools' have been founded. These are small private institutions run by expatriate teachers who, inspired by countercultural ideals in the 1970s, now embrace the pedagogical task of education under globalizing conditions. In Ibiza, the largest of these schools had 180 students and 18 teachers in the early 2000s. Yet, considering the remoteness of the island and the smallness of its population (under 50,000 during the 1970s), their presence indicates the importance of expatriate life on the island.

Currently, these international schools embody broader issues of education, citizenship and globalization. One of them displays the suggestive slogan: 'An education in our school is the passport for your child's future.' Nonetheless, while providing a relative alternative to the national education system, most of them cater for families of a single nationality (German, English or French), although never exclusively. While most children in these schools are born in Spain, over 80 per cent of their parents are foreign expatriates. Half of the kids have parents of the same foreign nationality, and the rest have parents from differing nationalities. These families are drawn from middle and upper social strata in Europe who decided to migrate to semi-rural Spain in search of a better quality of life.

Spanish families of equivalent income level do not seem as interested in international schools, and favor public schools when registering their children. One reason is financial, as monthly tuition fees at international schools ranged from US$300 to US$500 in the early 2000s. This topic requires more investigation; nevertheless, since Spanish parents also pay for tuition in national private schools, it can be suggested that they do not value international education in the same way that expatriate parents do. In any case, international education in Ibiza contradicts common assumptions about globalization as a homogenizing force: whereas the 'local' embodies the mass standardization of national public systems, the 'translocal' embodies small-scale, personalized care with an eye on global conditions.

However, in order to comply with state regulation at different levels, international schools regularly negotiate their legal and curricular status with official authorities locally and abroad. For a reason, parents worried about the validity of school certificates across national borders. Even those parents with a more alternative orientation sought to avert this problem for their children. Thus, school principals sought to make sure that their curricula were kept in line with Spanish and alien legislations. In the meanwhile, insular authorities also pressed for a more locally oriented curriculum, with a higher share of classes in Catalan disciplines and language. This was a contended issue among expatriate parents. Many considered that an excessive regionalization of the educational grid would impose an unnecessary burden on their children, since Catalan was deemed secondary in the arena of international opportunities. In sum, international schools have to accommodate multiple pressures, interests and orientations at the local, national and transnational levels.

Despite the relatively cosmopolitan orientation of these schools, several parents envisaged them as a space for forging a certain national character in alien lands. Scorning Spanish ways as lax and inefficient, they expected these schools to instill 'proper' German or English values in their children. Teachers often noticed such expectations with apprehension, and worried about their arrogant, imperialist-like attitude in Spain. Charlotte mentioned a couple who, annoyed with local bureaucracy and manners, moved in and out of Spain and then back again in a short period of time, thus 'upsetting the educational and emotional needs of their children.' Ignasi and Barbara agreed, and such a critical view was not circumscribed within expressive expatriates. The Spanish press warned about German enclaves that developed apart from local life in southern Spain. Sun and cheap prices (as well as tax evasion and money laundering) were some of the main reasons that motivated wealthy aliens to purchase real estate in Costa del Sol and the Balearic Islands.

Conversely, expressive expatriates are more appreciative of Spain, sometimes manifested in the form of a reversed ethnocentrism: rather than disdaining the Other, they charge against their own homelands. Their stories have become recurrent throughout this chapter: dissatisfied with their life in the metropole, their hopes for a more fulfilling lifestyle brought them to the warm periphery. In Ibiza, they seek to detach themselves from homeland identities, while experimenting with idiosyncrasy and sensual engagements with the present. In the long run, their self-identities unfold through spiraling cycles of estrangement and re-identification with biographic and cultural references of the homeland.

In the case of expatriate children born in Ibiza, the blurring of national identities complicate the terms of allegiance. To ask, 'where are you from?' triggers short-circuited answers at the logical, dialogic and semantic levels. The questioner is inadvertently positioned in the position of a naive outsider, as expressive expatriates are ambivalent toward national references, while valuing exotic combinations. The difference between being *from* and *of* somewhere reveals the ways by which these post-national subjects can creatively articulate origin and identity. Nora was 'from

America' rather than 'American,' as Barbara was 'from Germany' rather than 'German.' As a generalization, two main social types can be distinguished in the overall population of expatriates on the island: the nationalistic utilitarian, and the cosmopolitan expressive, each being informed by distinct principles of identity: fixity or metamorphosis, as theorized in Chapter 1.

Expressive lifestyles

In contrast with the rush at the Eivissa–Sant Antoni axis, the northern area of the island was praised by expatriates for its pristine woods, magnificent landscapes and bohemian villages. As an effect of their predispositions, time there seemed to flow more slowly and pleasantly, entailing a wholesome feeling of connection with nature and humanness. At a material level, housing was more affordable. Squat punks from the mainland (known as *okupas*) were able to discover a few abandoned huts for temporary residence. Public transportation was virtually nonexistent, yet hitchhiking was relatively successful, at least for the time being. The main town of Santa Eulária boasted an elegant marina, and, while undergoing mild gentrification, its tourism was considerably calmer and better organized than rowdy Sant Antoni.

Alternative events, such as hippie markets, spiritual retreats, drum and trance parties, tended to concentrate in the northern region, whereas in the south they had to confront the harsher realities of mass tourism. But before examining these complex interrelations with the political economy of tourism, this chapter further elaborates on the patterns and meanings entailed in expatriate lifestyles, particularly focusing on their expressive and cosmopolitan orientations. The cultural substrate of expressive expatriate life on the island is further examined in the following sub-sections upon examples of yoga classes, Osho disciples and bohemian encounters.

Self-techniques: yoga, Biodance, neo-sannyasins

New Age healers play music during sessions, aiming at engendering special moods in the one being treated. Ethnomusicological studies have tried to ascertain whether such states result from the physicality of structured sounds, or from the cultural beliefs of participants (Takahashi 2004; Becker 1999; Fost 1999; Gerra *et al.* 1998; Greer and Tolbert 1998; McCraty *et al.* 1998; Forsyth *et al.* 1997). Though such a question lies beyond the scope of this research, I would argue that the efficacy of musical sounds upon the subject's affective states stems from a peculiar combination of physical and cultural factors: structured sounds stimulate certain neural responses, which, in turn, are amplified or hindered according to the cultural predispositions of the subject (in turn, a product of biographic and socio-cultural factors). This topic will be resumed in Chapter 5. The goal at this point is to analyze significant correlations of art, culture and subjectivity commonly verified in countercultural sites.

The music Nora played during yoga and massage sessions was deeply melodious, with slow rhythms and deep base lines. It is intended to relax the subject or take them out of ordinary patterns of thought. One of the New Age CD albums she often played was 'Walkabout' produced by musician Patrick Walsh. The CD booklet describes it poetically: 'If such seclusion is desired, within us all there is a territory unreachable by anything in the external world ... sanctuary from society ... sabbatical from stresses ... unmolded identity' (omission points are original). By exploring music from widely diverse cultural traditions, Walsh seeks to create a cosmopolitan aesthetic of universal spirituality:

> Walkabout is an album that merges instruments from several cultures and regions of the earth. The result is a unique blending of instruments and melodies spanning from the royal courts of India to the 40,000 years old culture of Aboriginal Australia. [. . .] These compositions are my attempt to create music evocative of a feeling of which few poets write ... music that would allow the mind to journey within a state where other considerations of body and physical reality become purely remote. [. . .] Seemingly boundless horizons can be created in this realm of being through means of the international language and harmony we call music.

Along the same lines of liminal sentiments, Nora played a one-track CD of tamboura music during yoga classes. A string instrument from India, the tamboura produces a highly reverberating sound, of 'hypnotic quality' according to the CD cover:

> The attention to its prolonged resonance absorbs the yogi into the space of Consciousness, attaining the state of the self. Its sound resonates with the primordial sound Om, from which all melodies arise and into which they subside. Melodies are no longer separate notes but blend together into an ocean of sound that quiets the mind and soothes the heart.

With other practical purposes, this music is to be played 'during meditation, as it aids concentration by screening out distracting background noises.' At Nora's apartment, constant music was necessary during yoga classes, due to the noise of young tourists at the hotel across the street. More broadly, music was part of her life, as she also enjoyed playing the guitar, creating her own songs with bucolic lyrics and devotional fashion. In her former work as a musician in tourist resorts, Nora learned that people of different nationalities react specifically to certain musical patterns: 'We had different repertoires depending on the nationality of tourists. If they were English, our selection was more melodic, with lots of la-la-ri la-la-ra. But if they were German, then it was tum-tum-tum,' drawing her fist in mechanic movements.[12]

As it is predominant in conventional yoga practice, Nora's classes followed the *hatha* structure, meaning, a sharp emphasis on body discipline and resilience. Most of her students were women, as I also verified elsewhere (Strauss 1996). The first hour was dedicated to slow yet demanding physical exercises through repetitive movements that stretch and position the body in challenging poses (*asanas*). Nora showed the position, and participants followed. The ensuing thirty minutes were dedicated to gentler positions of meditation and relaxation. Finally, Nora conducted a complex 'Sun salutation,' coordinating ample body movements with the chanting of Sanskrit verses, in richly melodic and monotonous fashion.

Nora sometimes drove to Santa Eulária (about 20 km northeast of Sant Antoni) to deliver a massage therapy or to attend some social event. We arranged to meet her friends, Biodance therapists Nadi and Ishwara. In town, as we walked along the main boulevard, Nora stopped to greet a man running a tent selling handcraft products. Originally from Barcelona, Alfonso sold decoration items in hippie markets. He was also the main coordinator of the Siddha Yoga chanting group which he founded in Ibiza in 1991, and delivered *satsangs* (chanting meetings) at his house located in the countryside near San Carlos, comprising a small group of expatriates and alternative Spaniards.

As in other individual cases shown in this chapter, Alfonso's lifestyle interrelates an ideology of self-development with practices of mobility in space and interest. Alfonso had been to India five times, where he stayed from three to five months each time, for spiritual (Siddha Yoga) and economic reasons (bringing exotic goods to the West). In Ibiza since 1987, Alfonso nonetheless revealed a certain wish to 'move on' with his life: 'I want to learn something new, like a therapy, and practice it.' He was considering Barcelona for the possibilities of learning and delivering alternative practices. On the other hand, he regretted that such a move would imply giving up the seductive conditions that kept him and others on the island: autonomous flexible labor, within a community of cosmopolitan, spiritual and aesthetic interests, in a semi-natural insular landscape. A few years later (in 2003), he completed the apprenticeship of an exquisite healing-mystical system which he learned during several visits to Barcelona. He then attempted to live in both places.

We left Alfonso, and while walking by the marina sidewalk, we soon met another acquaintance. Rejane – also known as Umani – was a Brazilian expatriate, married to Baghat, a Spanish musician. The couple sold his paintings and exotic clothes in the hippie markets. Originally from the Canary Islands, Baghat was very involved in his work as a percussion teacher and played in a salsa band in beach bars. He was a regular

Biodance practitioner, whereas Umani imparted séance sessions in an herbalist store in Santa Eulária.

Umani and Baghat were spiritual names which they acquired in India, as disciples of Osho. Umani grew up in Porto Alegre, main southern city in Brazil, and was studying history at college when she met Baghat, then a communard in an Osho center nearby. They moved to the Canary Islands in the early 1980s, and after a year in Germany, they settled down in Ibiza. Umani said that they were thinking about moving again, perhaps to Madrid or Brazil. But, like in many other cases I noticed, they remained in Ibiza, mostly for the special conditions that it provided with regard to the lifestyle they pursued. Umani was very enthusiastic about the island, and exclaimed in a blend of Spanish and Portuguese: 'Ibiza is very cool! It is a lovely place to live in. People from all over the world come to live here. All very interesting people. You are going to love it!'

Nadi and Ishwara arrived in Ibiza in 1996 and were living in a terrace apartment with a nice view of the marina of Santa Eulária. Nora excelled in various languages, and we agreed to speak Portuguese. From a German ethnic background, Nadi spoke with a southern Brazilian accent (like Umani, she was also from Porto Alegre). Tall and suntanned, Ishwara spoke with a swingy accent from Rio de Janeiro.

Nadi worked as a Biodance therapist and New Age healer. Since the 1970s, she had been interested in integrating Western psychotherapy and Eastern spirituality in her work. In Brazil, she was a yoga teacher before getting involved with Biodance, which she continued to organize in Brazil during the 1980s. She then went to India, and, by the time of my fieldwork, Nadi worked on Biodance and spiritual massage. Ishwara was a chiropractitioner, specializing in craniosacral therapy. He mostly assisted Nadi during Biodance sessions, controlling the sound system or monitoring body exercises. Ishwara was explicit about the reasons why they came to Ibiza:

> Ibiza is great. It has sea, beaches, and also rich people who pay you very well for your services. It is close to Europe, yet rent and taxes are low; good prices for everything. Also, lots of interesting people . . . It is very good indeed.

His bluntness reflected the couple's identity as Osho sannyasins, renowned for their spontaneous, often outspoken attitude, usually developed during confrontational therapies. To wit, Nadi and Ishwara are spiritual names bestowed on them during initiatory rituals at the Osho commune in Pune, India. They have taught Biodance and craniosacral workshops at the place, which Ishwara describes:

> It is a meditation center; an AIDS-free and drug-free zone; a community of ten thousand people where you can do anything, literally

anything you want, do you understand? ... But India, man, India is a mess! It has completely different life concepts. It is either take it or leave it.

Due to its centrality in the social life of expressive expatriates in Ibiza, the Osho commune and the cultural system it embodies will be examined in the next chapter. Yet, the nature and meaning of Biodance must be noted at this point. Culled in the 1960s countercultural experimentalism, Biodance is a body practice that applies concepts of medical anthropology, and was originally developed by psychiatrist Rolando Toro in Chile. In weekly group meetings, each Biodance session lasts about ninety minutes, combining music, movement and expression in a supportive setting. In a structured sequence of body exercises, the therapist explores one of the five 'basic dimensions of life' according to Biodance: vitality, sexuality, creativity, sociability and transcendence. Due to the physically intimate and emotionally expressive nature of some Biodance exercises, I sometimes witnessed newcomers silently leaving the room. Regular practitioners, however, report positive benefits which outlast the session: wellbeing, vitality, relaxation, increased sociability, spontaneity and insight.

The profile of Biodance practitioners in Ibiza is quite revealing of their expressive and expatriate features. I identified 32 people over the course of six years of participant observation at Nadi's group. There were 16 foreigners and 16 Spanish citizens; 9 were Osho sannyasins who worked as hippie traders and artists; 6 occupied more conventional (mainstream) social positions, such as a taxi driver, a clerk, housewives, a teacher, a computer technician and a fireman; the remaining 17 stood somewhere in between while clearly demonstrating an interest in alternative lifestyles; they were a DJ, a clown, handcrafters, a dancer, a yoga teacher, organic gardeners and a vegan cook.

The smallness of most samples presented in this chapter is highly significant, rather than dismissive of scientific merit. New Age settings are constituted by means of primary ('warm') and reflexive relationships which unfold upon the paradox of togetherness and individualism (Maffesoli 1988). Rather than large 'molar' aggregations, alternative settings are sustained by 'molecular interactions' (Deleuze and Guattari 1980). The myriad of micro-groups is integrated into fluid webs of exchange and support integrating a multiplicity of spaces, groups and symbolic references. In this chapter, I locate yoga teachers, Biodancers and Osho sannyasins within the social landscape of expressive expatriation which lies at the core of alternative life in Ibiza, yet always pointing outward.

Blind spots of New Age enlightenment

As expressive expatriates mutually interact in typical spaces, their ethos is crystallized in mental patterns that are not free of tensions, and even of contradictions. For example, their xenophile cosmopolitanism may collide with implicit ethnocentric assumptions that they hold about non-Western cultures. Particularly in Romantic imaginaries, alien cultures have been exoticized in a dialogic relation that is constitutive of Western identities (Airault 2000; Hutnyk 1999; Pratt 1992; Parkes 1991; Said 1978); however, such dialogism is often imbricated with forms of domination that contradict cosmopolitan claims on the surface. This sub-section analyses this question in reference to the reception and interpretation of media representations by a group of expatriates.

A small group of Biodancers, sannyasins and other friends gathered at Nadi's apartment to watch three documentary films about New Age spiritualities. The video tapes were given to Lourdes by hosts of her countryside hostel, which catered to spiritual and therapy groups vacationing from Europe. She managed *El Jardin de Luz* ('The Garden of Light') with her ex-husband Tom, a Dutch expatriate and Osho sannyasin. Originally from northern Spain, Lourdes fell in love with the island during a holiday: 'I felt that I could be very free here and do whatever I wanted. Besides, it was here where I healed from a chronic illness, and that was a miracle. Ibiza is a very special place indeed.' Lourdes has been to Pune, but no longer used her sannyasin name because she was also involved with other spiritual groups. 'I am always looking for a guru,' she said while showing me the brochure of a yoga retreat she planned to attend in Germany.

It was a sunny evening and about twenty people gathered in the spacious living room. Wearing light summer clothes, they were therapists, hippie traders, New Age businesspeople and retired housewives who practiced yoga or Biodance, in addition to several Osho sannyasins. They were all expatriates or alternative Spaniards from the mainland. Only one person was born on the island (a young lady whom I would meet by chance in Pune years later). Since several people spoke only poor English, Nora provided simultaneous interpretation of the movies into Spanish.

The first film titled 'The Temple of Humankind in Damanhur' featured the architecture of an underground temple located in the Italian Alps. The edification belonged to a spiritualist cult called Damanhur (Damanhur Federation 2006). Richly decorated with large crystals, mirrors and white marble, the temple in classic style was carved in a massive granite formation. Its iconography combined Renaissance and Ancient Egypt motives, resulting in a syncretism which sought to represent the 'ecumenism of the twelve ancient civilizations.' Following some principles of chromotherapy, each room was colored and designated for specific body organs. Yet, the temple was also devoted to healing the entire planet, since it was built upon 'a mine of rare minerals, 300 million years old,' in a location that 'interconnects the three magnetic lines of the Earth, in the geographic link between the Euro-Asiatic and African plaques.' With such grandiose ideas of 'ecumenism,' 'twelve races' and 'geological plaques,' the temple of Damanhur expressed a certain perception of colossal globalization.

However, such multiculturalism was contradicted by the fact that all of the members were white European, as was the iconography on display. The project presented itself as a Romantic pastiche, cultivating an 'Other' that was entirely absent, or, at most, as a lost reference from ancient times.

Most of the people who watched the film remained silent. While it is not possible to assess their perceptions at a deeper level, it can be said that expressions of critical 'judgment' are commonly rejected among New Agers, at least in public or ritual spaces. However, a few of those present made cheerful comments on the temple's beautiful iconography. A Frenchman tried to answer questions about the cult leadership and healing practices. While an enthusiastic woman suggested that 'we should all go there,' another made a remark on the considerable financial resources that must have been spent in the construction of such a magnificent structure.

The next video, 'The Miracle of Waters,' focused on the alleged healing powers of specific water springs located in India, Germany, Mexico and Kenya. Each case featured comments by spring proprietors and believers, who praised the supernatural effects of the wells. The Kenyan case was peculiar for its messianic overtones. In a poor rural area, an old black woman ran the well, angrily fending off a crowd of excited onlookers. Suddenly, the camera turned to a tall Semitic man wearing a turban who walks toward the well and delivered a speech (his voice was not on audio). The narrator enigmatically noted that he claimed to be 'Maytrea, the Esoteric Jesus.'

Unlike professional documentaries, the film provided no alternative explanation for the alleged powers of springs or to the Maytrea apparition. As a matter of fact, Lourdes informed us that the tape was actually produced by a group of Maytrea believers who had recently stayed at her resort for some spiritual retreat. The reaction at Nadi's room was again apparently uncritical, or relatively blasé. Two women, however, somehow revered the spooky avatar fearsomely. I also noticed that two other women had laughed at Kenyan peasants trancing in spasmodic fits. Since laughter indicates tension or paradox, their reaction begged the question of what was the underlying assumption confronted by those apparently disturbing images. These women could not explain why, but at a deeper cultural level, their laughter was effectively symptomatic of a discrepancy between Western idealizations of oriental civilizations as carriers of ancient wisdom, and the African trancing peasants who introduced an element of disorder into the frame of ordered Eurocentric spirituality.

The last video, 'Peace and Healing Celebration of North American Indians,' documented a cross-national march of Native Americans riding horses and meeting in the US mid-West. Abundant in ideals of 'Mother Earth' and 'the Creator,' the video represented them as naturally peaceful and ecologic beings, in the lines of the Rousseaunian *bon savage*. What passed unnoticed was the fact that 'mother earth' and 'father sun' are notions borrowed from eighteenth-century Franciscan priests in their attempts to convert Native Americans to Christianity. Similarly, the audience missed issues of land repatriation that underlie the Native American agenda as it intersects New Age misrepresentations. The film's noble idealism was irresistible, as even Nora, who was usually critical about America, sighed in enchantment, 'Ah, I wanna be there. You know, that is my land too.'

Following the screenings, Lourdes suggested a few silent moments in a prayer for global peace. The group held hands in a chain and remained with eyes closed for about ten minutes. Afterwards, it gradually broke down in multiple conversations, as people dispersed and left. Driving the car, Nora asked my opinion and why I did not speak about the movies. I reminded her of the lack of receptivity for intellectual claims in New Age gatherings, and she agreed. As Osho has jokingly said regarding the proper attitude for attending his lectures, 'leave your shoes and minds outside.' As these video screenings indicated, there were blind spots in the dialogic process of identity formation of expressive expatriates – aesthetic forms can fascinate the subject, making them ignore categories of exclusion and consistency. New Agers remain open to new perspectives, insofar as these do not hinder their will to self-cultivation.

Expressive at night – bohemian connections

Social leisure for expressive expatriates must be meaningful, pleasurable and preferably carried out in locales of natural beauty. Rather than 'killing time' for 'de-stressing,' it is seen as an opportunity to joyfully socialize with like-minded individuals, sharing the same concerns with ecology and expression. In a previous session, I described the exotic parties that Rochelle organized for friends in her property by the sea. In a beautiful setting, expatriates desultorily talked about life on the island, absent friends, future trips and spirituality.

In one of her parties, I was introduced to Deep and his wife, Argentinean expatriates who traded exotic clothes at hippie markets. They had been living on the island since the early 1980s. As a hint of their spontaneous, slightly eccentric personalities, they were, as a matter of fact, veteran sannyasins who had engaged in multiple countercultural experiments. Our conversation about spirituality drifted toward psychedelic experiences, in particular about an Amazonic neo-shamanic cult named Santo Daime. Interestingly, Deep was not only a sannyasin but also a main organizer of the cult in Ibiza. Multiple affiliations were common among expressive expatriates, exemplifying a type of post-traditional religiosity typically seen in the New Age. The Santo Daime revolves around a sacramental drink named *ayahuasca*, a hallucinogenic tea collectively ingested during an overnight ritual, which also comprised a highly monotonous dance, the chanting of hymns and periods of silent meditation. Participants report to have visions of a mystical, sacred nature during the ritual. Due to the religious context of consumption, the legal status of *ayahuasca* has remained undefined in various countries, although state authorities have been typically hostile toward the cult. In the case of Spain, the socialist governments of the 1980s and 1990s decriminalized drug consumption, while maintaining drug trading as a criminal offense (Escohotado 1998).

Deep explained that, for a while, Daimistas were able to bring the substance through airport checkpoints in twenty-liter containers, declaring it an 'energizer drink from the Amazon.' But customs officers demanded them to stop the transaction, and the group began to import *ayahuasca* instead from Holland, overland and by ferry. However, the cult ceased its operations in Ibiza for other reasons. According to Deep, participants gradually lost interest in the cult, as their attention drifted toward other self-development practices. They sporadically conducted Daime rituals, based on special visits or requests. But the original enthusiasm had apparently faded.

This story illustrates the life cycle commonly verified in New Age forms of religiosity. A ritual practice is sustained for as long as the participants remain genuinely interested. Yet, because of their avid curiosity in trying new possibilities, without an influx of new members or organizational creativity, a group often disintegrates, as former members gradually become involved in other spiritual systems. New Age affiliations are thus non-authoritative and temporary, with personal affiliations lasting from a few sessions up to several or many years, until the subject feels that it is time to move on (Maffesoli 1988). In this case, religious 'tradition' is not an authoritative grid that determines personal roles and choices, but rather a tool for the reflexive cultivation of the self in its axiological, corporeal, social and cosmological dimensions (Beck *et al.* 1994). In sum, the New Age expresses the shifting, contingential needs of post-traditional subjects, who are seeking magical gain or ethical development (D'Andrea 2000; Heelas 1996; Luckmann 1991). New Agers are therefore nomadic in their engagements with spiritual or self-development systems, varying according to time, opportunity and need.

Other expatriates actualize their expressive drives in secular or artistic fashion rather than in religious spirituality. The following example illustrates a different type of expressive individualism. Patricio was a plastic artist and event producer, a Chilean expatriate based in Brussels who regularly visited Ibiza. I first met him at a small gathering that Rochelle organized for screening his internationally awarded short film titled *Flood*, featuring the sculpting of a sandman by Patricio near the waves of a rising tide, which finally destroy the sandman. On that occasion, a motorcycle manufacturer hired Patricio to co-produce an exclusive promotional party in one of the mega-nightclubs of Ibiza.

We scheduled an informal interview in Ibiza town: Monday midnight, a peculiarity that clubbers and bohemians largely ignored or celebrated.[13] Patricio and I met at the old jazz bar and joined his group at one of the many open air bars at the marina located beside the medieval fortress. In an article titled 'The Floating Nightclub,' the Catalan reporter notes:

> The night of Ibiza has always been, and above all, a state of mind that is born from a strange combination of hippiness, circus-like modernity, electronic music, hedonism (sometimes light, sometimes wild), and an ensemble of extreme peoples and sexualities.
>
> (*El Temps* 2000: 19)

Patricio introduced me to his daughter and friends, all of them Belgian. Sophie was a film producer who lived in Ibiza. As I mentioned my research work on 'alternative lifestyles and spiritualities,' she spontaneously began to talk about her own experiences with Santo Daime. Sophie complained that the ritual had too many disciplinary rules and that she felt very stomach sick (an expected side-effect of *ayahuasca*). She paused for a moment and reconsidered her affirmation about never trying *ayahuasca* again.

The conversation dispersed as the group began to speak a fast French which I was not able to understand. As a perceptive expatriate, Patricio remained speaking Spanish only. As previously mentioned, these polyglots often changed over three or four languages in a single conversation topic, usually to emphasize aspects of a narrative. Yet, as an implicit rule, veteran expatriates sought to speak in the language that most participants could understand.

Patricio came to Europe in 1973, right after the military coup of Pinochet in Chile. He was neither involved in politics nor in imminent danger, but felt very disappointed with the situation. Then, he was a cinema student at the University of Santiago. Upon leaving, he first considered to ask for exile in the US, but 'the government was denying our entrance, because they were worried about having to host masses of Chilean refugees.' He added with a laugh, 'but the situation flipped over when they began to think that we were millionaires jet-setting around the world, and began to offer one-year visas to any of us for free!' This comment denoted a pragmatic perception that expatriates have about the shifting circumstances that characterize international environments, and which they must consider when trying to actualize their strategies of mobility. After decades of conservative Christian rule in Chile, the rise of democratic socialism in the late 1960s was paralleled by a culture of experimentalism amid the urban youth in the realms of art, therapy and sexuality. Thinking of the fact that Biodance was born in Santiago de Chile, I asked Patricio if he had ever heard about it. He stared at me flabbergasted, and said: 'You mean, Rolando Toro?! Of course I know Biodance! I participated in his original groups, when he was still trying with it.' Then, Toro was a researcher at the Center of Medical Anthropology at the Medical School of the University of Santiago. Patricio seemed touched, as he recalled:

Those experiments were very strong . . . Emotional expression, expression of your body . . . Touching each other with lights off, then everyone naked with lights on. There was lots of face-to-face confrontation, and aggressive stuff coming out, yeah. Those exercises were really shattering . . .

He shook his head as if returning from a mild trance. Since he left Chile, however, Patricio had not heard about Biodance again. The 1973 coup resulted in the suppression of all forms of cultural experimentalism. Toro fled to Brazil, and then to Italy. Patricio was glad to learn that Biodance had flourished in several countries, and that there was a group in Ibiza.

At 3:00, Patricio drove a young Belgian photographer and me to the nightclub *Privilege*. On Monday night (into Tuesdays), the venue was rented out to UK promoters of *Manumission*, a party that attracted 10,000 mostly British clubbers each week throughout the summer. Patricio parked the car and walked with us to the entrance, but curiously halted and refused to enter: 'No, no. If I begin, nothing will stop me,' he ominously said, and left. His friend nonetheless insinuated that I could get him in for free. Though sometimes I sought to attend such requests, my own entrance as a club ethnographer was never assured. In any case, he disappeared in the crowd, while I entered through the line queuing for the guest-list. An hour later he found me inside. 'I just told the guy at the door that I am a photographer, showed him my press ID, and he let me in,' he said shrugging his shoulders.

This apparently trivial anecdote contains some curious yet relevant aspects of Ibiza's nightlife, as experienced by bohemians. Patricio's refusal to attend *Privilege* indicated the familiarity of expressive expatriates with the famous Ibicencan nightclubs, historically imagined (and sometimes actualized) as orgiastic spaces of self-derailment. Second, free admittance was a delicate issue for these expatriates, not only because the cover was deemed quite expensive (about US$35 or €30, excluding drinks) while they enjoyed moving freely across different clubs over the week and even in the same night. Free entrance also reaffirmed the personal and collective status of those who had effectively engendered the charisma of Ibiza's nightlife: well-connected bohemians and clubbers who, nonetheless, had to learn to navigate the increasingly commodified environments of the leisure industry. The complex interplay between underground and mainstream formations in Ibiza constitutes the main topic of analysis of the next chapter.

Conclusion: the aesthetics of centered marginality

The diaspora of expressive expatriates illustrates important social and cultural issues of globalization. The distinctiveness of this globalized formation resides less on its geographically and synchronically multi-sited nature, and more on the way that it is globally constituted: their practices of displacement and connectivity acquire special significance in the constitution of identities that value not sameness but continual variation, not local roots but translocal interests.

As such, the study of expressive expatriates must confront a methodological challenge. As an island, Ibiza would seem to materialize the ethnographer's dream of a remote, tightly bounded entity that separates a pure and elucidative 'in here' from the contaminating influences of the 'out there.' However, mobile expatriates dissolve the certainties associated with the analytical privilege of the 'local.' The investigation of transnational phenomena occurring in a place must consider the local conditions and historicities that contribute to the development of grounded realities. Yet, the meaning of such cosmopolitan formations can only be grasped with reference to the translocal circuits and forces that these peoples, practices and imaginaries constitute and refer to. The study of particular, delimited sites is a necessary element in the study of translocal processes; however, it is not sufficient for understanding the wider processes and historicities that affect the 'local' and that constitute formations not entirely connected to or dependent on it. Although situated in localities, the 'site' of a research on hypermobility lies beyond the 'local' and requires a methodological apparatus informed by a nomadic sensibility capable of addressing such formations beyond local immobility.

Despite their need to make a living, expressive expatriates did not migrate to Ibiza looking for 'better jobs and wages,' nor do they isolate themselves in ethnocentric 'expat' communities. Many have abandoned favorable labor conditions in the homeland, in order to search for something that they deem more meaningful. Others, in dire straits, just did not want to go on struggling with neo-liberal pressures any more. In either case, their material conditions – favorable or not – did not determine why they chose to develop alternative careers, often in even more unstable economic conditions. They have prioritized existential goals of actualizing expressive, spiritual and/or epicurean values. They become handcrafters, food artisans, gardeners, New Age entrepreneurs, hippie traders, musicians, DJs, body therapists, masseuses, yoga teachers, healers, etc., as well as jet-setting bohemians of the affluent class.

Beyond welfare and neo-liberal conditions, they inhabit a cosmopolitan culture of expressive individualism that, at a wider theoretical level, fully instantiates Foucauldian notions of subjectivity formation. While attempting to break apart from biopower regimes of state, market and morality, the subject is confronted with a basic question: how to conduct one's life under conditions of ethical freedom? These expressive expatriates have sought to respond to this challenge with an aesthetics of existence that operates as an ethics of self-mastery (Foucault and Lotringer 1989). This is not aestheticism, but rather the basis of a political ethics of the self that seeks autonomy by dissociating systemic normativity from life politics (Giddens

1992; Hacking 1986). Whereas the regime of biopower/'sexuality' have forged the modern subject of interiority and control, countercultural formations sustain experiments that point toward the possibility of a post-sexuality age, defined as a specific arrangement of power relations and truth claims about the subject and sociality. This counter-hegemonic apparatus would enable and legitimate alternative experiences of the self and identity formation in which pleasure, reflexivity and metamorphosis may play a larger role.

Ibiza itself determines the possibility of this aesthetic lifestyle. It is visible that a variety of cultural organizations (cooperatives, schools, museums, art galleries, etc.) dedicated to the betterment of Ibiza have been founded or revitalized by expressive expatriates as they fall in love with the island. And, thus, two paradoxical consequences are to be noted. While they flee the mainstream, Ibiza's utopian imaginary, which these expatriates have in essence created, has paradoxically placed these self-*marginalized* people at the *center* of its creative life, a charismatic populace crafting much of the seductive charm of the island. However, though mass tourism also affects other Balearic islands and southern Spain, nowhere else has leisure entertainment gained such an intensity, reputation (and notoriety), for having expressive expatriates as a pivotal magnet of tourists and celebrities. As a consequence, the gradual commodification and surveillance of alternative spaces, practices and imaginaries have threatened the sustainability of such countercultural formations. Expressive expatriates have to reassess their position by resisting, accommodating or assimilating larger systems. How they relate with the captive machine of state surveillance and leisure capitalism is the central topic of the next chapter.

3 The hippie and club scenes in Ibiza's tourism industry[1]

'*Qué habéis hecho con mis hippies?*'
'What have you done to my hippies?'
    Prince Juan Carlos to Ibiza mayor, 1973

Counterculture and commodity

Ibiza is a unique place in terms of its materiality and symbolic projection. It displays some of the highest rates of tourist activity and income-per-capita in Spain and the Mediterranean. The tiny island is also known as the 'clubbing capital of the world,' hosting the biggest and the best night-clubs on the planet (Dancestar 2004; Guinness 2003). Likewise, because of the longstanding presence of bohemians, the international media have represented Ibiza as an icon of utopia and liberation. However, the growth of mass tourism has led to the chaotic urbanization of the island's coast and even its hinterland, and also resulted in pressing environmental problems. In the meanwhile, the leisure capital juggernaut of Ibiza has under-cut the countercultural elements of nightclubs, submitting these venues to a logic of predatory profiteering. The press now benchmarks Ibiza as a saturated tourist trap or decadent paradise, even though alternative scenes do persist in more secluded areas of the island. Considering this problematic scenario, it can be asked, what are the conditions that sustain Ibiza as a utopian space and party capital? How does the massification of tourism interrelate with such utopian imaginary?

The special status of Ibiza cannot be explained on the basis of its pleasant climate and leisure amenities alone, since similar conditions prevail across most of the Mediterranean. My main argument in this chapter is that the charisma of Ibiza stems from the significant presence of expressive expatriates, who have been arriving on the island since the 1930s: artists, naturalists, beatniks, hippies, gays, sannyasins, clubbers and freaks (D'Andrea 2004; Stratton 1994; Scheurmann and Scheurman 1993; Rozenberg 1990; Paul 1937). As seen in the previous chapter, they have migrated to the island to shape an alternative lifestyle that integrates labor, leisure and spirituality within a cosmopolitan community of mobile expatriates dedicated to practices of expressive individualism. In Ibiza they actively promote and participate in the nightclub, the hippie and the gay scenes with various transnational connections. In other words, supposing their absence, Ibiza would likely remain as a tourist destination, yet without the charismatic reach projected internationally.

In this connection, a paradoxical situation follows the presence of such expatriate charisma. Although fleeing the mainstream, these expatriates are soon followed by growing numbers of tourists, business developers and migrants. While tourism creates economic opportunities for expressive expatriates, the excessive growth of mass tourism along with state surveillance gradually promotes, captures and stifles, in commodity and legal form, those spaces, practices and imaginaries that were formerly circumscribed amid expressive expatriates. Not only does such modernization undermine the utopian project, it also damages the social and environmental landscape of the island in the context of growing competition among Mediterranean resorts. In face of price inflation, pollution, overregulation, overwork and social stress, expatriates must reassess their situation, and decide to capitulate to modern regimes of labor and law, to move elsewhere, or to develop more ambivalent strategies of accommodation without assimilation.

In order to examine how leisure capital captures countercultural formations, this chapter focuses on the hippie and the nightclub scenes considered in their symbiotic interaction with the political economies of tourism and entertainment industries. The next section sets the tone of the chapter with an example that describes the social and environmental transformation of a pristine nude beach into a tourist attraction. A large section is then dedicated to an analysis of the hippie scene, discussing various cases that evince how alternative markets, parties and music capitulate under capitalist formations and the ambiguous rule of law. The third section analyzes the structure of the mighty nightclub oligopoly, as the environment in which underground clubbers navigate. The final chapter section discusses the diasporic nature of alternative Ibiza: both utopian ideals and flexible capitalism propel expressive expatriates seasonally to leave the island, particularly toward exoticized locations in South Asia and Latin America.

As an analytical remark, rather than an approach of economic determinism, I elaborate on the pivotal role that expressive expatriates have played in triggering the outstanding popularity of the club and hippie scenes, which then become contested sites for the play of capital and law. It is against this backdrop that the dichotomy 'mainstream-counterculture' must be reconsidered. It provides a cognitive reference that informs the decisions of alternative subjects, authorities and tourists, and has important economic and cultural consequences. Yet, political economies and counter-hegemonic formations rearticulate in ways that contradict folk claims and expectations about such dichotomy. My analysis, therefore, does not seek to find the truth about what is 'countercultural' or 'mainstream.' Rather, it seeks to keep the productive tension between economic and cultural logics, which may contribute to understanding these marginal formations as ambivalent sites of struggle and identification (Grossberg 1997; McRobbie 1994a).

Utopian sites under siege: Punta Galera

Nora took me to a rocky beach formation dearly appreciated by expressive expatriates. Although located just a few kilometers north of Sant Antoni, Punta Galera *was* a relatively secluded space. Suiting commonsensical images of paradise, it was an outstandingly beautiful place where nudists and snorkel divers could enjoy spectacular Mediterranean scenery. Environmentalists have long tried to keep it as a 'secret beach' among well-connected residents only. Road signals were destroyed every time a local authority sought to promote Punta Galera as a tourist attraction. Though buses could not run on the steep curvy roads down to the place, rental cars – a massive presence during the summer – and even an excess of boats could have an impact on the area.

A few discreet paintings, of a spiritual nature, could be seen on the rocks. First, the outline of a yogi in lotus position was carved on a rock plateau by the sea. Nora explained that it was a *mandala* (sacred icon) representing the 'ecumenism' of cultural and spiritual traditions in Ibiza. It was carved in 1993 during the visit of a neo-shamanic healer from Brazil. New Age healers were always an attraction for curious expatriates, and a group followed him to Punta Galera to practice meditation and drink

Figure 3.1 Punta Galera, formerly a nude beach.

ayahuasca. For years to come, Nora, Rochelle and others remembered the 'beauty' and 'power' of that event.

Other marks of the New Age could be seen inside a cave hole on a cliff. Hardly noticeable, it nonetheless had the words '*no entre*' (do not enter) hand painted. One had to stand on tiptoes to look into the hole. There was enough room for one person to sit or lie down; a thin mattress, a red candle, a matchbox, a notebook and a picture of the Hindu god Shiva. The place was occupied by a Peruvian handcrafter who sometimes stayed there for shamanic retreats during the off-season. During sea storms, he would stand and face the big waves with his arms open, 'just to feel the power of nature,' Nora explained. In my few interactions with Ari, I noted that, despite living very modestly, he had traveled to the Himalayas. I sometimes spotted him in nightclubs, which he attended for free, like most of the island's alternatives.

Finally, the words '*Cala Yoga*' and the symbol 'om' were hand-painted on a large standing rock. The word 'cala' means beach estuary in Ibicencan dialect. Nora explained that a yoga teacher, her acquaintance, made the painting in the early 1990s, 'to express his feelings that Punta Galera is a spiritual place.' Staring at the horizon Nora sighed, 'Yes, this place is really very special . . . '

Since I first visited it in 1998, Punta Galera has undergone a dramatic transformation. Every high season (from May to September), a growing number of tourists rush to the site, clearly associated with increasing volumes of litter and erosion. On weekends, new urban residents add to the crowd, while jet-skis, tour glass-boats and yachts noisily cruise at a swimming distance. Due to such invasion, nudism is rarely practiced. In addition, there are rumors about business plans for 'developing' the area, as has happened to many other urbanized beaches. Finally, a growing number of summer houses have been built on the previously green hills that surround Punta Galera, despite government attempts to curb the seemingly unstoppable urbanization of the island.[2]

This picture suggests the end of Punta Galera as a 'piece of paradise on earth,' as expatriates once described it. It has become another attraction – and victim – of mass tourism and real-estate development, following the harmless presence of expressive expatriates on the beach. In the meantime, while expatriates look for more secluded beaches, similar patterns of tourist massification and urbanization can be verified in other parts of the island, such as Benirrás beach, as discussed on p. 89.

The hippie scene: autonomy and tourism

Marketing campaigns promoting Ibiza tourism depict images of smiley 'hippies' playing drums, juxtaposed with sunny beaches, an exciting nightlife and ancient folklore. Although Ibicencans no longer praise the

Figure 3.2 Drum party at Benirrás beach.

friendliness of hippies, their presence has long caught the attention of both tourists and businessmen. An influential hotelier declared in an interview for a British TV documentary:

> Hippies made Ibiza known internationally. Thanks to them the island became famous. Hippies did more for Ibiza in a few years than ministries of tourism could do during their entire lives.
>
> (*Ibiza Uncovered*, Sky TV 1998)

Nonetheless, such media overexposure came with a price. The seasonal pounding of mass tourism affected the rhythms of social life, compelling alternative subjects to reassess their position. The tip of the balance between labor and leisure dramatically turned toward the former, and usually in an undesired manner. A relatively free and autonomous lifestyle thus became dependent on exogenous, disciplined and intensified labor practices, all of which caused expatriates to flee their homeland in the first place.

On the other hand, the circulation of hippie images may attract a specific segment of curious tourists, dissatisfied with their lives at home. As seen in the previous chapter, it is often during a holiday in Ibiza that they have a glimpse of utopia, prompting them to migrate. The transition, nonetheless, is not always immediate. An intermediary state between tourist and expatriate, to be examined in this chapter, is embodied in young bohemian workers who seasonally come to the island to 'work for party.' This group ambivalently oscillates between nationalist ethnocentrism and cosmopolitan experimentalism, revealing an identity that is neither sedentary nor nomadic.

This section, in sum, provides further evidence and analysis of how alternative sites, practices and subjects are gradually shaped and incorporated within larger regimes of leisure capital and state surveillance, with a focus on what can be economically referred to as the 'hippie scene.'

'Hippie markets': for tourists

Many expatriates (including Spaniards from the homeland) worked at one of the three main 'hippie markets.' Las Dálias is a rustic farmland property by the road to San Carles, which hosts a hippie market every Saturday of the tourist season (from May to October). Dusty parking lots head to the patio of a farmhouse where some 100 stalls display a variety of exotic goods: ethnic/hippie clothes, handcrafts, paintings, gems, jewelry, incense, tattoos, fruit juices; there is also a *chai* shop. Besides expatriates and Santa Eulária residents, the market is mostly frequented by tourists. In pleasant sunny weather, longhaired vendors sit by their booths, reading or informally interacting with anyone willing to chat or buy. As the press recurrently notes, the atmosphere in Las Dálias is not 'touristy' (commercialized), but rather 'hippie': relaxed, lively and intimate.

Opened as a rustic roadside bar in 1954, Las Dálias improved its facilities to host barbecues for organized groups of tourists. But this system dwindled throughout the 1970s, with the growing competition posed by Eivissa and Sant Antoni. Ironically, such demise transformed Las Dálias into a secret hangout bar for pop stars and their entourages, including Robert Plant, Nina Hagen, the Rolling Stones, Led Zeppelin, Judas Priest, Queen, UB40 and Simply Red. Daytime auctions at the garden encouraged an expatriate woman to organize a regular 'hippie market' from 1986 onward. Alternative residents could sell their artisan products to new waves of tourists within the general upsurge of tourism in Ibiza that began to take place in the late 1980s. Even so, perhaps due to its relative distance to main urban centers of the island, Las Dálias hippie market was able to maintain a somehow peaceful and relaxed ('chilled out') atmosphere into the 2000s.

Differently, Es Canar 'hippie market' happens every Wednesday in summer, and very clearly caters for tourists since its inception in the early 1990s. Located at Santa Eulária, it emerged from an agreement between area hoteliers and an excess of hippie traders who were dissatisfied with

Las Dálias. Much larger than Las Dálias, it hosts more than three times the number of stalls and perhaps ten times the number of tourists. Many alternatives work on both markets, although Spanish and Senegalese traders are a visible presence in Es Canar. In addition to alternative products (hippie clothing, leather, jewelry, etc.), there is a large amount of African wooden craft and cheap manufactured goods, such as toys, watches, sunglasses, regular clothes and CDs. In any measure, Es Canar seems less 'hippie' and more 'market' than Las Dálias.

As I kept returning to Las Dálias, some hippie traders eventually greeted me with smiles and *holas*. In several instances, I had never spoken to them. I remarked this occurrence to Nora as we wandered through the market. She did not seem surprised:

> Of course, they are recognizing your face. You know, they see you walking with me. And they see so many people during the season, and tourists disappear. But some faces stick around and begin to stand out from the mass. So, yeah, you are becoming more familiar. You are becoming part of the family!

These comments point out a sense of solidarity that identifies hippie traders internally. In fact, several of my main informants (Nora, Rochelle, Barbara) were known as regulars in the alternative scenes of the island. During the late 1980s Nora sold tofu in Las Dálias. Thus, whenever she greeted any of her many acquaintances, Nora introduced them to me, or later gave me a summary of their lives. Such communal bonds can be noticed in relation to many alternatives that did not work at the market, yet showed up to socialize and get updates about upcoming events. Las Dálias was, in sum, a space of socialization for expressive expatriates (including Spanish 'expatriates' from the mainland).

In contrast with a conventional sales mode (impersonal, reverential, forceful), expressive expatriates candidly interacted with potential buyers. They gestured spontaneously, made lively comments about any triviality and joked (between themselves) about tourists. Many of these hippie traders displayed flamboyant personalities, wearing exuberant clothes, hairstyles and jewelry. Donovan sold his paintings at Las Dálias. Originally from Italy, he had lived in California (US) during the 1960s. He was a masseur, but preferred to work as a house painter and, like Nora, complained about tiredness. He poked fun at everything, including himself working as a masseur in hotels, or about his daughter's boyfriend who lived in Japan. Nora sighed, and we kept walking.

Strolling through the farmhouse archway, we found the recently opened *chai* shop. The exotic beauty of the room was outstanding, in a word, 'orientalist.' A scent of sandalwood incense pervaded the air. The room was dimly lit by two candles and the natural light through a small window. Long silk sheets crossed the ceiling. A large kasbah-like display of exotic products covered the right wall: Moroccan mats, drapes, cushions, silver pots, incense, a crystal ball and statues of Hindu gods, such as a magnificent Nataraj (dancing Shiva). On the left side, a rustic bar combined Moroccan decoration with an Ibicencan peasant-style kitchen lined by tall bar chairs. At the end of the room, ground-level tables were surrounded by various sitting cushions. In contrast to the tourist frenzy outside, the *chai* shop was tranquil and relatively empty. A group of youngsters smoked in the table area; two tourists were browsing. A flamboyantly dressed couple managed the place. The *chai* shop reminded me of a Romantic painting of Eastern motives, such as *The Snake Charmer* by Gérôme (depicted on the book-cover of Said's *Orientalism*).

As we sipped some *chai* (spiced tea), Nora whispered that she could not remember the owners' names, and left to talk to someone outside. I initiated a conversation with the woman, Marol, who was tall, blond, fit, and wore a long flowery skirt and a white top with puffy short sleeves. She lived in Ibiza, but frequently left the island during the winter, going to Holland, Morocco or India, from where she brought the exotic merchandise on display. A Dutch expatriate in her early thirties, Marol had four children 'spread everywhere' as she jocosely remarked; two lived with relatives in Holland and Spain, and the youngest ones stayed with her. I saw one of them running barefoot around market stalls, playing with other children and tenderly watched over by hippie traders. Despite working hard to promote the exotic events she co-organized, Marol seemed to enjoy that lifestyle. Charismatic and expressive, she could step onto an empty dance floor and loosely dance, while the crowd silently watched, until a child grabbed her long skirt in order to say something.

As a potential buyer approached Marol, I turned to the man over the counter. Mediterranean in appearance, he wore a simple medieval-like shirt and red turban. As a Spanish expatriate, his adopted name was Alok, a sign of his discipleship to Osho, like many other expatriates that I met. Accordingly, he had also been to the Osho commune in Pune, India. (On a different occasion, he told me that he was a real-estate broker in Barcelona following an existential crisis. Someone suggested that he should travel to India, where he incidentally heard about Osho. He decided to try the commune and was radically transformed, as he put it. Upon return, he realized that his life in the city was 'unbearable' and moved to Ibiza after a vacation on the island in 1996, settling down with the help of connections he had at the hippie market.) Alok invited me to the grand opening of their weekly party *Namaste*, a 'very special night with a surprise dinner and magic shows,' as he described it, to be examined next.

Namaste: *freak business and seduction*

Over the course of a few years, *Namaste* grew from an uncertain experiment into a key event in the hippie nightlife and a successful tourist attraction just the same. It takes place in the garden area of Las Dálias restaurant every Wednesday night throughout the high season. Tourists sit in the restaurant area watching the exotically dressed hippies and artists. In the chill-out garden, gregarious 'freaks'[3] and elder bohemians lie on cushions around low tables, drinking *chai* and discreetly sharing hashish joints. A number of exotic performances take place in a small circular patio, including flamenco guitarists, Latino poets, opera punk singers, North African dancers, fire acrobats, Indian musicians, belly dancers, and there is even a Biodance demonstration.

A dance room with psychedelic decorations, named 'trance room' due to the Techno trance music being played, was added at *Namaste* in 2001. Inside the farmhouse, the trance room began to attract a horde of young freaks arriving late at night. In contrast to such freakness, Las Dálias's owner, Juanito, is an Ibicencan man of more conventional tastes. Although hippies sometimes persuade him to wear a white tunic, his main concerns were attendance and noise levels, as police drive up and down the road, watchful for compliance infractions. Like his relatives running the property, Juanito is not engaged with alternative culture, and he delegated the artistic component of the business to Chris, a Canadian–Spanish musician and event producer.

In between the seasons of 1999 and 2003 (research period), *Namaste* crowds increased from 200 to about 2,000 per party, and so did its prices. Dinner cover increased from Ptas 1,200 to 3,000 (US$7–18), in addition to a new entrance fee, which also increased from Ptas 1,000 to 2,500. The new euro currency pushed these figures up. Tourists prevailed during the evening, while alternatives arrived later, looking for a combination of *chai*, hash and trance. As *Namaste* gradually catered for tourist demands, the more underground crowd drifted toward the Sunday night parties organized by *Tribe of Frog*, a new contender from Bristol (England). Freaks certainly preferred free parties in the countryside, and thus insisted on free or largely discounted entrance at Las Dálias.

During wintertime, *Namaste* promoters organized a few low-profile dance parties at *El Divino*, the most elegant nightclub in Ibiza. This venture evinces a connection between hippie and jet-set scenes – which will be detailed in the next section. Nevertheless, Alok and friends aborted plans for a summer season in the nightclub, since Las Dálias reissued its own party license; moreover, the stiffly competitive club industry represented an overwhelming challenge for any club party promoter, with the risk of financial losses. Curiously, Alok and I chatted about *El Divino* as we unexpectedly met in a chill-out bar in Goa, India, a few years later.

Namaste has succeeded as a lively, profitable event offering orientalist exoticism for hippies, freaks and tourists. In addition to the entrepreneurial skills of its promoters, *Namaste* has relied on the extensive word-of-mouth among hippie traders, attracting a large number of tourists. In the Ibiza context, *Namaste* has also benefited from the peripheral location of

Las Dálias in relation to the island's mighty club oligopoly, in a period when the utopian imaginary of Ibiza has become internationally marketed as a tourist commodity. Despite hinging on the commercialization of alternative formations, *Namaste* cannot be properly characterized as a commodified process, because of the transparency of social relations still found among cultural producers and alternative consumers, thus conferring an air of 'authenticity' to the event.

Mediated by exotic events such as *Namaste*, the utopian imaginary of Ibiza exerts a seductive influence upon segments of mainstream tourists, particularly the existentially ambitious youth. A short vacation on the island may trigger a latent crisis of self-identity, which may soon subside or lead to a critical decision to move to the island more or less indefinitely. The 'Ibiza bug' is an expression from the 1960s that aptly captures the infectious character that traveling through exotic lands may have on the victim. How such orientalist events entice tourists to risk a new lifestyle is a question that requires further investigation. Nonetheless, it is not uncommon to witness young tourists inquiring about alternative gigs on the island, who later 'drop out.'

Hippie markets: for hippies

In contrast with Es Canar and Las Dálias, other markets were predominantly attended by expressive expatriates. Located at a modest ranch in the northern countryside, the 'organic market' of Can Sort took place every Saturday morning, during most of the year. Narrow dirt roads lead to the house with some sparse parking spots amid bushes and stone barriers. Usually about a dozen vehicles were parked in the bucolic setting, ranging from rusty old vans, to economic sedans, to luxurious sedans and even an American-style SUV.

Under a modest barn, Miguel and Marta (Barbara's housemates, see p. 56) sold organic produce and breads. With effort, a Scottish woman ran the ranch with the assistance of two younger women in the kitchen. They cooked vegetarian food and served plates over the counter, directly to the visitor who then sat on the patio outside. Most of the two dozen people present were expatriates: a German belly dancer accompanied by *Matrix*-looking companions (wearing dark leather clothes, sunglasses and trimmed haircuts), a few American hippies, South American teenagers, etc. Eating vegetarian food in a simple rural setting seemed to be an attractive element in bringing them to socialize at Can Sort.

But not all of them were countercultural or expatriate types. As an illuminating exception, José was a modest working-class man from mainland Spain, who attended Biodance sessions for a few months. He was employed in the construction industry, a well-paid sector because of the unstoppable urbanization of the island. In contrast to answers typically given by expressive expatriates, he bluntly said that good wages were the only reason that brought him to Ibiza. In our conversations, I never detected any of the aesthetic or existentialist references that punctuate expatriate explanations of Ibiza's 'beauty,' 'energies,' 'freedom' or 'cosmopolitanism.' Likewise, he differed from the expressive or stressed profiles that attend Biodance circles. In a sense, he was the only 'conventional' individual at Can Sort, seemingly enjoying the gathering as much as expressive expatriates did.

The 'flea market' of San Jordi took place in the deactivated hippodrome at the outskirts of Ibiza town, every Saturday morning throughout the off-season (November to April). At a distance, it resembled a gigantic kasbah, marked by a variety of banners spontaneously raised by participants, depicting prevalent themes of the alternative world: the Jamaican flag, anarchism, Tao, fractals, Hindu symbols, etc. Many old cars and caravans were parked behind the stalls, displaying license plates from various Western European countries. Mohican-haired freaks wore leather clothes and boots due to the winter chill. A Babel-like mix of languages, dialects and accents could be heard. Dispensing with permits, anyone could set up a stall, usually second-hand objects: clothes, home antiques, books, kitchenware, toys, electric appliances, music records, etc. Several handcrafters sold jewelry and clothes, while senior Spaniards sold shoes or groceries. In addition to alternative types and expatriates, there were a smaller number of Spanish urbanites in search of some weekend amusement. With no tourists during winter, the island became quiet, and the general atmosphere at San Jordi was relaxed and enjoyable – sunny and chilled like the weather.

The market also resisted commodification. Economic exchanges occurred in an environ that enabled people to interact more personally. Most of the crowd were regular visitors who often claimed that their purchases were incidental. Rather than a sea of standardized and universally priced commodities, each object appeared to possess a unique patina, which onlookers speculated about. It was the affective link (a 'magic click') between object and buyer that prompted a transaction, which was then negotiated. In contrast with the compulsive consumerism of impersonal shopping malls, the social function of the flea market was as, or more important, than its economic function. The diversity of peoples and situations at San Jordi constituted not only a market but also a space of socialization and mutual acknowledgment where participants shared experiences, stories and plans about previous and future seasons.

In this connection, two seasonal peaks at the flea market indicated the level of mobility among expatriates each year. The first one occurred in late November, when they rushed to sell stock leftovers and other unwanted belongings, a final opportunity to generate extra cash that would help to fund winter unemployment or journeys overseas. The second peak occurred in April, when expatriates again concentrated in Ibiza, preparing for the coming season. As usual, they chatted about visits to their parents, adventures in faraway lands and expectations for the coming months. This mobile community of hippie traders also validates a theoretical claim about the dialectic of mobility/moorings as a key component of complex globalization (Urry 2003: 126): rather than wandering endlessly (as mistakenly assumed about nomads), expressive expatriates have to obey a period of rest and refueling, as a condition for further displacement.

Drum and trance parties, and the logic of state surveillance

Besides hippie markets, expatriates also gathered at more intimate music events taking place in secluded areas of the island, beyond the reach of tourists. Drum parties typically occurred on beaches before sunset, a small circle of drummers and their troupe improvising on shifting rhythms. The largest of the drum parties congregated a few thousand people, scattered in a myriad of candle-lit groups on the beach of Benirrás, at the northernmost coast of the island, every last Wednesday of August. It began in 1991, as a spiritual protest against the Gulf War I, and grew in numbers each year.

However, the event has suffered under the political feuds and business interests ruling the island. In 2001 the Socialist-Green government prohibited it, claiming issues of public safety and environmental protection. A group of artists then prepared a report that disputed the official decision on technical grounds, but to no avail. As a French expatriate told me, the event fell victim to rivalries between Socialists in Eivissa capital and Conservative mayors in northern towns. Yet, after the left-wing coalition collapsed in 2001, weekly drum gatherings were tacitly allowed in Benirrás provided they did not attract large crowds.

Lack of coherence and organization among public authorities prevail. As in Punta Galera, larger numbers of tourists have been arriving at Benirás each summer anyway. Moreover, to the dismay of drummers and environmentalists who fought for their right to promote the annual gathering at Benirrás, a local mayor, seeking to promote tourism in the area, granted a permit to a group of British party promoters, allowing them to organize massive barbecues for clubbing tourists in summer 2003. But the project failed due to financial and logistical issues, as well as because the British clubbing 'elite' of DJs, promoters and industry workers based in Ibiza town (rather than Sant Antoni) disregarded such dance barbeques as unfashionable ('uncool').

Finally, trance parties are a critical reference among alternative peoples of Spanish and expatriate countercultures. Also known as 'Goa parties,' these events secretly thrive in highly secluded areas of the island's coast and countryside. Their secrecy is a marker of subcultural identity and exclusivity, in addition to being a tactic of evasion from state and market regulation. Official authorities argued that such events violated the law on the environment and public order. Countryside residents would call police whenever they noticed an unusual flux of vehicles by their properties or heard the digital stomping afar. On the other hand, if held in a more accessible location, the party could grow too large, attracting unwanted tourists, resulting in police raids mobilized by powerful club barons. Trance freaks claim that they are persecuted because their parties beset the economic interests of the mighty club industry. This seems unlikely or at least grossly exaggerated, since trance freaks and mainstream clubbers do not mingle, although 'underground' clubbers are often seen with trance freaks.

Ironically, it is such criminalization of countercultural practices that enhances the mystique surrounding trance parties, which, in turn, contributes to make Ibiza such an enigmatic and charismatic place, attractive for leisure capital and consumption. As an example of how tourism seeks to exploit these transgressive subcultures, large-scale trance parties were only possible by means of an official permit granted by some remote city hall in the north of the island, or within the patronage of the MTV festivals held in the bedrocks of Sant Antoni throughout the late 1990s, until political intrigue forced the corporation out of the island. A detailed analysis of the ritual and politico-economic dimensions of the Techno trance scene will be provided in Chapter 5.

In conclusion, the hippie scene must be considered in the context of capitalist predation that marks the socio-economic life of the island. For a long time, political and economic elites seem to have agreed with a shortsighted strategy of development that maximizes immediate profits at the expense of any consideration with the environment, quality of life and social justice. More and more tourists is usually the basic measure of economic 'success,' even though an organized model for tourism development has shown its first signs. Under specific legislation, Ibiza has been slowly upgrading its tourism infrastructure and facilities, hoping gradually to substitute mass tourism with a more gentrified orientation.

In addition to the economic imbrications between the hippie scene and tourism, the action of state surveillance and major moralities further complicate their situation. As mentioned, hippies claim that their events are prohibited because they do not contribute to the economic interests of local oligarchies. On the other hand, the authorities and local population complain that hippies disobey the law and offend morality – to which, hippies respond by pointing out that the state and authorities are hypocritical for being complicit in allowing drug consumption in the nightclub/pub sector. However, what both sides fail to perceive is that such mechanisms of surveillance and mutual accusation inadvertently enhance the charisma of countercultures and, by extension, of the island, as an effect of the imaginaries of desire that biopower/sexuality reproduce.

Commercializing spirituality: Café del Mar, El Divino *and* Buddha Bar

Having examined the action of market/state systems upon the hippie scene, this sub-section more closely considers how alternative practices, artifacts and imaginaries are actually reprocessed within the strictly commercial schemes of entertainment in urban Ibiza.

Within the rise of mass tourism, *Café del Mar* grew from a tranquil coffee bar attended by daytime bohemians in the late 1970s into a tourist attraction hosting hundreds of weekenders each day of the summer in the late 1990s and early 2000s. The hippie concept is repackaged for economic ends: by the sunset you and your friends sip drinks (purchased at the bar) while listening to a gentle mood-altering music. The formula was then effectively imitated by neighboring bars, all along the coast, and even internationally.

In addition, *Café del Mar* CD album compilations of 'ambient' music became international bestsellers, to the point that consumers in foreign markets ignored the fact that *Café del Mar* was actually a café by the sea. 'Daytime DJs' – such as legendary José Padilla – were hired to create the musical ambience, with discreet loudspeakers facing the beach strip. Their skills evolved to the point where the music was somehow matched to the position of the sun in its final descent. The music goes deeper and slower, and those who get in tune become silent, feeling ethereal, almost uterine. As the sun touches the sea, the melody climaxes and remains on a plateau of subtle emotional undertones before fading like the sun behind the sea line. The sky becomes a blanket of shifting colors, altering from orange, to pink and violet. This is a bio-musical assemblage that engenders exquisite, even if ephemeral moods, as noted in desultory conversations and direct observation.

The more alternative crowd at the 'chill-out' bar *Kumharas*, located at the opposite side of Sant Antoni bay, considers such sunset ritual to be 'very spiritual,' a 'cosmic moment of transition.' It allows people to get in touch with their inner moods, which is facilitated with ambient music. Some of them will be quietly smoking a hashish joint, while a few others will bring their hands together in a prayer position. Conversely, the massive crowd of British tourists at *Café del Mar*, *Mambo* and *Savannah* keeps photographing, talks loudly and cheerfully applauds the sunset, culminating with beer bottles thrown at the sea. (I snorkeled in that area, and saw dozens of beer and *breezer* bottles lying at the shallow bottom.)

Even *Kumharas* underwent sensible gentrification since its opening in 1997. No longer a straw-made bar with rustic tables for longhaired youth, *Kumharas* has upgraded its facilities, increased the number of tables, and installed a touch-screen cashier system for its staff. The price of its drinks has significantly increased while catering to middle-class tourists and various agents of the record industry from overseas. As bar owner and cultural promoter Miguel once told me with mixed feelings, 'I used to have friends here, now I have a clientele.'

One of these friends was ambient music producer and DJ Lenny Ibizarre, a Danish-Dutch expatriate who has been living on the island since childhood. At a younger age, Lenny enjoyed throwing trance parties with friends in the countryside. Committed to ambient music, Lenny developed a personal studio in his house located in the northern countryside. His talents in producing ambient music led him to sign a contract with *Sony Records*, which acquired the rights to globally market his music label (*Ibizarre Records*). In the meanwhile, UK magazine *Cosmopolitan* included Lenny in a list of 'young, rich and available men' in the year 2000. In contrast, Lenny seemed aloof to such allure and success. In an interview for *Pacha Magazine* in 2003, club celebrities (mostly top DJs) were asked what they wanted to be doing in ten years. While most answers revolved around doing more and having more, Lenny, in his early thirties, replied differently:

> In ten years I would like to have the same life that I now have. I am perfectly happy. Living in my house in the countryside, where I compose my music during the day and take care of my garden during the afternoon. That's what I want to be doing in ten years. No changes.

The spiritual aesthetic of expressive expatriates has been also incorporated at high-end venues of entertainment business. *El Divino*, consensually seen as the most elegant nightclub on the island, provides a classical example. Located at the marina of Ibiza town, the former veranda restaurant enjoys a spectacular view of the medieval fortress. Yet, its history illustrates how expressive expatriates have paved the way for the subsequent massification of clubbing in Ibiza and even globally. In 1992, interior designer and DJ Charles Challe, businessman Claude Frederich, and Felini's set designer Paolo Galia purchased a rustic dockworker's bar and transformed it into a classy marina restaurant. In a plush physical setting, *El Divino*'s distinctive character essentially stemmed from its post-dinner party concept, incorporating ambient music and catering to a very special clientele.

The three partners envisaged *El Divino* as a special venue for wealthy flamboyant friends of the 'golden triangle' – a jet-setting cohort circulating across Ibiza, Morocco and Goa. Many within the former circle were Osho sannyasins actively involved in this expressive diaspora. It is significant to note that the sannyasin Alok threw hippie parties in this venue, which he told me about when we met in Goa (India) by chance. In connection with previous observations, it seems that sannyasins constitute a relevant node of expatriate experiences wherein spiritual, hedonist and transnational features overlap organically, as will be examined in Chapter 4.

Charles Challe quit his partnership in 1993 and returned to Paris where he subsequently opened the internationally acclaimed *Buddha Bar*. Like the Ibiza sibling, *Buddha Bar* was devised as an upscale bar–restaurant with an orientalist 'lounge' ambience, and soon became a reference among foreign yuppies and wealthy tourists visiting the city. Similarly to *Café del Mar*, *Buddha Bar* also released CD compilations featuring 'lounge,' 'world' music, a successful enterprise that suggests the striking inequalities associated with the commodification of Third-World art: whereas cassette tapes of Pakistani singer Nusrat Ali Khan are sold in India for about US$1, the same songs remixed within a deluxe *Buddha Bar* CD are priced in the West at about US$50.

With the exponential growth of mass tourism in Ibiza, *El Divino*'s dance floor became more profitable than the restaurant. As the exotic glitz of veranda dinners gave way to the flashing buzz of dance music at the veranda, chic hippies and sannyasins disappeared against the massive wake of Euro clubbers. As executive director Antonio, an experienced restaurant businessman originally from Galicia, explains, 'El Divino seeks to attract a more sophisticated clientele of quality clubbers that stay in Ibiza town. But of course everyone is welcome.' By 'everyone' he was indirectly referring to the rowdy British working-class tourists hosted in Sant Antoni. On the other hand, 'real' or 'underground clubbers,' typically connected with the global club scene, favored more 'messy' nightclubs (see p. 101).

Converted into a nightclub, the profitability of dance parties became the exclusive criterion for managing the business, as pointed out by Antonio. Far from driven by any underground idealism, Ibiza nightclubs constitute a highly competitive industry with international ramifications. Nonetheless, Middle-Eastern businessman Khaled Rodan bought *El Divino* in 1996, in part for his own enjoyment (as he was regularly seen at the VIP veranda). *El Divino* continued to attract celebrities, as well as upmarket manufacturers who eventually rented the main venue for promotional events. In the early 2000s, *El Divino* had most of its weekly night slots allotted to party promoters from the UK, Italy, Russia and the US.

Nevertheless, discreet but distinctive traces of New Age Orientalism still characterize *El Divino* and *Buddha Bar*, and likely underlie their commercial success. Staircases are lined with incenses and candles, while an impressive Buddha statue rests at the VIP area of both venues. *Buddha Bar* CD booklets quote Gautama, whereas *El Divino* postcards depict belly dancers on site, and its elegant invitations for the annual 'opening party' also depicts Buddhist motives and the infamous club logo: halved-faces of the sun and the moon in unity, symbolizing the meeting of night and day – a concept aptly explored by nightclubs in their subliminal communication.

In sum, the hippie scene is a charismatic magnet for tourists, largely subsumed under the logic of leisure capital. Advertising materials explore images of hippies. Drum gatherings are forbidden, soon replaced by commercial barbecue parties. Trance parties are suppressed by police, while crowded sunset bars employ the hippie taste for nature to their own economic advantage. Alternative musicians sign millionaire contracts with record companies, adapting their music to 'Ibiza' branded CDs for global consumption. In the meanwhile, high-end venues in Ibiza and Paris embody elements of New Age spirituality as a stylish pretense of distinctiveness. In all of these cases, it is noticed that alternative spaces, practices and lifestyles previously circumscribed to expressive expatriates are repackaged for mass consumption. Within this process, modernization as commodification undermines the material and cultural conditions necessary for the reproduction of alternative lifestyles as such.

The club scene: underground and industry

During the summer, Ibiza also becomes a hectic laboratory for hundreds of DJs to try new records on the dance floor, and to network with colleagues, party promoters, music producers, journalists and agents of the record industry. Record companies have scouts infiltrated in the scene, watchful for unlicensed records that electrify the island, then contracted into commercial 'Ibiza' CD compilations that are annually released onto the global market. In such an environment, 'being underground' is often just a rhetorical gesture by music producers aiming at a contract with a large record company that will catapult their careers. More widely, drifting away from its origins among expressive expatriates, the club scene has become a mighty sector of the entertainment industry, within the general activity of tourism on the island. The seven mega-nightclubs and about 100 disco-pubs amassed an officially declared amount of US$110 million in the year 2001, about 11 per cent of the gross tourism revenue of the

Figure 3.3 Privilege, the largest nightclub in the world, with a 10,000 capacity.

island (Govern de les Illes Ballears – Conselleria de Turisme 2002), contradictorily oscillating between their countercultural origin and voracious
commercialization.

This section examines how the unique charisma of Ibiza's nightclubs
stems from the strategic position that expressive expatriates have occupied within the political economies of tourism, media and entertainment.
More specifically, I assess how countercultural, capitalist and moral formations dynamically converge and clash within regimes of capital and desire
that regulate the club scene, considered as an analytical unit. As a caveat,
rather than exclusive categories, the binary 'mainstream-counterculture'
must be seen as contingent folk references that simultaneously inform the
maneuvers of self-fashioned alternative segments, while also feeding the
symbolic logic of consumptive capital. The point is not to define the truth
about such claims, but to examine the cultural motivations and economic
implications of such dialectic.

Initially, I present the individual trajectory of a Buddhist DJ who
worked in clubbing sites marked by hedonism and illegality, thus making
explicit some of the ethical challenges that must be confronted in the
highly predatory environments of the Ibiza club scene. Second, by means
of a description of a typical night in the largest nightclub on the planet
(*Privilege*), I delve into a micro-ecology of social types that reflects and
speaks to wider social hierarchies of class and distinction. The empirical
findings tend to reaffirm classical claims of the Birmingham school of
cultural studies (about the correlations of social class, style and resistance),
which have been dismissed more recently by the 'post-subcultural' critique
(Bennett and Kahn-Harris 2004; Muggleton and Weinzierl 2003). Third,
considering these biographic and ritual cases in the context of the political economy of the nightclub industry, I describe the economic structure,
corporate strategies and political ramifications of the seven mega-
nightclubs that determine the nature of Ibiza's nightlife. Finally, after identifying the basic dynamic of the club industry, I illustrate the play of desire
and morality upon concrete sites of the leisure capital, with an analysis
of the 'largest dance party in the world' (allegedly, *Manumission*), focusing
on how its meteoric growth has mutually amplified a media scandal of
transnational proportions.

A Buddhist DJ in the land of hedonism

Every early June, Gary drove his car loaded with hundreds of vinyl[4]
records, all the way from Kent in England to Ibiza island, where he stayed
until mid October. Over the years around the millennium, DJ Lucci (as
Gary is professionally known) regularly played at *Manumission* parties
held at the nightclub *Privilege* each Monday, and daily worked as a
'daytime resident DJ' at *Bar M* in Sant Antoni, besides playing at other
parties on occasions. In contrast with the multinational orientations of

expressive expatriates and underground clubbers, Gary's daily life was predominantly encapsulated in the highly ethnocentric British club scene in Ibiza. I first met him at Nora's place, as he had learned about her massage therapy work through an article published in a club magazine (*DJ Magazine* 1998).

From a working-class family background, Gary struggled to become a professional DJ. Like many of the same generation, he lived with his parents or shared a place with friends. At a younger age, he decided to quit school, as it was more pleasurable to work as a delivery driver in London. In the meanwhile, he went clubbing with 'rough types,' as he puts it, elements from the youth working class or unemployed friends, enduring the harsh social transition into the neo-liberal world of disman-tled labor and welfare in the UK. Gary first went to Ibiza in 1989 in his mid-twenties. In reply to my question 'how was Ibiza back then', he said:

> I remember that there was much less people, and definitely much less British people. It was fantastic! *Privilege* was then *Ku*; and we danced in the open air, under the stars, as nightclubs had no roof back then. People was marvelous, and the atmosphere was just incredible. It was the first time that house music was playing, because it had just been created. So, nobody knew its direction or how long it would last. It was something new, and we wanted to enjoy all that as much as possible because we did not know what was going to happen next.

Gary thus conflates Ibiza with clubbing, while emphasizing the extra-ordinary nature of its nightlife. Its 'fantastic' atmosphere is shaped by 'marvelous people' who 'dance under the stars.'[5] He also underlines the newness of house music, what engendered a subliminal anxiety regarding future uncertainties as well as their desire to enjoy the present, a nostalgia founded on the prospective of a lack. Wonderful and uncertain, these nightclubs propelled Gary to return to Ibiza almost on a yearly basis throughout the 1990s. In 1998 he got the position of 'daytime resident DJ' at *Bar M* (M for *Manumission*).

Considering the risk of petty crimes and scams that infested Sant Antoni during the summer, both Gary and I were looking for reliable flat-mates. We thus rented the small ground apartment located in the same building where Nora lived. With odd working schedules, we often talked overnight.

Unlike most biographic trajectories described thus far, Gary was not a typical 'expressive expatriate.' Despite the many repeated stays on the island, he never cared about learning Spanish. Moreover, Gary adhered to identity references that were markedly national, male and working class. On the other hand, he was very interested in forms of spirituality more commonly verified among alternative expatriates. A Reiki master, Gary also practiced Buddhist meditation every day. Not only that, he consciously sought to live his everyday life according to his ideas of 'inner peace,' 'compassion' and 'positive thinking.' The house music he played was characterized as 'uplifting,' with cheering lyrics and sounds that promoted a sense of well-being. He also created a record label named *Planet Love Records* under which he produced and released his own records, sometimes with explicit spiritual themes, such as 'Journey to Enlightenment,' a progressive house record with a sample of a popular Buddhist prayer. By all means, much of what Gary did in his professional and personal life sought to reflect his beliefs in Buddhism.

His interest in spirituality grew during a career transition in the late 1980s. Gary mentions the impact that an astrological reading had on him, 'triggering off things that I knew deep inside.' He still worked as a van driver, when the astrologer spoke about his inclination toward communication and underlined his need to 'express myself and motivate people through music.' In 1995 he joined a Mahayana Buddhist retreat, which represented a turning point in his life:

> I noticed that the meditation and the monk's teachings were helping me a lot. I remember that the monk said that only a few would remain in the retreat; and I wondered about myself. I was so much into it that I stayed until the end, whereas my brother who had asked me to join the workshop left in the middle. I was much more focused. I then realized that what I really wanted was my own career as a DJ, despite problems with money and with my parents who didn't understand my decision. I gained a peace of mind that I never had before. I gave up my job as a van driver to dedicate myself to become a professional DJ. I was already playing for friends in small raves. It was also around that time that I decided to stop with all the heavy drinking, smoking, drugs, and other crazy things that me and my friends did all the time [. . .]. It was just too much! Acupuncture also helped me to stop smoking; I became more focused, and it gave me much more energy. And since then, I have been trying to learn more about meditation, Buddhism and Reiki.

What does it mean to be 'spiritual' while working in the predatory environments of the Ibiza club scene? As a professional DJ and Buddhist practitioner, Gary's ethical values regularly clashed with typical situations of the club scene: blunt interactions, dodgy offers, decadent temptations, endless postponements, unfulfilled promises, endemic backstabbing, etc. These vices seemed to be drastically amplified in Ibiza's transitory settings of hedonism. Furthermore, Gary refused to engage with predominant forms of networking practice, which revolved around ongoing party and drug indulgence. Instead, he envisioned himself as a 'focused' DJ and music producer, evoking cases of successful producers who, according to him, thrived on a sober and even anti-social work ethic. His kind personality thus sharply contrasted with what was expected of a '*Manumission* DJ' (eccentric, excessive, blunt, etc). In sum, Gary's attitude simultaneously was an ethical bonus and a subcultural handicap – in any case, an anomaly in the scene.

Nonetheless, his spirituality did not result in his rejection of the club scene for its highly mundane nature. It rather entailed a reformed stance in this regard. Gary's explanation was both evasive and pragmatic:

> In Buddhism, we learn to accept things with compassion, and not to judge them. When someone is stupid at me, I feel compassionate about their ignorance. [. . .] When I am working as a DJ, I try to send love through the records I play. This is why I like playing soulful and uplifting house, because I know that this music affects people's moods, and so many people in clubs are depressed, on drugs, with problems and stress . . .

In conclusion, Gary seeks to overcome the derailing and anomic sociability of clubbing with a more ethical form of individualism that soberly integrates personal and professional pursuits. In order to understand the meaning of this effort, it is necessary to consider Gary's position as an artistic producer against the backdrop of clubbing hedonism in Ibiza. The next subsection provides an ethnographic description of a typical night in the largest nightclub on the planet *Privilege*. By means of an organic assessment of clubbing as a ritual practice, an ecology of subgroups that populate the club scene can be discerned.

Ethnography of the world's largest nightclub

With a 10,000 capacity, *Privilege* is 'the largest nightclub in the world' according to the *Guinness Book of World Records* (Guinness 2003). The venue is located by the main road, near the village of Sant Rafel, at the very center of the island. Owned by Spanish businessmen, *Privilege* hosts parties organized by promoters based in England, Italy, Germany and Spain each day of the week from June to September. Monday nights were reserved for *Manumission*, arguably the biggest weekly party in the world, as its promoters claimed. To wit, *Manumission* secured turnovers that often surpassed *Privilege*'s capacity limit. DJ Lucci and I agreed to meet at *Bar M* to go to *Manumission*, where he also played. As he did not show up at the bar, I decided to try to find him inside *Privilege*.

Hundreds of taxis and cars dashed around its gigantic structure overhanging a smooth hill. Thousands of British kids queued at the main entrance. Their dressing style was quite uniform: boys wore shirts buttoned to the neck and wrists, black pants, leather shoes, and had trimmed haircuts; girls wore skirts, Lycra tops and high-heels, carrying small purses, cheap jewelry, and visibly polished nails and make-up. In a sex ratio of 80/20, they comprised the absolute majority of clubbers in Ibiza. However, another segment of elder clubbers, apparently more eccentric, international and experienced in fashion and attitude, would arrive later in the night, often without paying the expensive cover. They are known as 'smart,' 'real' or 'underground' clubbers.

Inside, *Privilege* is a colossal hangar-like structure in steel and glass. Sections of the dance floor were built upon and around a swimming pool (the premises belonged to a sports club until becoming the nightclub *Ku* in 1978). The presence of security agents attempted to dissuade a few enthusiastic kids from jumping in the water, but the lifeguard had to assist them out of the pool, and out of the club. The DJ station was nested on a concrete crossway, positioned at the very center of the swimming pool. A green laser drew geometric shapes on and through a curtain of rain falling behind the DJ. Despite multiple turrets of loudspeakers, due to the huge room dimensions (25 meters high) and the massive compact of human bodies, the sound quality was hampered, to the dismay of professional DJs. Nevertheless, the crowd raved anyway, aloof to technicalities. Go-go dancers performed on podiums. By the sidewalls, red banners featured Che Guevara, but, as I surveyed around, nobody knew who Che was.

As the night unfolded, the gigantic room overcrowded, heated up and felt uncomfortable. A second-floor balcony provided a more comfortable overview for anyone willing to pay €300 for a bottle of vodka on a table. Clubbers could breathe some fresh air in the multilayered garden or at the dome-platform outside. In addition to the main room, there were two minor dance rooms where other DJs played simultaneously. The human ocean peaked around 3:30, when early comers initiated to leave. In the meanwhile, 'real' clubbers, bohemians, hippies and queer characters began to arrive. They gathered in the smaller dance rooms, called 'Candy Bar' and 'the back room.' Their assertive appearance as well as the dance music styles played in these rooms engendered an 'underground' atmosphere that curiously kept mainstream crowds away.

I found DJ Lucci playing in the bathroom, one of the many eccentric ('crazy') ideas that characterized *Manumission*. Later in the night he would play again in the veranda room reserved for entertainers, *Bar M* workers, DJs and friends. The music in the bathroom was earsplitting. I tried to greet him and screamed to no avail. From behind the turntables, Lucci calmly said something. I showed my helmet, which he placed under the turntables. He showed the palm of his hand wide open: finish at 5:00. I span my finger in a cone and pointed at the floor: I will walk around and come back later.

With five different dance rooms, *Manumission* hired about 15 DJs per night. Each room played a specific sub-genre of dance music as a general policy. The main dance room played commercial house music with ephemeral labels ('Euro-trance,' 'progressive,' etc.): formulaic songs with catchy melodies and sentimental lyrics. Groovy flashback songs of old disco and funk music were played in the bathroom and veranda.

At the Candy Bar and the back room, DJs played underground sounds, such as big beat, deep house, fucked house, industrial, tech-house and new oddities, which not only provided a subcultural reference but were also considered important in triggering psychedelic states and visceral reactions.

This spatiality of sounds also corresponded to visible differences in social class and taste. The majority of British working-class kids were crammed into the main area, whereas wealthy outsiders and media agents enjoyed the exclusive balcony area. In the meanwhile, highly intoxicated clubbers, jocose revelers and drug dealers gathered at the oddly lit back room. The Candy room, in turn, hosted a compact of 'smart' clubbers, 'industry' workers and bohemians, aloof to the transvestites who danced on the top of the bar counter, while stoned hippies banged their bongo drums to the rhythm of the groovy house music being played by a black DJ wearing sunglasses and beret.

The consumption of drugs in the club tended to vary according to class habitus, intermixing economic difference, network contacts and cultural distinction. The working-class clubber drank beer or 'vodka red-bull,' often simultaneously with pills of 'ecstasy.' The wealthiest strata rejoiced in discreet overdoses of champagne, cocaine and ecstasy. Among underground clubbers, the attitude was of performed carelessness, yet they were usually narcotic connoisseurs: stimulants, tranquilizers, hallucinogens, erotogens and its various combinations, for the desired effect and mood. Ecstasy was the drug of choice across all social strata. In the early 2000s, a small beer bottle cost €8 in a club, while a pill of ecstasy could be purchased for as low as €5, depending on the quantity of the pills and familiarity with dealers. By comparing the economic cost for altering one's mood over the night, clubbers often concluded that, 'In Ibiza ecstasy is cheaper than beer.' Despite the impressive levels of drug abuse in Ibiza, death overdoses are surprisingly rare. A paramedic working at *Privilege* disclosed in private:

> For every ten thousand people in a party, ten cases reach the nursery room. Seven are due to alcohol intoxication, and three to glass cuts. Sometimes, alcohol is mixed with ecstasy. But I have been working here for four years, and I have only seen three freak cases, which were not related to ecstasy alone but to a mix of everything: alcohol, cocaine, hashish, ecstasy, acid . . . *una locura* . . .

As the night advanced, more underground clubbers arrived. Many were arriving from bars and restaurants where they worked during the season, bringing along friends who they sought to get in for free by persuading the security at the door. Often from a relatively educated, middle class from Spain and the rest of Europe, in Ibiza they favored easy jobs that allowed them to party and socialize intensively. As will be discussed later, they were a segment of bohemian workers whose rationale can be summed up in the motto 'maximum party, minimum work.' Another segment of self-fashioned smart clubbers sought to spend as many summer weeks as possible in Ibiza, while living in main urban centers overseas, in occupations related to media, art, public relations and fashion. By all means, these culled clubbers saw themselves as a special cohort that cultivates cutting-edge music and fashion through an attitude that values cosmopolitanism and transgression. They abhorred mainstream clubbers, who they deemed boring and unsophisticated at all levels.

Unlike mainstream clubbers, the underground expressed no excitement about going to conventional popular parties, such as *Manumission*. They disregarded them as commercialized and tacky, seeing most of the DJs who played at them as 'crowd pleasers,' pushing formulaic tunes as a means of moneymaking. Underground clubbers attended a few of these parties, granted that their entrance was free of charge and that they could gather with peers of style. Instead, they favored messier, more exclusive parties at *Amnesia*, *Space* and *Pacha*, or at smaller nightclubs that emerged before they were shut or incorporated by the mighty nightclub oligopoly. In addition, a share of underground clubbers cultivated close connections with freaks (neo-hippies) and could be seen at trance parties taking place at remote coastal cliffs.

I returned to the bathroom at 5:15. Gary was packing his headphones and vinyl records in a metal case. The toilet sound system was off. He did not meet me at *Bar M* because of a VIP dinner that had overextended. We grabbed a drink by the garden, before his next gig at 6:00. We chatted about the history of clubbing, and I mentioned the role played by Argentine DJ Alfredo in the Ibiza scene back in the 1980s. Garry reminded me that Alfredo was a resident DJ at *Manumission* and usually played the final session in the main room every Tuesday morning. Wearing a funky beret and sleeveless shirt, and sipping some champagne while waiting for the next record to be mixed, Alfredo was renowned for his ability to engender an exquisite dancing atmosphere with the 'Balearic beat' he is reputed to have created: a seamless sequence of records overlaying house music with remixes of classic reggae, Euro pop and rock (e.g. Bob Marley, The Eurythmics, Pink Floyd, U2, etc). His trajectory and personality will be examined in the next sub-section.

It was Tuesday morning when Alfredo played the last record. The sunlight inundated the gigantic room where a few hundred diehards persisted. Other rooms were being shut, yet a messy crowd concentrated at the Candy Bar. By the swimming pool, a young entertainer incited the remaining people to attend the 'Carry On *Manumission*' party at *Space*, the infamous 'daytime club' located at Playa d'en Bossa (a beach located about 9 km away). *Privilege*'s buses waited on the parking lot. *Manumission/Bar M* entertainers, resident DJs and promoters would soon resume their activities at *Space* until about 14:00. The 'carry on' was smaller but highly eccentric, as clubbers displayed some impressive endurance and enthusiasm, fueled by variegated forms of substance intake.

From Monday to Monday, the island hosted about sixty nightclub parties, some of which began in the morning, in a series repeated each week. By taking advantage of such schedules, it was possible to indulge in clubbing marathons virtually around the clock, insofar as the clubber possessed the economic, social and biological resources to do so. Holiday-makers and bohemian workers boasted about how many parties they could attend in a row. By means of drug buildups and sleep deprivation, 'headstrong' clubbers pushed their limits, disrupting bio-rhythms and cognitive references. Many nightclubs featured names that captured such derailing experiences: *Amnesia*, *Space*, *DC-10*, *El Divino*, *Eden*, etc.

DJ and shamanism: charisma and bricolage

Among veteran clubbers, DJ Alfredo was a living legend. In 1984, he revolutionized *Amnesia*'s dance floor with his 'Balearic beats.' Back then, the club was no more than a rustic farmhouse with a sound system and people danced on an open-air patio under a starry sky, an experience that these clubbers deemed magic. Alfredo developed his style by playing endless sessions to dancing crowds that were more eclectic in terms of nation-ality and taste. According to a club journalist, 'The way Alfredo put it all together captured the indefinable magic of the island after dark, the hippie legacy, and the hedonistic present' (Collin 1997: 50; see also Reynolds 1998). As it is retrospectively romanticized about *Amnesia*, 'At night the hippies and Bhagwan *sannyasins* would gather and dance around lit bonfires outside, and you might spot flamenco guitar hero Paco de Lucia or one of the Pink Floyd crouched around the embers' (Collin 1997: 49). Whether or not such depictions are historically accurate, they capture the spirit of bohemian life in Ibiza, in part enjoyment of the present, in part nostalgia about a real or imagined past.

Like hundreds of South Americans (mostly from Argentina and Uruguay), Alfredo arrived in Ibiza in 1976. He did not come as a polit-ical exile, although the military dictatorship restricted his activities as a journalist and rock concert promoter. In Ibiza, he used to organize open parties in the countryside. DJing was just an emerging occupation, thus granting a competitive edge to Alfredo as a talented pioneer. According to DJ José Padilla (author of several *Café del Mar* compilation albums): 'Alfredo just got the right place at the right moment and he put his balls on the line and said: "this is how I think it should be"' (Collin 1997: 50). Alfredo also produced various club-sponsored albums compiling summer dance hits throughout the 1980s and early 1990s. But his popu-larity declined after the British party promoters took over the Ibiza club scene in the mid-1990s. Backed by the fact that over half of the clubbers on the island were British tourists, these promoters were able to impose their own rules, connections and tastes, largely favoring top DJs based in the UK.

Nonetheless, by the early 2000s, DJ Alfredo was still revered by several promoters, clubbers and Argentinean expatriates. He was a charismatic celebrity, according to many clubbing insiders, particularly women. Every now and then, a woman would persuade the security officials to allow her into the DJ decks in order to greet and kiss Alfredo. On one occasion, two young acrobats tried to capture his attention by spontaneously pole-climbing in erotic positions at *Privilege*. Argentinean clubbers regularly cheered him from the dance floor. He eventually responded with a quick smile, submerging again into his record collection.

However, other party promoters considered Alfredo as a potential troublemaker. As I have witnessed, he could engage in verbal harangues with more irreverent DJs inside the booth during the gig transition, a delicate and potentially contentious moment of interaction between two DJs. Likewise, other than brief informal interactions, Alfredo rarely agreed to structured interviews. On a different but significant note, like many other expressive expatriates, Alfredo had attended the Osho commune in Pune, an experience which he regarded tenderly, although he did not fashion himself according to sannyasin precepts.

In an anthropological vein, it can be ascertained that his professional techniques and personal traits, enveloped in the social belief in his charisma to engender collective states, suggest that the work of the DJ is similar to that verified in traditional shamanism. Under the light of classical studies about the magician, Alfredo's disruptive personality can be better understood as constitutive of his persona as a legendary DJ, just as shamans are characteristically anti-social and neurotic (Mauss 1904). Likewise, both DJs and shamans employ ritualistic devices of bricolage and improvisation in order to create an impression (Lévi-Strauss 1962). Their repetitive drumming and expressive gestures are devices for engendering states of collective effervescence – 'taking the crowd on a journey,' as DJs put it – and, in the last instance, personal wellbeing, as clubbers often report. A discussion on the ritual and experiential features of DJing will be resumed in Chapter 5.

Club structure and strategy – the mega seven

'These nightclubs make more money than an African nation.' This anecdotal yet significant comment discreetly appeared in the Ibiza magazine supplement of British *DJ Magazine* in summer 1999. Ibiza's nightclub/pub sector declared an official income of €110 million in 2001 (Govern de les Illes Ballears – Conselleria de Turisme 2002), which must be considered in the context of the larger tourism industry, which comprises 80 percent of the gross wealth and labor force of the island. Every year 1.7 million tourists spend €1 billion while on the island, in addition to €0.4 billion that remain overseas (Govern de les Illes Ballears – Conselleria de Turisme 2002; Maurel 1988; see also note 2, p. 229). As seen in Chapter 2, most tourists are British and German (and Spaniards increasingly so), massively concentrated in coastal areas, and during the summer months almost entirely. Though resulting in considerable environmental and social pressures, mass tourism has transformed Ibiza into one of the wealthiest places in Spain, following the presence of expressive expatriates as a trend-setting reference (Rozenberg 1990).

Even though nightclubs have become feverish money-making machines, a segment of underground clubbers were still able to attend these disputed venues without having to pay admission. It was once noted that, out of a total of 11,000 people in a *Manumission* party in 1999, there were about 2,500 names on the guest-list, including not only clubbers of the local scene but also media and record agents and their entourages, mostly from the UK. Such a figure was unusually high, but a conservative margin of 10 percent of non-payers can be ascertained for any club event on the island (including *Manumission* itself, after *Privilege* directors found out about the episode). As a gross estimate, the club industry concedes free entrance worth more than €10 million each summer, which begs the questions: How does the club scene reproduce itself as a gigantic economic machine? Who joins the clubbing elite that enjoys certain privileges of consumption and status within this machine?

In order to understand the nature of Ibiza's club industry, it is necessary to identify its main structure and strategy forms. *Space*, *Pacha*, *El Divino*, *Amnesia*, *Privilege*, *Es Paradis* and *Eden* are the seven main nightclubs, which regularly rented out their premises to external party promoters (mostly from the UK, Germany, Italy and Spain) willing to accept rigorous contractual conditions. With capacity limits varying from 2,500 (*El Divino*) to 10,000 people (*Privilege*), these clubs appropriated most of the ticket revenues and bar sales. Party promoters had their remuneration based on a one-off amount or on a share of ticket sales, depending on the projected size, weekday of the event, expectations of success throughout the season vis-à-vis contending parties and other contractual agreements. Party promoters were usually well-established nightclubs headquartered in main European cities. As a basic reason for coming to Ibiza, while expanding vertically into record, media and merchandise, these foreign club corporations employed Ibiza as a special venue for showcasing their brands at an international level.

Each of the Ibicencan mega-clubs sought to organize a portfolio of seven weekly parties that promised to be most profitable and successful in the short and mid-term. Each of the seven nights was rented out in a seasonal basis, comprising around fifteen weekly parties over the course of four months. The external promoter was almost entirely responsible for promoting and executing their parties, whereas the host nightclub provided the venue, multimedia equipment, and basic services of security and bar. Mega clubs also promoted their own 'homemade' parties, employing 'resident DJs' and PR (public relations) staff. With a few exceptions, nonetheless, homemade parties resulted in lower-than-average turnovers. The exceptions will be discussed below.

As an example of how a party portfolio is constituted, every year *Amnesia* lined up a diversified set of weekly parties, seeking to encompass the main national and party audiences on the island. The club was thus able to attract crowds varying from 1,000 to 5,000 people each night during the 1990s and early 2000s. In 2001, *Amnesia* featured the following party mix: On Mondays, it hosted *Cocoon*, a techno party based in Frankfurt (Germany) led by top DJ Sven Vath who played minimalist techno music for a mostly Germanic crowd. On Tuesdays, *God's Kitchen*, a nightclub from Birmingham (England), delivered hard house music for a young, apparently teen British audience. On Wednesdays, the tremendously successful *La Troya Asesina* was a homemade party strongly supported by the gay community of the island, and it played house music for a mixed crowd in terms of nationality, style and sexual orientation. In the meanwhile, a foam dance party named *Espuma* took place in the internal room, attended by young tourists. On Thursdays, *Cream*, a leading nightclub from Liverpool (England), played commercial trance house music for a massive yet slightly diversified crowd of British clubbers. On Fridays, *Dance Valley*, a rave festival in Amsterdam, provided variations of house and techno music for continental, mostly Dutch, German and Scandinavian crowds. On Saturdays, *Zenith* was an event organized by an Italian–Spanish team, playing percussive (Latin) house for a Mediterranean crowd, which also indulged in the second *Espuma* foam party of the week. Finally, on Sundays, *Kamasutra* was a minor homemade party in partnership with a local strip-club, playing house music almost as a background pretense for voyeuristic crowds of young males and Spanish tourists on a low budget. This weekly schedule was relentlessly repeated over the course of four months, just like all of the other mega-nightclubs. According to club journalist Ronnie Randall, 'with this portfolio, *Amnesia* is the best and the closest of what a real club should be, catering to a wide range of national tastes.'

The spatial location of a nightclub in the urban and tourist landscapes of the island largely determined its party mix, and agreements with party promoters were accordingly made in order to optimize given opportunities. In Sant Antoni, *Es Paradis* and *Eden* hosted less expensive parties for the British working-class youth. By the marina of Ibiza town, *Pacha* and *El Divino* struck deals with high-end promoters that catered for clubbers from the middle-to-upper strata of various countries. Within the German resorts of Playa d'en Bossa, *Space* hosted several techno parties and was the only venue with a daytime license, thus attracting highly eccentric clubbers on their way to the beach or directly from an overnight party. Equidistant from Ibiza town, Sant Antoni and Playa d'en Bossa, *Privilege* and *Amnesia* diversified their portfolios in order to increase the overall number of clubbers, all coming by rental cars, scooters, taxis or 'disco buses.'

Beyond the clubbing business, these mega nightclubs also developed complex partnerships with the record, entertainment and tourism industries locally and abroad. *Space* utilized its brand and resident DJs in promotional tours across German and American venues, in addition to opening a branch in Miami (US). In its turn, *Pacha* constituted an international franchise, lending its cherry logo and expertise to a number of sister venues in Barcelona, Marrakesh, London, Munich, Hamburg, Budapest, Vilnius, Buenos Aires, etc. The club also explored its close connections with the world of fashion, and commercialized a line of *Pacha*-branded clothes and wear accessories on its website and across small merchandise stores. As a step further, in 2003 *Pacha* opened a boutique hotel just across the street from the main nightclub, hosting top DJs, celebrities and pampered wannabes. In their turn, Sant Antoni nightclubs developed joint ventures with tour operators, employing a variety of sales techniques in local hotels and travel agencies in England. In Ibiza hotels, tour guides skillfully ostracized teenagers who declined to purchase the 'ticket pack' for clubs and 'pub crawls,' as predefined in an obscure economy of commissions and kickbacks (Butts 1997).

This nightclub-tourism association engendered a type of highly fabricated party that epitomizes the commodification of clubbing in Ibiza. Consider the following example. Each week, a tour/club association would bring groups of 2,500 British young people to the island, then take them on coaches from hotels to pre-assigned parties, back to hotels and to the airport a week later. This cycle was relentlessly repeated throughout the summer, amassing hefty profits in pre-sold tickets, commissions and other expenses. Despite the fun elements (music, drinks and 'mates'), these teenagers sensed that they had been sheepishly taken into 'fake parties,' as some insiders put it. This was a product of dubious quality, for it lacked the aura of spontaneous authenticity that animates nightclubs as spaces of communion and expression.

Party promoters faced daunting challenges when managing their party series against the highly competitive arena of Ibiza clubbing. Financial results were a source of anxiety, and executive managers were glad to break even at the end of the season. Nonetheless, during the golden years of corporate clubbing (during the 1990s), foreign clubs have afforded, and even foresaw, financial losses from the operations in Ibiza. Despite heavy expenses from booking top DJs, the main corporate goal was to have its brand name associated with the tremendous media exposure generally given to Ibiza during the summer at an international scale. As a result, the 'Ibiza factor' supposedly contributed to increase the overall revenues at the homeland and globally: club attendance at the headquarters, advertising sponsorship, discounted purchases, sales of CD compilations, merchandise, magazines, etc.

In terms of operational activities, the party promoter placed an executive manager who had to strike a deal with rapacious club directors, while getting acquainted with the intricacies of local life. Throughout the season, their main task was to manage locally a series of about 15 parties, seeking to increase sales revenues and containing operational expenses. In addition to some autonomy to hire minor DJs, they had to ensure effective street promotion. Usually, they concentrated their efforts on neighborhoods where tourists were most likely persuaded to attend the party. As previously noted, the spatiality of nationalities is a critical aspect in the allocation of promotion teams and resources, because, as a rule, mainstream clubbers attended events of their own nationality, regardless of other interesting attractions.

Comprising about half of total tourists and club parties on the island, the nationalism of young British clubbers is a phenomenon that requires some attention. During my fieldwork, I noted dozens of Union Jack flags being intentionally displayed on hotel balconies of Sant Antoni. T-shirts, towels, caps, bikinis and other media evoked the colors and shapes of English, Scottish and Welsh, as well as of Irish national symbols. These tourists try cheap *paella* only once, and for the remainder of their stay, they feed on 'English breakfasts' and 'fish and chips' in British-styled pubs frequented by British youngsters. They will not miss football matches on British cable TV at pubs and hotels. They will only go to British-promoted nightclubs and hang out with 'mates' who, as they find out, live in nearby towns back in the UK. Many hesitated in identifying Ibiza as a part of Spain. They tended to fear, albeit excitingly so, the island as a lawless zone that entices indulgent behavior. For most tourists, as well as mainstream expatriates residing on the island, Spain is little more than home-plus-sun or home-plus-cheap-prices. Upper strata foreigners seemed more considerate of cultural differences (whether or not they were actually interested in them). Based on these pieces of evidence and fieldwork among residents and tourists in Sant Antoni and the rest of Ibiza, it can be suggested that these assertive expressions of nationalism stemmed from the gregarious nature of leisure amid these young British tourists coupled with low levels of education (deduced from personal accounts, in addition to crass mistakes in basic geography, history and contemporary issues, as well as relatively poor English writing skills and vocabulary).

Exceptional parties were able to break through the nationalism that underlies mainstream clubbing in Ibiza and became exciting references in the global club scene. Without tapping into the segment of tourist clubbers, their attendance comprised an apparently eclectic mix of styles, types and nationalities, evoking queerness and cosmopolitanism. Around year 2000, the main successful examples on the island were *La Troya Asesina* (at *Amnesia* on Wednesdays) and *We Love Sundays* (at *Space* on Sundays). According to international clubbers, these were the best parties on the island. In fact, these events attracted self-fashioned clubbers arriving directly from the airport, as well as freaks (neo-hippies) who regularly disdained nightclubs. More will be said about these two parties in the final section of this chapter.

Underground clubbers, particularly those 'residing' on the island, refused to pay entrance at nightclubs. Price tickets were deemed expensive, varying from €30 to €60 in the early 2000s, and particularly so for those many who clubbed several times a week. Free admission was thus imperative and demanded good networking skills. It was actualized by having the name on the guest-list, by possessing a season pass, by befriending the door staff, or by taking advantage of a trick or serendipity. Pop or scene celebrities and their entourages could regularly enjoy this perk, as did physically attractive women who cast their charms on door 'bouncers.' On the other hand, club directors sought to restrict these possibilities by putting pressure on managers and door staff. Guest-lists and season passes were temporarily cancelled during peak months (July and August), when clubs overcrowded with thousands of young tourists.

At a symbolic level, free entrance marks the special status of the clubber – and of the nightclub – in the scene. It indicates the prestige that is accrued by adhering to a distinguishable style of mobile bohemianism (to be further discussed at the end of this chapter). On the other side, by allowing desirable 'underground' types in, the club also gains in charisma, thus propelling the belief that the venue is indeed a place to attend, to see and to be seen, or 'miss out' and be ostracized. In sum, this play of seduction and privilege is an indicator of countercultural activity on the island. As exchange tokens in an economy of favors, influence and prestige, free entrance exposes the basic contradiction that underpins the club scene: between its countercultural origin as a 'community' and its capitalist orientation as an 'industry' (Buckland 2002; Stalnaker 2002; Reynolds 1998; Thornton 1995).

Freedom from slavery – the Manumission scandal

By the turn of the millennium, while *Amnesia* and *Space* hosted the 'best' parties on the island (respectively, *La Troya* and *We Love Sundays*), *Privilege* arguably hosted the largest one, *Manumission*, with an average turnover of 9,000 people each Monday of the season. Among the causes of its outstanding success, British promoters have noted that, during the 1990s, parties did not succeed on Saturdays and Wednesdays, 'changeover nights' for British tourists arriving or leaving the island. The fact that *Manumission* was one of the first foreign promoters to arrive in Ibiza, back in 1994, represented a strategic advantage over other parties. Furthermore, *Manumission* promoters sought to cultivate a special relationship with the press: 'We wanted to use the media to our advantage and it was quite easy because we were in Manchester and they were all in London. So we could create a mystique out of nothing' (*Mixmag* 1999).

The popularity of *Manumission* stemmed, in part, from its 'party concept.' As envisaged by brothers Mike and Andy and fiancées Claire and Dawn, *Manumission* is a Latin metaphor that designates freedom from slavery. With catchphrases such as 'the craziest party that you have ever been to,' the press portrayed *Manumission* as a 'yearly bacchanal' where you could 'liberate yourself.' By the late 1990s, its fame was such that North American clubbers actually believed that *Manumission* was a physical nightclub in Ibiza. Sons of a military officer and a therapist, Andy studied engineering in Manchester, while Mike worked as a model in New York. Dawn was an architecture student when she met Andy in 1993. Together they promoted exquisite parties at the gay nightclub *Equinox* located in Manchester. Instead of DJs, they placed sex dolls in the DJ booth, playing dance music on cassette, while volunteer entertainers wore provocative costumes on the dance floor. As Mike explained:

> We knew nothing about club land so we made it up as we went along. My inspiration was cabaret and performance rather than music. [. . .] We were doing more blatant, explicit gay-themed fly posting than any of the gay bars or clubs could do. I think that helped us to get the support of the gay community.
>
> (Ibid.: 52)

They decided to cancel their gigs at *Equinox* after suffering a violent criminal assault. But a visit to Ibiza in 1994 enticed them to change their minds about party promotion. As expatriates who trivially enthuse about Ibiza, Mike romanticizes it as a space of pluralism and tolerance:

> Ibiza is paradise on earth. A tiny island in the Mediterranean with more nationalities living there than anywhere else in the world, the best parties, no racism or homophobia or ageism . . . You don't even get judged on your clothes. You're judged on you. And if you are a nice person then you'll be welcome.
>
> (Ibid.: 52)

They approached *Privilege*, still recovering from the 1991 roof collapse that led to its bankruptcy, and agreed to promote a weekly party known as *Mad Mondays*. In a collaborative effort with other minor promoters and friends, they were able to attract large crowds of British youngsters, arriving on the rebound of tourism in the mid-1990s. The event was renamed *Manumission*. In addition to cultivating good press relations, they hired an inexpensive team of young amateurish dancers, mostly dressed as kitsch entertainers. Claire was leafleting in the streets of Sant Antoni when she met Mike. Due to their outgoing personalities, Mike and Claire represented the public side of *Manumission*, whereas Andy and Dawn looked after finance and logistics.

Attendance grew from 500 to 6,000 over the course of a few months. Aggressive discounts were then canceled without hindering attendance. As a club magazine observed, '*Manumission*'s anything-goes approach had clicked with the island's tradition of hedonism and the newer habits of traveling European youth who had been weaned on the acid house lifestyle' (Ibid.: 54). But what accounted for such an explosive growth?

> It has never been about the music so much as the feeling of the night. We have to keep pushing it, doing something new ... to surprise people. All we ever wanted was to put on the sort of parties that we wanted to go to ourselves, so it couldn't just be a room with a DJ. The name *Manumission* means 'freedom from slavery,' and the idea has always been that you could do whatever you wanted.
>
> (Ibid.: 50)

The explosive edge came from sex shows performed on the dance floor, commenced in the second season (1995). Recently returned from New York, Mike and Claire not only proposed the idea, but decided to be the main sex performers, thus shocking the crowd with an air of authenticity. In addition to lesbian and heterosexual orgies, they also hired a male stripper who practiced self-fellatio on a tall podium, leaving thousands of mouths wide open with well-articulated 'Oh-my-god ... '

In Britain, *Manumission* became a scandal overseas. The tabloid press (*The Sun* and *Daily Mail*) published embarrassing pieces about the sex shows alongside interviews with intoxicated teens bragging about their sexual encounters at Sant Antoni's 'West End' pub district. Yet, the situation gained a dramatic overtone when Sky TV broadcast the documentary series *Ibiza Uncovered* (1997, with a second edition in 2000). While focusing on the ordinary life of British clubbers visiting or residing on the island, it brought to the fore in filmic form what the tabloid press had been doing on printed paper. While *Manumission*'s explicit hedonism resonated with the erotic fantasies of the mostly male working-class youth in sunny lands, the UK cultural attaché for Ibiza resigned, claiming to be ashamed about the behavior of this vacationing youth. A conservative politician requested that measures should be taken to prevent British tour operators from promoting sex tourism overseas (British Parliament 1999). In Ibiza, the main local newspaper *Diário de Ibiza* reacted, by publishing innumerable editorials and outraged letters criticizing the TV documentary for months to come. And the British-oriented publication *Ibiza Now* (see Chapter 2, p. 58) also questioned the TV series in the editorial titled 'What has "Ibiza Uncovered" to do with Ibiza?' from September 1997:

> Thus far the series has revolved around a rather depressing parade of youths getting drunk and bragging about how often they have had

sex. Apart from one or two sequences shot in the countryside and in some of the more recognizable parts of Ibiza town, it could have been filmed almost anywhere on this planet. [. . .] It says absolutely nothing about Ibiza. It does say a lot about the English media, England, and the English. [. . .] If the series had provided any sort of evidence to those of us living here it is to remind us of why we choose to live here, and not in England!

(*Ibiza Now* 1997)

Pornography was, in sum, a quite efficient way to boost attendance and publicity for *Manumission*. It also launched Mike and Claire as outrageous celebrities of the club scene, cheered by a highly eccentric entourage, including a dwarf doorman, porno actresses and self-fashioned junkie DJs. But the sex-for-the-masses formula was also being questioned inside *Manumission*. In *Ibiza Uncovered 2* (Sky TV 2000), whereas Mike and Claire praised sex shows ('It is incredible what the show does. The sexual energy lifts the party!'), his brother Andy complained, 'It is difficult to relate as brothers and as business; we don't know what the other does. But we [Andy and Dawn] don't value that sex helps *Manumission*.' In a magazine interview, Andy stated that, 'Our main concern is to give people the best experience we can. [. . .] People don't think of us as very moral but actually there is a very moral element to *most* of what we do' (*Mixmag* 1999: 55, italics added).

In fact, sex shows were no longer staged from 1999 onwards, but they were never declared over as such, thus keeping rumors that sustain certain expectations among the male young crowd. To wit, two years later, as I walked through *Privilege*'s parking lot, four Swedish male teens excitedly commented that they had come to see the sex shows. I told them about well-behaved strippers but suggested to them to be skeptical about the rest. Their smiles faded, and one disappointedly noted, 'But the guy who sold us the tickets promised us that there would be sex show . . .'

Several factors contributed to the end of pornography in *Manumission*. Mike and Claire had a baby, and settled down in a *finca* house in the countryside. In later interviews, they praised the marvels of bucolic life, and actively downplayed their previous eccentric persona. Moreover, economic pressures provided the final blow to the sex shows. In a casual encounter with the self-fellatio performer on a bus, I asked him why he had stopped sucking his penis in public. 'Well, it was *Orange* who asked us to stop it, you know . . .' The telecommunications corporation was the exclusive sponsor for *Manumission* from 2000 to 2002, and did not want to run extra risks by outraging parents and politicians in the UK. The male dancer still performed low-key stripteases, but could no longer expose his acrobatic genitalia.

While keeping some soft lesbian shows at the margins of the party, *Manumission* no longer hired the expensive erotic performers that it brought from New York and hosted in the soon-defunct *Manumission Motel* located just outside Ibiza town. Instead, it offered modest gigs to strippers who worked at a local strip-club, working for much lower rates. Their discreet, and only suggestive performances agreed with Claire's perception that, 'It is softer if it is girls, it is not so offensive' (*Mixmag* 1999: 54). In fact, it seemed that, in contrast with sexual penetration, soft lesbian erotica better connecteded with the MDMA (ecstasy) experience, as clubbers reported highly pleasurable sensations pervading the entire skin surface, rather than a concentrated focus on genital stimulation.

The bottom line was that average attendance at *Manumission* parties was already overheated, frequently exceeding *Privilege*'s limit capacity. Some de-marketing was thus necessary, as local authorities expressed concern over safety issues. Once more, ticket prices increased, with a minimal impact on attendance. Dressed in white, Mike and Claire would wander through the hangar room upholding a standard banner with the *Manumission* logo, and later socialize with friends in more exclusive areas of the club. Party profitability was, after all, the basic criterion in the club industry, even among outrageous promoters.

Manumission sought to maintain its charisma by re-emphasizing entertainment. In addition to naughty entertainers, it hired fire and trapeze acrobats who staged short spectacles in the club's main room. The acrobats were freaks (post-punk neo-hippies) who sought to revitalize a culture of itinerant art, and were regularly seen in hippie markets, trance parties and rundown bohemian bars. In their turn, wearing nurse and cavemen customs, the kitsch entertainers wandered about teasing male clubbers as a way of creating a fun atmosphere. As will be examined in the next section, these youth were bohemian workers whose main purpose on coming to the island was to party in the extreme.

Finally, *Manumission* developed special musical shows performed during the dance event. On a large stage, dozens of amateur dancers, goofy villains, and Mike and Claire as the main heroes performed cartoonish versions of Broadway-like spectacles, with a vintage-style narrative that visually and musically reread pop icon stories, such as 'Popeye *Manumission*' (2001) and 'Sherlock Holmes Singing in the Rain' (2003). These shows were performed in multiple short acts interspersed from 3:00 to about 4:30, with a special music in the background. It was frustrating for main room DJs to have to interrupt their gigs in order to run the playback and wait.

However, at a deeper level, *Manumission* was actually departing from club and rave cultures which had inaugurated a postmodernist art genre of blurring the lines between performer and consumer (Reynolds 1998). In them, the dancing crowd became the spectacle, to be seen and engaged with interactively, with the DJ merely facilitating the collective assemblage, taking 'the crowd on a journey.' However, by promoting conventional shows (either as pornography or musicals) and hiring pop

DJs, *Manumission* interrupted such machinic experience, reintroducing the modernist separation: disenfranchised from their expressive productivity, the clubber – markedly, the British working-class male youth – was positioned, again, as a passive consumer (observer) of pop art.

Bohemian working class

Located on the sidewalk of Sant Antoni by the bay, *Bar M* was one of the main 'pre-party' bars on the island in terms of activity, publicity and symbolic importance. The 'pre-party' concept refers to a meeting point where revelers socialize and drink before leaving for another more hectic leisure destination, usually a nightclub. Resident DJs (like Lucci) played 'warm-up' music (gentle house music played at mid volume), contributing to a lively ambience that anticipated an exciting night.

A brief description of *Bar M* illustrates the situation of the bar scene as ancillary to the club industry. It physically encompassed a small patio lined by bars and a DJ booth, in addition to a veranda bar with jacuzzi. Catering to a majority of young British clubbers on vacation, it operated daily from 10:00 to 4:00 (18 hours) over the tourist months. Most of the bartenders were young women, 'to keep the blokes drinking,' as manager Yolanda explained. On Mondays, *Bar M* hosted the pre-party for *Manumission*, selling drinks and tickets to a lively crowd attracted by DJ stars that came for quick demonstrations. Geared toward profit maximization, *Bar M* also delivered the pre-party for other nightclub parties during the rest of the week, and sold tickets to all of the parties of the island (including Monday competitors of *Manumission*). The bar was

Figure 3.4 British bar workers at the pub district of Sant Antoni.
Source: Courtesy of Ronnie Randall.

co-owned by Andy (*Manumission*) and Willie, a Spanish businessman who grew up in California and Mallorca. Willie was assisted by Yolanda, a Spanish–Australian who traveled from Sydney each season to manage the bar. She was particularly open to my research, for a reason: she had a degree in anthropology. The bar employed about 40 workers overall: British DJs and bartenders, Spanish busmen, Filipino cooks, and many other workers from Eastern Europe, Latin America and Australia, working as street promoters ('proppers'), 'watchers' (on police, for noise control), manual helpers or party entertainers.

Before detailing the social life and motivations of these young workers, it is necessary to outline this phenomenon more widely. A few thousand youth come to Ibiza each year looking for jobs in bars, restaurants, party promotion and nightclubs. In 2001 *DJ Magazine* estimated that 6,000 people fell under this situation, an apparently realistic figure, considering the number of bars in Sant Antoni (about 130) and an average non-Ibicencan staff (of about 10), in a town that corresponds to a third of the tourist activity on the island (Govern de les Illes Balears – Conselleria de Turisme 2006: 100). In addition, there were '300 DJs and 400 reps [tour agents]' (*Ibiza Uncovered 2*), and about 200 street promoters for the sixty weekly nightclub parties, besides the staff hired by nightclubs. The figure thus totals about 5,000 people, but does not include a high turnover, which, if realistically estimated at about a third throughout the season, would take this estimate up to the order of 6,500 people.

Quite anomalously, their main goal while working for the bar/club scene is not to obtain the best possible wages, but rather to secure free access to nightclub parties. They can tolerate being economically exploited by greedy bar owners, as long as their hedonist drives can be somehow fulfilled. The term 'bohemian working class' coined by club journalist Matthew Collin seems very appropriate to designate this youth segment:

> In the eighties, as unemployment grew in Britain, a new breed of tourist reached the island. These weren't backpackers or two-week booze cruisers, but bright, inquisitive youths for whom the prospect of slaving low pay or subsisting on the dole held little appeal; better to get out there, see the world and catch some sun and fun than stay in rainy, depressing Britain. They traveled to Tenerife in the winter, Ibiza in the summer, with perhaps a stopover in Amsterdam [. . .]. They would survive by doing odd jobs, serving behind bars, giving out promotional tickets for clubs, or running credit card scams, doing petty robberies and selling hash. This bohemian working-class update of the hippie trail was hardly a luxurious existence, but better than stagnating at home.
>
> (Collin 1997: 48)

As historical accounts in rave/club studies affirm, back at home these youth sought to recreate the 'Ibiza vibe' in 'acid house' parties held in pubs, gyms and warehouses (Reynolds 1998; Collin 1997; Kempster 1996). Though constituting an exclusive clique, their upbeat, expansive attitude was a sparkle for the explosion of rave parties throughout the UK. However, rave was criminalized, and virtually disappeared from Britain after 1994. Still, several of those Ibiza fans developed ascending careers in the record and entertainment industries.

DJ and music producer Paul Oakenfold provides the classical trajectory, as the story has been overly repeated in the club press to the point of acquiring mythic overtones. Originally from a middle-class background, Oakenfold was a young party promoter in London around the mid 1980s. As the story goes, while on holiday in Ibiza in 1987, he underwent a narcotic-induced epiphany upon first trying MDMA in *Amnesia* (a less glamorous version asserts that it was in the Sant Antoni pub district). Because of the liberating intensity of the experience, he decided to devote his career to disseminate house music throughout the world, as a self-appointed apostle of the electronic dance gospel. Former 'warm-up DJ' for U2 tour concerts, Oakenfold became a highly perceptive music producer, cleverly adapting underground genres – such as the Balearic beats from Ibiza and Goa trance – to more conventional tastes of the commercial mainstream. Not only that, anticipating the decline of corporate clubbing in the UK by the early 2000s, Oakenfold moved to Los Angeles (California) where he has been booked to compose sound tracks for movies (*Matrix Reloaded*) and video games (*EA Soccer Manager*). By late 2002, *CNN World* featured Paul Oakenfold as 'the most successful DJ in the world.'

Despite the insightfulness of the term 'bohemian workingclass,' Collin did not develop it conceptually, nor did he explore the productive tensions that it embeds. While referring to issues of social class in the context of labor decline, the expression 'bohemian worker' appears as an oxymoron in a classical Marxist analysis. Marx depicts the proletarian as an ascetic or brutalized being, subjected to the discipline of labor under inhuman conditions. Their income barely covers the level of material subsistence, let alone the pleasures of an unregulated lifestyle. Moreover, though a bohemian himself, Marx assessed ethylic and sexual laxity as an index of decadence among the lumpen proletariat, this dark nebula of marginal types deemed unsuitable for disciplined work. By all means, the working class lacks the material conditions that could enable existential categories associated with the notion of 'lifestyle.'

The notion of 'bohemian' is, therefore, negatively assessed in Marxist theory. Alternatively, it refers to the Romantic bourgeois or parasite nobility who have renounced or missed their position in the system of productive forces. Although these subjects claim individual freedom, according to Marx, nonetheless, identity is defined by labor as the mediation between social class and life conditions. The 'self' is thus defined by its position in the class structure, and, as such, bohemians can only occupy a marginal position in relation to the productive base, in a form of idle aristocracy, which is one of its historical sources. Within a Marxist perspective, therefore, the bohemian identity can be only defined as a residual extension of bourgeois individualism.

Under the communist ideal of a social utopia, leisure is envisaged by Marx in prosaic, not to say, puritanical terms. After an enjoyable multi-task workday, the worker goes fishing, reads poetry and contemplates nature. Pleasure is thus largely over-coded by labor, deriving its meaning from creative work, whose value is measured not only by its capacity to foster a rounded development of the self, but also, and perhaps mainly, for the aggrandizement of the human species. In no instance, pleasure is considered as a force that potentially transforms self-identity, let alone the life conditions that sustain it. Nor is pleasure accepted as a way of problematizing dominant normativities, since these are considered as crystallizations of conflicts at the level of relations of production. In sum, there is no politics of pleasure in Marx.

However, it is important to consider that, rather than rejecting labor (as in the bourgeois case) or being unable to find it (as in the proletarian case), the bohemian is rejecting the very conditions of labor. The move, therefore, is not for a revolutionary assault on the status quo, but rather a tactical withdrawal from the sphere of industrial labor. By refusing both bourgeois individualism and proletarian puritanism, the bohemian seeks to engender a work ethic that is based on non-commodified, autonomous and expressive forms.

Ironically, the bohemian ethic, either in its subcultural or popular variations, has been largely favored by higher levels of economic productivity that characterize the affluent societies of the postwar era. The welfare model of labor protection (reduction of working hours, paid vacations and unemployment insurance) has allowed wider segments of the population to spend more time in other spheres of life and enabled the emergence of mass tourism in the late 1950s. However, higher levels of education have amalgamated the frustration of the youth middle-class segments with the unfulfilled promises of modernization, thus contributing to the counter-cultural upheaval of the 1960s (Roszak 1995; Wallerstein 1989). Likewise, the rave movement of the 1980s emerged as a reaction to neo-liberal agendas implemented in advanced societies, particularly the UK and US. Contradictorily, the decline of labor and welfare has also fostered an underground ethos that often reflects a new combative individualism proposed by neo-liberalism, differing, for example, from the collectivist traits of hippie communalism. 'In the 1960s the young dropped out, in the 1980s they are dropped out' (McKay 1996: 52; see also Reynolds 1998).

Toward an empirical analysis, it is necessary to consider how segments of the working-class youth in Ibiza seek to conciliate labor with their bohemian drives. The study of bar workers at *Manumission* and *Bar M* provide a privileged window into the world of bohemian workers. In tandem with its reputation as the 'craziest' party on the island, *Manumission* hired the most eccentric individuals looking for a job position in the scene. To wit, these workers often arrived at work directly from a party, sleep deprived and still recovering from drug intake. Along with excessive working hours (about 48 per week), poor diets and the warm weather, these youngsters developed mood swings and chronic tiredess which escalated throughout the season, culminating in the 'August blues' syndrome. Yet, those who survived could then enjoy the highly expected 'closing parties' of late September.

Bob and Rob[6] were very close friends who illustrate typical trajectories of British bohemian workers in Ibiza. College students with part-time jobs in England, they used to come to the island every summer to work at *Bar M*. While employed as bar staff, they eventually played as substitute DJs. Their connections in the party scene enabled them to play as warm-up DJs at *Amnesia*'s terrace, still at a very young age. They were usually involved in adventurous situations involving girls, drugs, room-mates, records, scams, etc. Although often late for work, they were usually more responsible than the rest of the staff. But after five seasons, they decided to take different paths. One of them gave up the clubbing lifestyle entirely, while the other became a DJ in his neighborhood in England, sporadically visiting Ibiza in the condition of a well-connected clubber.

Victor illustrates another type of bohemian worker. A globetrotter from Mexico, he worked for *Bar M* and *Manumission* during two seasons. He had been traveling extensively across the US, Europe and the Middle East for over three years, and worked at bars, hotels and restaurants in order to add funds to his travel endeavor. From a middle-class background, Victor was a student of economy (in leave of absence) at a top university in Mexico. He extended his global traveling for an extra year, because he wanted to return to Ibiza and experience more 'crazy parties' and 'crazy girls,' as he put it. In Ibiza, Victor and workmates decided to spend the following winter in India, before he returned to Mexico for good. As a matter of fact, a year later I met him in Goa (India), where he also met his future wife, with whom he later went to live in Australia.

Bohemian workers were subjected to exploitative labor conditions, earning wages as low as Ptas 700 per hour (US$4.00) and working as many as 48 hours per week. In addition to wage delays, nothing upset them more than the sudden cancellation of their weekly day off. Yet, besides the seasonal nature of these jobs, they accepted such hardships for two main reasons. First, main bars, pubs and restaurants provided free night-club tickets and even season passes for reliable workers. These tickets were circulated as 'gifts' or promotional items among nightclub directors, party promoters and bar owners, and then passed on to their favorite employees.

Second, bohemian workers felt themselves as special members of an exuberant club scene, a party elite amid masses of tourists. They were very much aware of their privileged condition, whereas their tourist counterparts, often vacationing friends, were confined to trivial life and labor routines back at home. As an envied cohort, bohemian workers forged bonds of solidarity, sharing homes, drugs, experiences, affections and dilemmas at a young age. These bonds sometimes survived into wintertime, consolidating a web of contacts that extended back at home or into interesting places, notably Thailand, India, Dubai or Hong Kong.

Despite their familiarity with traveling practices, they remained within the same 'expat' community, which reinforced their ethnocentric assumptions, tastes and references. In fact, their experience of Ibiza was very much restricted to clubbing and Englishness (or Germanness) transposed to a sunny setting. For example, once I suggested a *bocadillo* (sandwich) to *Bar M* worker Bob (already on his third season on the island), and he did not know what the word meant. A staggering number of mistakes about local culture, and even about the most basic elements of history, geography and international topics, Ibiza, Spain and Europe, suggest a worrisome level of ethnocentric alienation. With a few exceptions, bohemian workers cultivated no interest in Spanish life, let alone culture and history (or unless a significant other turned out to be a local). The only locals they interacted with were bosses, landlords and taxi drivers – all of which had to speak English. Moreover, they were unable to think monetarily in any currency other than their own. The Spanish word they most joked about was *mañana* (tomorrow), which was what they often heard when carrying out their errands with local shopkeepers. They represented Spanish people as being 'warm' and 'fun' as well as 'nervous,' 'greedy' and 'rude.' They did not openly criticize Ibicencans, but treated them with strong reservations. Like their tourist counterparts, Ibiza was tacitly considered a lawless zone, prone to adventures, easy access to cheap alcohol and hedonistic indulgence (in addition to the fact that Spain's legislation on drugs was comparatively liberal).

While bohemian workers integrated labor and mobility in order to primarily actualize hedonistic interests, their self-identity as citizen and subject could be transformed at different degrees. More schematically, three typical arrangements of mobility, labor and identity can be noticed in the universe of bohemian workers. This model is not linear, mechanic or evolutionist, for its variants may overlap or recede into one other, depending on the individual case. Yet, such arrangements can be graded in terms of deterritorialization, periodicity and cosmopolitanism, and are better seen as ideal-types: analytical filters that enable meaningful inferences upon the empirical realm.

The first arrangement is typically seen among the youngest bohemian workers, usually from Britain, but also Spain, France, Italy and Germany. Their mobility is circumscribed by the pattern *move–work–home*. They travel from their hometown to Ibiza, work on the island during the summer, and then return home. (Some will instead go to work in Andorra or Dubai, driven by the same bohemian interests.) Back at home, they often resume a conventional lifestyle in terms of class, education, taste, personal aspiration and national belonging. An eventual winter trip to Asia can undermine their personal references, but, more often than not, the transformative potential of travel experiences is diluted in their ethnocentric dispositions, reinforced by the influence of traveling compatriots. This pattern of homeland-centered mobility can be sustained for several years, usually terminating when the subject enters adulthood, confronting the realities of family and labor regimes which they had previously scorned: the university or office for the middle class, the factory or chronic sub-employment for the working class. The development of alternative lifestyles seems to be easier among those from higher social and better educational backgrounds – but this is not an iron rule. In these cases, bohemian workers may enter the fast lane of deterritorialization and cosmopolitanism, as schematized in the two following types.

The second arrangement is seen among long-haul travelers, such as Australian and Latin American youth of the middle class who usually arrive in Ibiza by chance or hearsay. They follow a *move–work–move* pattern, differing from the previous type in terms of more complex trajectories in space and time. Propelled by sheer curiosity, they meander from country to country over the course of several years, stopping for local reconnaissance and some menial work. Like migrants in general and British bohemian workers in particular, they are still tied to conventional notions about the homeland and personhood, which can be inferred from their statements and intention to return home, to actualize aspirations of family, labor and citizenship.

Finally, the third arrangement is seen among the expressive expatriates of Ibiza (detailed in Chapter 2). Although combining features of the arrangements above, it actually results in a quite different arrangement, outlining a *move–live–move* pattern. Propelled by a blend of actual dissatisfaction and utopian hopes, they leave their homeland, aiming at establishing a new home elsewhere. They migrate to inexpensive and sunny locations, where they can interestingly socialize with like-minded expatriates and romanticized natives. This strategy is reinforced by life-transformative trips to South Asia (Chapters 4 and 5). In order to materially sustain such expressive lifestyles, they set an economic function to spiritually motivated trips (Chapter 2). In terms of identity, their practices of spatial mobility usually coincide with post-national orientations and experiments of subjectivity formation (meditation, therapy, spirituality, psychedelia). In the limit, they feel at home wherever they are – the epitome of the universal cosmopolitan. In practice, however, after having resided in three or more countries, they settle down in one, at most two, homes in alien countries.

Ibiza imaginary: transgression, nostalgia and diaspora

As the end of the season approaches, the social life of hippies and clubbers – expressive expatriates in general – gains a nostalgic undertone, particularly noticeable during ritualized gatherings, such as the mega-club 'closing parties,' the hippie market final days, and more intimate sessions like Biodance. While interacting in such settings, they evince a more reflexive mood, pondering over summer experiences and anticipating their next 'moves,' both of a traveling and learning kind.

More widely, the island's socio-economic life declines sharply in October. Tourism will be virtually nonexistent for the next six months. The airport silences and hundreds of rental cars are relocated to mainland Spain. Hotels, bars and restaurants close en masse. The Spanish population will then rest with the support of unemployment allowances provided by the state.

In tandem, the 6,000 or so bohemian workers pack and leave, promising never again to return – just as they said in the previous season ... The majority flies back home, to follow the conformist schemes outlined above. But a few others will be soon traveling to Asia, maybe as an expression of a new and engaged interest in alternative occupations and more cosmopolitan exchanges. After all, at a subjective level, cosmopolitanism indexes the heightened interest in searching about one's own self, its origins and conditions of being (see Chapter 1). They may be thus emulating the first steps of a trajectory more typically found among expressive expatriates.

This final section examines how the spatiality of Ibiza is appropriated into a utopian imaginary, attracting various peoples to the island. When the island hibernates, its insularity and seasonality reinforce the centrifugal drives of mobile expatriates. Feelings of 'isolation' and the need for 'rejuvenation' propel them to periodically leave the island, taking them to exotic countries and original homelands in a geographic triangulation. The following sub-sections summarize how self-fashioned gays, New Agers and clubbers envisage Ibiza's utopian and centrifugal features that affect stylistic socialities and flexible subjectivities alike.

Gay Ibiza: 'You are repressed!'

Many 'real' clubbers considered *La Troya Asesina* to be the 'best,' 'hottest' and 'wildest' party on the island. Every Wednesday, crowds thronged *Amnesia*'s entrance throughout the night and, for hours after sunrise, a continuous influx of cars still arrived at already overcrowded parking lots. The party was regularly well alive beyond 11:00 on Thursday morning, neglecting official warnings and compliance fines. *La Troya*'s tremendous success hinge on how the gay community captures the imaginary of Ibiza as a space of transgression and liberation from moral codes. In this case,

Figure 3.5 Postcard of Ibiza.
Source: Courtesy of Ekki Gurlitt.

nightclubs and Ibiza reinforced each other's symbolic power to address utopia in a synergic manner.

La Troya moved from *Privilege* to *Amnesia* in 1999, and then to *Space* in 2006. Its successful formula as well as main promoters, DJs, characters and fan base have, nonetheless, remained essentially the same. Indifferent to road billboards and magazine ads, the popularity of *La Troya* stemmed from word-of-mouth across venues of the gay scene: trendy bars, boutiques, beaches, saunas and art galleries of Ibiza town. However, it would be a mistake to label it a 'gay party,' because, ironically, it was its 'sexy' and 'transgressive' overtones that attracted a larger variety of clubbing types: underground clubbers, model wannabes, bohemians, hippies and jet-setters, in addition to less eccentric segments of mainstream clubbers. The general absence of British kids was positively seen by regulars, and this post-gay queer party thrived without needing to tap into mass tourism. Para-doxically, *La Troya* succeeded commercially because, rather than a structured business enterprise, it fashioned itself as a messy, orgiastic event organically integrated to the counterculture.

In contrast with other weekly parties at *Amnesia*, musical styles at *La Troya* were essentially the same in both main room and terrace: house music with sexy vocals and percussion, leaning toward an underground blend of big beats and Euro pop remixes during morning hours. However, despite this musical uniformity, the distribution of peoples over the two areas was differentiated in terms of style and sexual orientation. The majority of apparently 'straight' clubbers danced in the darker main room, located inside, where a huge foam party took place around 5:00. In the meanwhile, gay men, model-like women and eccentric clubbers preferred the glass-roofed terrace, sipping drinks, socializing and sizing up exposed bodies (the 'talent on offer,' as some would put it) by the *Coco Loco* bar.

It is important to identify the social types that locally reproduce such imaginary of transgression. *Coco Loco* was the most revered and pivotal bar in *Amnesia*. Its gay staff served a potent drink made of vodka, coconut milk and a 'secret substance' confidentially mixed by bartenders loyal to club manager Brasilio, who created the drink as a variation of the caipirinha from his native Brazil. As a residue of club solidarity, coco loco drinks were given free of charge to 'bar friends,' while strangers and tourists were asked to pay Ptas 1,000–2,000 per drink (US$6–12). 'It depends on their face and the way they talk to me,' explained Italian transvestite Tirry, an artist who has run the bar for many years. Tall, thin and blond, Tirry usually wore a sex android outfit in leather, high stiletto heels and a black stripe painted across her eyes. During the night she eventually took a break to literally fly over the massive crowd by means of suspended parachute chords, swinging to and from a giant smoke machine.

Having arrived from Brazil in the late 1970s, Brasilio (his real name) opened the original *Coco Loco* bar in the narrow streets of Ibiza town port area, serving just this one mysterious drink, offered for free, although patrons were invited to make contributions. The bar, staff and drink were transposed to *Privilege* (known as *Ku*) in the early 1980s, and then to *Amnesia* in 1999. While socializing with outrageous celebrities such as Freddie Mercury and Grace Jones, Brasilio brought an invaluable know-how of carnival production, derived from personal connections with TV stars and media barons in Brazil. He has long arranged an annual July parade through the streets of Ibiza town as a promotional call to his one-off *Brazil* themed party in *Amnesia*. The parade featured a musical float, accompanied by some 100 figurants, percussionists, *capoeira* fighters and transvestites, all camply dressed in light feathered costumes. They were mostly Italian and Spanish gay men, and Brazilian samba musicians who lived in Madrid or Barcelona. Though it is a mistake to compare carnival with clubbing, Brasilio's background, enthusiastically backed by the gay community, was a key element in making Ibiza's nightclubs into major references on the global club landscape.

Inspired by Ancient Greco-Roman imaginary, *La Troya*'s decorative theme evoked the idea of orgiastic bacchanalias. Muscled-up gladiators and sexy slaves danced on podiums, amid the imperial scenario which included a king-size bed where clubbers could rest. The original party title was *La Vaca Asesina* ('the murderous cow'), an argot among Brazilian transvestites referring to the insatiable sex drives of a hyperactive queer. But since a local businessman copyrighted party names aiming at money making, the promoters then renamed it *La Troya*, granting a penetrative and ambush overtone to its already bestial references.

By 5:00 in the morning, the party was still growing strong, as underground clubbers and other bohemians were just joining the crowd already high on music and stimulants. Hundreds of shirtless males rubbed on the dance floor, while 'cool' punters and androgynous types hung out by *Coco Loco*. An unusual musical shift – a hot techno of the type favored by drag divas – heralded the arrival of a fat drag queen walking on stilts. All in black and breasts hanging out, she mesmerized the audience with a provocative style of tongues and faces. Through a wireless microphone, she stood overhanging the dancing crowd and sang in Spanish:

> You are oppressed. You are repressed.
> But I am your solution.
> To make all of your fantasies come true.
> Your desires. Your perversions.
> Come with me. Come with me.
> I am Ibiza. Ibiza . . . Ibiza!

Yet, Ibiza not only liberates, it also derails. By the *Coco Loco* bar, I listened to a regular punter complaining about having the blues about minor disappointments. The bartender, a Brazilian transgendered performer, exclaimed, 'Hey, babe, this is Ibiza! It is exactly like that. One day you feel like you are on the top, the next day you are at the bottom. Ibiza messes up with your mind. I know it, babe, that's Ibiza.' That was not an isolated remark. Expressive expatriates regularly evoked Ibiza, the island itself, as the main cause of certain moods and ordinary events taking place in their private lives. *La Troya* thus illustrates one way by which musical and ritual texts are weaved into the social life of alternative subjects. Besides self-fashioned gays, New Agers also represented Ibiza as a space of transformation, and gave their own view about the mysterious 'vibration' of the island.

New Age Ibiza: the Scorpio island and its sun mercenaries

Late at night, on my way out of a hippie party at Las Dálias farm, I came across Aurora, an alternative 'expatriate' (originally from northern Spain) who worked at the hippie markets. She was involved with New Age forms of Mexican shamanism and Maya astrology, and organized study groups and ritual dances about them. However, melancholic about her recent separation, she spoke about future traveling plans. I asked why she chose to live in Ibiza after all. She corrected me:

> No, no. It is not you who choose Ibiza. It is Ibiza that chooses you. Yes. It is the energy of the place, you know. It attracts all these types of people that have to be here. Ibiza is like a magnet, and this is really very curious.

Many expatriates, particularly those of a more mystical proclivity, described their presence on the island as a blessed mystery. Those into astrology claimed that Ibiza is ruled by Scorpio, a zodiacal sign that represents intense sensuality (and materialism), mysticism (and selfishness) and radical change (and betrayal). In the same vein, the sea rock of Es Vedra has been an object of fantastic stories due to its peculiar standing shape and luminosity, its 'powerful energies.' And, while some residents jocosely commented on alleged predictions by Nostradamus that Ibiza would survive a nuclear war, others recalled rumors about geo-magnetic streams that could account for the 'special nature' of the island.

Likewise, they have fueled fantastic beliefs as a result of archaeological findings of Phoenician colonies. Their gods were worshiped on the island around 700 BC (Kauffman 1995; Planells 1994). Bes is a dwarf deity borrowed from Ancient Egypt associated with sleep protection and sex, and likely explains the word 'Ibiza,' since the Phoenicians called the place *I Bes*. Tanit is the goddess of the Moon, fertility and war, sometimes evoked to account for the charismatic nature of 'Ibiza women,' to say, expatriates whose personalities were deemed specially independent and assertive.

Above all, Ibiza is believed to be a place that directly influences personal dispositions as well as relationships. Couple separations are often interpreted with reference to Ibiza as an intervenient cause. Nora claimed that all the expatriate couples that come to the island together break up sooner or later, although she also remarked that long-lasting couples were possible as long as they were formed *on* the island. During a body workshop, we learned about the separation of a couple of sannyasin therapists after ten years. The therapist spoke about the 'rhythms of life' that bring people together and apart. Later in the car, Nora observed, 'They were one of the last couples still together. But now, you see, that is the "curse" again.'

Both in secular and magical versions, the basic assumption is that Ibiza accelerates the influx of life, deeply affecting people's values, interests and desires. Expatriates' impetus for self-transformation certainly derives from a previous disposition to flee their homeland. Upon arrival, a new occupation, along with the possibility of a significantly different lifestyle, in a refreshing environment populated by interesting subjects, inspires the hopes and possibilities for self-actualization in an unprecedented manner. Initially sensed as a 'thirst for living,' the subject feels compelled to experience independently a variety of physical, social, cultural and spiritual possibilities, all of which are deemed fully legitimate in alternative Ibiza. In the case of couples, both partners tend to link their relationship with homeland memories which they are trying to disentangle from. Their relationship is then seen as a hindrance to their personal development and separation follows. In future, both individuals may reassess what has been gained and lost since separation, and they may even resume their relationship, but as reformed selves. In any circumstance, expressive expatriates sustain the highly individualistic idea that one first needs to come to terms with oneself, in order to become able to develop a legitimately fulfilling relationship. Such a perspective calls for an art of happiness in aloneness, whose capacity is continuously reassessed by means of reflexive self-examination. In sum, Ibiza stages an apparent paradox: through recurrent dramas of self-discovery, tragedy and transformation, the island victimizes its expressive residents by stimulating their belief in autonomous responsibility.

Likewise, the more somber aspects of Scorpio also affected the island, particularly during the summer tourist peak. Intense labor rhythms and hedonist practices predisposed expressive expatriates to manifest a more conspicuously selfish and materialistic behavior. As they often noted (see section on 'expatriate media' in Chapter 2), the intense modernization of Ibiza has led its residents to neglect nature, community and Being, the very elements that have brought expressive expatriates to the island in the first place. Rochelle once gloomily commented:

> This is Ibiza and the people who live here. If you are rich, healthy and strong, everybody likes you and comes to you. If you are down, with problems, overwhelmed, then everybody is gone. It is not a place for aging. It is a place for the strongest.

Her observation points to the potentially exclusionary nature of utopia. Neo-hippies (freaks) and clubbers often develop an assertive ethos of economic predation, aesthetic elitism and hedonist indulgence, which may verge on proto-fascism. Some of them were involved in risky or illegal activities, such as smuggling and drug dealing. In her book *Goa Freaks: My Hippie Years in India*, Cleo Odzer describes how a few days spent on organizing drug scams in South Asia could sustain an entire year of idleness and hedonist indulgence among a clique of flamboyant hippies living across the Goa–Bali–Ibiza circuit of the early 1970s (Odzer 1995).

Rochelle's comments resonate with a testimony by Tanit, not the Phoenician goddess but a notorious club bohemian. An African–French expatriate, he rented a trendy pre-party bar near *El Divino*. During the 1980s, Tanit (despite the name, actually a man) was a daring nightclub promoter (*Ku-Privilege*) who, among other things, could stand naked before the dance floor holding a lighter in circles. In a documentary about the club scene in Ibiza (Kinesis Films 1990), Tanit was asked why the island attracts hippies. He categorically replied in a mix of languages: 'Hippies are mercenaries. *Pi-ra-tas! Ibiza es una isla de mercenários*' (Pirates – Ibiza is an island of mercenaries). He added, 'people come to Ibiza because they look for energy. They look for sun, the energy of the sun.'

His references to mercenaries and sun seekers provide a powerful insight into a segment of expressive expatriates more directly engaged with the sensual, mystical and derailing aspects of Ibiza (the 'Scorpio influences'). Even though a subculture of agonistic gatherings persisted in the Ibiza of 2000s, those entrepreneurial scams Odzer refers to have long been replaced by complex narco-traffic networks. Hippie traders and bohemian workers could still be mercenaries surviving the predatory conditions of neo-liberal capitalism; nevertheless, they were more parsimonious in their expenses and exposure. In any case, Tanit's comments suggest a likely case of New Age reflexivity. Ibiza historically was a hideout and prey for various classes of pirates over the centuries.

An intrinsic contradiction lies at the core of utopian imaginaries. From Homer and the Bible, to Romantic countercultures and Hollywood, paradises are depicted as remote spaces of awesome natural beauty, endless joy and eternal youth (Delumeau 1992). However, these representations stand as an impossible myth, for decay, poverty and ageing remain as brute realities of human life. From a cosmological perspective (Geertz 1973), these conditions impose a logical challenge to religious ideologies that affirm the goodness of god and to secular variations of optimistic individualism, which in the New Age takes the form of a cosmic pantheism ('I am god, all is god, all is beautiful and just'). Nevertheless, a more balanced understanding of utopia could recognize such predicaments of life cycles, by translating them into meaningful lessons of modesty, temperance and wisdom. After experienceing a variety of life difficulties, to wit, mature expatriates may gradually develop a more stoic purview.

Closing party in the 'best club in the world'

Late September is the best time for clubbing in Ibiza, according to insiders. The weather is more pleasant and the number of mainstream clubbers declines noticeably. In addition, 'smart' clubbers flock from global cities to attend the highly anticipated 'closing parties,' particularly at *Amnesia, Pacha* and *Space*. Requests for guest-lists skyrocket, but only the well-connected clubbers will be able to dodge the money machine that nightclubs have turned into.

Amnesia's 'closing party' was an orgiastic pot similar to *La Troya* events, also producing massive traffic jams on the highway, as intoxicated crowds raved until 17:00 the next day. In the meanwhile, *Pacha*'s sequence of closing parties (thrown by different party promoters) was also overcrowded, albeit striving to keep its elegance. With multiple staircases conveying a catwalk atmosphere, 'to see and to be seen,' *Pacha* is renowned for hosting media celebrities and magnates accommodated in a VIP area absurdly larger than the common dance floor.

Space's 'closing party' epitomized the clubbing experience in the clubbing capital of the world. Ranked high in any international list of best nightclubs around the millennium, the venue enjoyed an outstanding situation in terms of location, structure, logistics, DJs and clubbers. Located between the beach and airport, it comprised a semi-open terrace and a dark inside room, both with impeccable sound and light systems. More importantly, the club was able to attract the 'best' DJs (according to club experts) which in turn reflected in a highly international crowd of 'smart' clubbers from Europe and beyond. The combination of all of these elements engendered a highly electrifying ambience, hardly matched anywhere else. In fact, *Space* was often chosen as the best nightclub in the world in those years (Dancestar 2004).

Among the mega clubs, *Space* customarily delivered the last 'closing party' of the season (around October 1), although smaller clubs have subsequently attempted to push the calendar a bit further with their own 'carry on' and 'closing parties.' *Space*'s finale was a unique occasion, able to attract party promoters, managers and DJs from competing clubs and bars locally and abroad. Clubbers often arrived directly from the airport. Jets roared over the club's dance terrace, enticing the crowd to cheer back. Others talked on cell phones, teasing their friends back in global cities, such as Barcelona, London, Frankfurt, Milan or Paris, on their way to bed or to work (depending on whether it was morning or night).

For those bohemian workers, clubbers and expatriates who have been on the island during the entire season, closing parties acquired a more specific meaning. Such events nostalgically marked the end of the hedonist dream, particularly for those returning to their homelands. Attending these parties – particularly by means of a free pass – crowned their sentiments of belonging to a privileged aesthetic community envied by the mainstream (or, at least, represented as such by the international media). They were, as the title of a *Space* CD compilation (1998) suggests, *Ibiza's Happiest People in the Morning*. As dawn arises, they bid farewell to buddies on the terrace, for most people would soon be leaving the island. By the DJ decks inside, *Space* owner Pepe signaled that it was time for the very last record. Around 7:00, the DJ played a significant record, not uncommon in house remixes of the late 1990s: a smooth dance track topped with Martin Luther King's voice, delivering the speech 'I Have a Dream.'

Freak diaspora: the centrifugal island and orientalism

Countercultural formations engage with politico-economic structures of Ibiza in complex and contradictory ways, also depending on the level of analysis. Though criticizing the hegemonic power of the state, market and morality, expressive expatriates have adopted a more pragmatic approach. Seeking to take advantage of economic opportunities, they do not oppose the encroachment of leisure capital in hippie and club scenes, as long as they can actualize expressive and hedonist values, at least in other more exclusive spaces. Thus, while working and enjoying bars, mega-clubs and hippie markets of mainstream Ibiza, they also attend highly secretive raves and trance parties, as well as body therapies and New Age workshops, which are self-fashioned as removed and autonomous practices not contaminated by biopower/sexuality regimes. The main problem is, de facto, the intensity and scale of systemic colonization, which transforms Ibiza's socio-environmental landscape to such an extent that rising inflation, overwork, overregulation and pollution levels undermine the material conditions of expressive lifestyles as such.

Such commercialization indicates the compensatory function that club and hippie venues play in consumerist societies. Leisure industries amplify the global circulation of media representations about Ibiza, by means of tourism advertising, club magazines, autobiographies, CD compilations, BBC on-site radio specials, celebrity news, movies and TV shows – all of which index 'Ibiza' as a brand of fun and youth, or as a space of utopian liberation. Furthermore, as a paradoxical example, the rise of corporate clubbing in Ibiza by the mid 1990s was propelled by the repression of rave parties in the UK. British promoters played a key role in reanimating the party scenes of Ibiza, Goa and US metropolises in the wake of electronic dance music (Ingham *et al.* 1999; Reynolds 1998; Collin 1997; McKay 1996). As such, facilitated by European integration, Ibiza became the rave suburbia of Britain and Germany.

More closely, nightclubs provide a space where countercultural, capitalist and mainstream moral forces dynamically clash and converge upon issues of sexuality. As seen, *Manumission*'s sex shows imploded under the pressure of politicians, media and corporate sponsors. Conversely, *La Troya*'s play on erotic outrage has thrived, largely because it remained circumscribed to non-heteronormative segments. In the meanwhile, at the apex of global clubbing, *Space* has attracted a multinational crowd of clubbers that cultivate more androgynous forms. In sum, nightclubs and hippie gatherings allure tourists (mostly young but not always so) to transgress the routines of daily life, although usually not extending beyond the weekend binge, thus reinforcing social conformism. In this case:

> Paradoxically [. . .], the more fully certain texts capture the feeling of modern alienation and anomie, the better they serve consumptive capital. [. . .] They become mutant messengers of hope and open a potential passageway [. . .] – even as they become part of the circuit of capital.
>
> (Povinelli 2000: 521)

However, it is often during a holiday or a temp job on the island that sedentary subjects are enticed to engage in an alternative lifestyle oriented by expressive, aesthetic and nomadic values. In addition to the logic of consumptive capital, countercultural projects must be assessed for their cultural resonance with the spatiality of Ibiza. Though suffering the deleterious impact of mass tourism, Ibiza still survives as an icon of pleasure and liberation. As seen, as the season fades, expressive expatriates rejoice about the possibility of rest, while nostalgically longing for utopia, whose inevitable finitude renders it an impossible dream (and an object of ephemeral consumerism).

On a subconscious level, expressive expatriates have chosen Ibiza (or 'were chosen by it') because of its very condition as an island. Its insularity engenders special moods modulated by feelings of isolation and community, tropes of the utopian myth that inspires their life aspirations. Indexing 'u-topos' as a 'no-place,' out of time and space, utopias are located on hanging gardens, mountainous valleys and remote islands (Delumeau 1992; Rozenberg 1990). Perhaps this explains (besides their low levels of education) why some tourists vacillate to identify Ibiza as being a part of Spain, while expatriates emphasize its uniqueness by affirming that, 'Ibiza is not Spain, but a world into itself.'

As another effect of such insularity, they also report periodic feelings of enclosure and suffocation, countered with a need to move and expand. The island thus propitiates a psychological cycle that compels them to move in nomadic patterns. While their will to move conditionally overlaps with the economic and climatic periodicities of the island (summer tourism/winter unemployment), expressive expatriates remit such insular moods to Romantic temporalities, something not at all verified among sedentary natives or mainstream 'expats.'

As work rhythms decelerate by autumn, expressive expatriates more desultorily attend the hippie markets. My informants stop by the stalls to greet and converse about the season's outcomes and impending plans. Hippie traders tell me that they will be soon departing for periods of several months: to visit relatives in mainland Spain, Western Europe or Argentina; or to pursue commercial and spiritual interests in Brazil, Mexico or Morocco. As a main finding, about half of the fifty hippie traders, bohemian workers and expressive expatriates I spoke to in a specific autumn revealed plans to go to India in the coming or next winter. And all of them knew about someone who was already on their way to South Asia.

In India they seek to integrate economic, leisure and spiritual interests. First, the country is an interesting market for purchasing exotic goods (clothes, fabrics, handicraft, jewelry, decoration items, incense and illicit drugs) to be traded in the West. Inexpensive accommodation facilitates their economic strategies, compensating airfare expenses insofar as they stay for many months. Second, they also attend ashrams and meditation centers as part of their interest in self-spiritualities, such as Osho sannyasins and yoga teachers reveal. Finally, they also indulge in leisure activities, visiting unknown regions, attending traditional festivals, and directly participating in trance parties (which rather hybridize leisure and religion, to be examined in Chapter 5). Likewise, their familiarity and pragmatism in relation to Spanish and Indian native cultures suggest that they should not be conflated with tourists, a hypothesis that draws on Hannerz's notes on expatriate cosmopolitanism (Chapter 1, pp. 15–17).

The pervasiveness of Asian artifacts, practices, symbols and representations – displayed in orientalist fashion – in Ibiza is closely entwined with the economic reproduction of alternative formations. However, beyond commercial needs, such orientalism is also constitutive of these expatriates' identity forms. Ibiza has been sometimes dubbed as 'the India of the West' or 'the island of sannyasins' (Rozenberg 1990). In the confluence of economy and culture, their exoticism performs an economic function, by granting charisma to expressive subjects, who, in turn, attract tourists and celebrities to the leisure circuit of the island, as this chapter noted in regard to the attractiveness of hippie markets, sunset bars, trance parties, exotic boutiques and New Age retreats.

Yet, the centrifugal drives of alternative Ibiza imposes a methodological challenge, leading me to reconsider the 'site' of my research. Considering the hypermobile and orientalist components of countercultural lifestyles, it became clear that to delimit my fieldwork to the perimeter of Ibiza would be empirically crippling. Transnational countercultures located in Ibiza are conditioned by social, economic and political contexts of Mediterranean Spain, but transcend the particularity of the island, since these formations are also shaped by the engagements and contexts of other localities (such as London and Goa). In methodological terms, although studying delimited sites remains a necessary stage in the investigation of translocality, it does not suffice for a proper understanding of the nature of hypermobile fluidic formations. It is thus imperative to address the global circuits that such formations refer to. In other words, although situated in localities, the 'site' of this research lies beyond the 'local' (see methodology section in Chapter 1). Therefore, at a pragmatic level, I was compelled to follow expressive expatriates during their winter journeys (or remain seasonally unemployed as an ethnographer, just like Ibiza tourist workers). Following these expatriates to India was a necessary condition for addressing globalized countercultures in their romantic mirroring of the Orient. After all, after telling me their stories about how traveling decisively transformed their lives (Chapter 2), expressive expatriates always asked me: 'Have you been to India?'

4 Osho International Meditation Resort

Subjectivity, counterculture and spiritual tourism in Pune[1]

Osho movement: counterculture and commodification

Ibiza island, late fall 2000: with the end of the summer/tourist season, expatriates left the island. My housemate Gary (DJ Lucci) returned to England, and Barbara's housemates Miguel and Marta departed on a caravan journey across Spain. We thus agreed that I would move into the spacious house where she lived, and, for another curious reason, we also found out that we shared plans to travel to India that winter. In this sense, both ethnographer and native were going to the field side by side. As seen in Chapters 2 and 3, India is a pervasive reference in the lives of expressive expatriates, who often talk about spiritual practices, exotic commodities, cuisine, art and traveling related to that country.

Figure 4.1 Main gates of the Osho resort in the early 2000s.

In the days before our flight to Mumbai, we stayed with Barbara's friends in Barcelona. In the movie section of a newspaper, I spotted a German film titled *Enlightenment Guaranteed* (*Erleuchtung Garantiert* in the original, or *Sabiduría Garantizada* in Spanish). I read the blurb to Barbara, 'Two brothers decide to travel to a Zen monastery in Japan in their quest for inner peace. But they get lost in Tokyo with no money or passports, and their daily life turns into chaos. Directed by Doris Dorrie.' Surprisingly, Barbara noted that she had worked with Doris years ago, a director renowned for creating insightful pieces on existential conundrums of modern life.

Enlightenment Guaranteed plays on dilemmas and hopes that lead Westerners to search for spirituality in Asia. In cinema *verité* style, fictional characters (two brothers) intertwine with real situations (monks in a Zen monastery) in plots that blend fiction and documentary. Gustav is a feng-shui consultant, who practices meditation and is boringly married. Uwe is a kitchen salesman, aloof to any religiosity, in a highly stressful marriage – until his wife unexpectedly departs. Desperate, he suddenly joins Gustav in his long-planned spiritual vacation in Japan. From hi-tech Tokyo to traditional Zen, the film humorously explores the diverging responses of the two brothers in alien environments. Surprisingly, Gustav becomes distressed with the discipline of monastic life, whereas Uwe finds great enjoyment in austerity and meditation. In the subway heading home, Uwe is clearly grateful for such a transformative experience, while Gustav notes that one should be authentic to oneself, and confesses that he must assume his veiled homosexuality. In anticipation of what I would soon find in India, this film accurately represents some of the unexpected feelings and outcomes that Western travelers experience when confronting their own inner realities in exotic lands.

As the plane descends toward Mumbai, the pilot announced a moon eclipse. Such astronomical events are highly valued by New Agers and Techno freaks. Coincidentally, the moon is one of the mystical symbols of Osho Rajneesh, whose commune in Pune was my first destination. Carrying Deleuze and Guattari's *A Thousand Plateaus* to inspire me during fieldwork breaks, I playfully speculated on functional meanings that an eclipse could unleash in setting the mood of thousands of travelers in India, in a sort of collective mind assemblage – virtual and translocal; or still, that functions may engender their own intrinsic meanings. In the meanwhile, jet lagging in warm thick air, we waited for the next taxi van toward Pune at 4:00.

This chapter examines the *Osho International Meditation Resort* (OIMR), a site dedicated to practices of subjectivity formation, typically verified among expressive expatriates and the New Age more generally. As seen in the previous chapters, many Ibiza expatriates are acquainted with Osho, and often participate in therapy and meditation sessions led by 'sannyasins' ('Osho disciples') who inhabit the island. A highly significant proportion of Ibiza expatriates have become sannyasins and visited the main Osho communes of Pune and Oregon (US, 1981–5). To wit, in her classical study about utopian lifestyles in Ibiza, sociologist Danielle Rozenberg has characterized Ibiza as 'the island of sannyasins' (1990: 82).

This chapter is based on ethnographic fieldwork of the 'meditation resort' located in Koregaon Park, a wealthy neighborhood of Pune, totaling six months during 2001 and 2002. Among the methods of data collection, I employed participant observation, reading materials (books and newspapers), unstructured interviews, daily interactions and email correspondence with sannyasins and Pune residents – prior to, during and after the fieldwork phase. While open to any relevant intervening issues, my focus primarily was on the globalized and individualist dimensions of the diasporic formation of expressive expatriates, as they personally engage, reflect and diverge with Osho institutional-ideological apparatus.

The chapter initially outlines the apparatus that sustains Osho's spiritual philosophy, as it is projected during the 2000s. To that end, after examining the gentrification of the resort (i.e. the replacement of former countercultural sannyasins by wealthier yet more culturally conventional visitors), I identify the central philosophical and religious tenets that underlie Osho's thought. The second section describes the main ritual practices and biographic trajectories, both of which resonate with a cultural project that seeks to criticize and transcend modern personhood, while legitimating 'authentic' self-determination, formalized, for example, in the conversion ritual for 'taking Sannyas.'

The third section provides a deeper investigation that detects and analyzes disruptive incidents that upset the order in the resort, thus exposing its problematic nature: the organization contradictorily stimulates and controls idiosyncratic behavior, and, in addition, it sustains a therapeutic apartheid tacitly imposed on Indians who frequent the resort. In analyzing these contradictions, I seek to reveal grids of power and ideology that not only reproduce the OIMR as a hybrid of 'total institution' and leisure resort, but also evince the Western specificity that marks the sannyasin ideology of subjectivity formation: a narrative of how selves are constituted, reproduced ('controlled') and transformed ('liberated').

The final section describes the main social networks that cut across the resort locally and transnationally. It examines how interests and motivations as well as historical circumstances enable the formation, scale, range and continuity of flows of sannyasins, travelers and expatriates who continuously interconnect Pune with other regions of India (particularly Goa and Mumbai), globally, and even, specifically, to Ibiza.

At a wider theoretical level, the anthropological analysis of sannyasin ritual and therapy settings provides empirical grounds for rethinking Western conceptions about the subject. The Western self is a crystallization of longstanding processes of social, religious and scientific institutions and

knowledge forms, which can be grasped through the notion of 'biopower/
sexuality' (Foucault 1976 – see the section on 'post-sexuality' in Chapter
1). This regime has overemphasized the notions of 'desire,' 'repression'
and 'confession,' which have become internalized by the modern subject
by means of multiple disciplinary mechanisms: family, school, church,
work, army and the nation. Biopower thus constructs and delimits a
certain experience of the self (centered on 'desire,' 'repression' and 'confession') in ways that are quite specific to the modern West. As Michel
Foucault remarks (1976), repression does exist but its status must be
reassessed in the context of power relations, for anti-repression discourses
of liberation have played a paradoxical role in sustaining the very biopower
modes of self-formation that they seek to overcome. In other words, utterances against repression may actually reinforce its force. In tandem, a
different arrangement of practices, relations and claims about the self
could possibly entail singular experiences of the self and sociality no longer
regulated by those tropes of modern sexuality. In this light, this chapter
inquires to what extent sannyasin formations reflect or depart from the
modern regime of biopower/sexuality.

Institutional and ideological contexts – the world's largest meditation center

Located 160 km southeast of Mumbai, Pune is the wealthiest non-capital
city of India, renowned for its gentrified neighborhoods, higher education
institutions and software industry (*Times of India* 2004a, 2004b). In travelogues, Westerners have depicted the overland journey from Mumbai to
Pune as a dramatic transition from chaos to order. Their descriptions of
harsh climate and social misery upon arrival in India enmesh with visceral
emotions of utter disappointment ('what am I doing here?!'). However,
as the traveler approaches Pune's uptown Koregaon Park, their narratives
change, as if recovering from the initial shock. Yet, as one perceives reality
according to inner categories of understanding, the traveler may well be
expressing an unconscious drive to move from psychological dystopia to
utopia. As they settle around the Osho resort, their focus will rapidly
shift from the objective misery of Indians to the subjective misery of
Westerners.

The *Osho International Meditation Resort* is self-fashioned as 'the largest
center in the world for meditation and personal growth. [. . .] this lush
contemporary 40-acre campus is a tropical oasis where nature and the
21st Century blend seamlessly, both within and without' (Osho International Foundation 2005). Amid lush bamboo gardens and pyramidal
buildings, maroon-robed visitors can enjoy leisure amenities, and participate in intensive therapy and meditation programs inspired by the work
of Osho. Previously known as Bhagwan Shree Rajneesh, Osho was a
polemical spiritual teacher who died in 1990. His books sold 2.5 million

copies in 40 languages in the year 2003 alone (personal correspondence with Osho International Foundation, July 2005).

Recent scholarship on the 'Rajneesh movement' nonetheless remains centered on the period of the 1970s and 1980s (Goldman 2005; Basnet 2002; Fox 2002; Aveling 1999; Urban 1996). These studies provide further nuance about established issues, such as the historical conditions that prompted highly educated individuals to join a charismatic cult; the communitarian and psychological dimensions of the master–disciple relationship; the flexible business model adopted to amass property (that included a Rolls-Royce fleet, as a 'joke on consumerism'); and, finally, how its short-lived community in Oregon (1981–85) clashed with the US establishment, leading to the extradition of Rajneesh and the reopening of the Pune commune in 1987. More contemporarily, Marion Goldman has briefly outlined the post-Osho diaspora of sannyasins, along with the decentralization of Osho-related organizations internationally (Goldman 1999). However, the lack of studies about the current movement suggests that, influenced by the media blitz of the 1980s, researchers have mistakenly 'assumed that the most interesting phase of the movement is over' (Palmer and Sharma 1993: 162; Van Driel and Van Belzen 1990).

From ashram to resort: meditating in the marketplace

At the gates, the visitor is directed to the 'Welcome Center,' an elegant marbled office sided by a bamboo pond with a Buddha statue. Over a desk, a maroon-robed volunteer checks passport visas into a computer and leads the visitor to the on-the-spot HIV-AIDS test. These procedures are mandatory for entering the resort. At the cashier's desk, the visitor purchases one-day stickers, pasted on the 'meditation pass' (photo ID card). During the early 2000s, daily entrance sharply increased from Rs. 100 to Rs. 330 (US$2–7.50 – Indian nationals pay 30 per cent of that value due to economic disparities). It includes free participation in hourly meditation sessions conducted at the main hall. Maroon and white robes, used in meditation and therapy, can be purchased in the resort's 'boutique' or with street vendors. Only a minority of visitors is accommodated in the resort, either as guests at the 60-room pyramidal hotel opened in 2002, or as workers in a small team of resident volunteers. Most people can find accommodation in apartments and hotels of the neighborhood, with prices in the range of $3–20 per day.

Despite official announcements, different people used the terms 'ashram,' 'commune' or 'resort' when referring to the organization. This semantic plurality is certainly prone to misunderstandings. The term 'ashram' confers a religious undertone to the place as a 'sacred dwelling for the guru and disciples' (Merriam-Webster). In its turn, 'commune' embodies the countercultural drives of a group that strives for self-sufficiency amid hegemonic adversities. Finally, 'resort' refers to the secularized notion of a space for recreation, more in tune with tourism and capitalism. As such, while marking different historical moments of the OIMR, these notions overlapped in a palimpsest of religious, countercultural and commercial connotations that express divergent forces, meanings and dispositions converging on this place. Such organizational mist is only enhanced by the highly reserved stance of the direction: my requests for a formal interview were ignored, and during the writing of this book, I was denied permission to use Osho postcards and screensaver slides to illustrate the chapter. It was under these circumstances that I had to dig information from the ground up, building the panoramic perspective along the way.

The OIMR has been marked by rapid transformations since its opening in 1974. From 'ashram' to 'commune' to 'resort,' as it was finally renamed in 2000, it has intensified a strategy of modernization, professionalism, and gentrification outlined by Osho during the late 1980s. The strategy is epitomized by the inauguration of the Mahakashyapa complex in 2002 (a large pyramid for meditation, comprising a hotel and sided by a business center). The directive board (known as 'inner circle') manages the resort within administrative parameters and has no religious authority.[2] Though based on voluntary work, the organization seeks to follow more strictly management criteria toward profitability, marketability and sustainability (Urban 1996). It has been increasingly catering to wealthier visitors rather than alternative expatriates, by means of sharply higher prices and upgraded amenities. While downplaying its cultic past, the main available end-activities (therapy, meditation, leisure, art and cultic practices) have been further compartmentalized, in order to please a wide variety of tastes in a free-choice system. In parallel, the editorial division based in New York City has outsourced the publication rights of Osho's books to a variety of large publishers internationally. As a result, over the period between 1990 and 2005, the number of visitors steadily declined from 3,000 to about 500 daily, whereas book sales have skyrocketed from 170 thousand to over 2.5 million annually (personal communication with staff of OIMR).

It can be estimated that about 12,000 people attended the OIMR each year during the early 2000s.[3] They ranged from ashramite workers who stayed up to six months (when visas expired), to backpackers passing by Pune for a few days, to the majority of visitors who stayed two to six weeks in Pune. About 50 percent of all attendees were white Westerners, 30 percent were Indians (mostly men), and some 20 percent were Eastern Asians (mostly women). During the monsoon season (from June to September), foreign attendance drastically dropped, resulting in a higher share of Indians beyond 60 percent. Black individuals wearing maroon robes were extremely rare (only two cases in six months). In an approximately equal sex ratio, ages varied widely but averaged in the mid-thirties. The main nationalities present in the place were, in decreasing quantitative order, Indians, Israelis, Italians, Germans and Taiwanese/Chinese; then

British, Japanese, Russians, Scandinavians, Latin Americans, Australians, North Americans and French, in addition to dozens of other nationalities (Osho International Foundation 2005).

Osho's Nietzschean Buddhism

Maroon-robed bodies wandered by black pyramids in jungle gardens in a bubble-like environment that provided a radical contrast with ordinary urban life outside. As some visitors have noted, they felt as if they were in a surreal scenario of science fiction – a spaceship landed in Pune. This experience of 'protective isolation' (Amitabh 1982: 40) allowed them to fully immerse in existential dilemmas. Moreover, sporadic rumors about cultic rapture, personal renunciation and sexual promiscuity still contributed to an air of mystery that pervaded the site, even if merely echoing a past of countercultural effervescence. As an example of such rumors, once, by the main gate, an Indian mother begged me in tears to take care of her American adult son, afraid that she would 'lose him to the ashram.' A veteran sannyasin (a German sannyasin who lived in Ibiza) aptly noted that, 'couples often break up when they come to the commune,' enigmatically explaining, 'it is the energy of this place.' Consequently, despite remarketing efforts to promote an image of a pleasant and conventional resort, a certain belief still lingered, although decreasingly so, that one had to be 'brave' (or 'crazy') to attend the OIMR.

The location owes its fame to Osho. Originally from a secular minority (Jain) background, he was a polemical spiritual leader who stunned mainstream audiences with his heterodox views on religion, sexuality and spirituality, coupled with therapy and meditation experiments in tune with 1960s counterculture. In Mumbai 1967, before the West discovered him, Rajneesh shocked a select Indian audience with a series of lectures in which he proposed that sexuality must be acknowledged as a step toward spiritual enlightenment (Osho 1967). Along with the embarrassment amid the religious elite, the national press readily labeled him 'the sex guru' (Mehta 1990). He retired by a close circle of influential admirers, but only temporarily so. In 1971, during a spiritual retreat ('meditation camp') in the Himalayan foothills, Rajneesh adopted the sacred title of 'Bhagwan' ('The Blessed One'). While justifying it as a way to formalize a ritual of initiation of his followers, the gesture certainly upset religious pundits. He responded that 'Bhagwan' must be understood, not as institutional religion, but as 'pervasive godliness' (Osho and Neiman 2000: 140). Westerners finally discovered Rajneesh in the early 1970s, and in 1974 a thin streak of visitors had become a flood of foreigners arriving in Pune in much larger numbers. Rajneesh began to speak more English and less Hindi, as the majority of sannyasins became whiter, younger and more countercultural.

There are innumerable biographic accounts about Osho written by sannyasins, journalists and scholars, usually tending to hagiolatry, sensationalism or summaries. A detailed and definitive biography is yet to be written, despite his own opposition to any systematic effort to register his life in a professional document. However, in light of the current organizational trends, two points must be made based on the biographic materials available.

First, Osho's way of reasoning must be considered in relation to his academic career, which extended from 1953 to 1966, first as a postgraduate student and then as an assistant professor of philosophy, likely his only formal occupation throughout his life. This period remains incredibly obscure, but it is possible to ascertain that Osho is fundamentally inspired by the philosophies of Friedrich Nietzsche and William James, as he indirectly admits. *Thus Spoke Zarathustra* tops his list of most important books (Osho 1985), and is the topic of a two-volume book based on Osho's lectures titled *Zarathustra: A God that Can Dance* and *Zarathustra: A Prophet that Can Laugh* (Osho 1987). The name 'Osho,' which Rajneesh chose in 1989, derives from William James's notion of oceanic experience, as Osho explains. Thus, rather than being mistakenly dubbed 'Tantra Hinduism,' Osho's spiritual philosophy – centered on a critique of civilization, the affirmation of the mundane drives as a step toward enlightenment, and the inscrutably experiential nature of religiosity – can be better understood in light of these Western influences on his thinking.

Second, underlying his deconstructive readings of mystical traditions, Osho insistently argued that meditation is the only valid path for spiritual development. As such, he reassessed the value of Zen Buddhism, affirming it as the most essential form of spirituality. 'Zen' is a translation of the Sanskrit word *dhyan* which means 'meditation.'

> I call Zen the only living religion because it is not a religion but only a religiousness. It has no dogma [. . .]. It is the strangest thing that has happened in the whole history of mankind [. . .] because it enjoys in emptiness [. . .]. For Zen, all that is, is sacred.'
>
> (Osho and Neiman 2000: 275)

In fact, the word 'Osho' also derives from a Japanese honorific title of a Zen master. By the time he chose the name, Osho was lecturing about Zen, before his death in 1990. His last book is titled *The Zen Manifesto: Freedom from Oneself*. Under this light, meditation is not a self-contained and ascetic body practice, but rather a total ethical stance in life – what Osho referred to as 'pure witnessing.'

In conclusion, sannyasin therapies embody this productive tension between Nietzsche and Buddha[4]. Since the early 1970s, countercultural therapists have assisted Osho in integrating cathartic (Dionysian) therapies with a mystical approach to meditation (Zen), although developed within an ideology that problematically celebrates the self 'beyond society.' In line with countercultural sentiments, Osho claimed that modern civilization imposes a repressive burden on the subject, obstructing its ability to meditate properly. The modern subject must first overcome a considerable degree of social conditioning and emotional suppression, in order to be able to develop the 'inner Buddhahood' to full capacity (Palmer and Bird 1999; Heelas 1996; Amrito 1984). In this connection, contemporary social life is marked by increasing levels of reflexivity, as moralities seem to lose their compulsory force to regulate the subject (Beck *et al.* 1994; Giddens 1989, 1992; Taylor 1991), which begs the question of how the subject constitutes itself under conditions of relative ethical freedom (Lash 1994; Foucault 1984c).

Osho International Meditation Resort: practices, trajectories and rituals

Considering that 50 percent of visitors in the resort at any moment are newcomers (Osho International Foundation, n.d.), the organization created an optional one-day 'start-up session' (upon a Rs. 500 fee, about US$10). My group with about 20 people gathered in a matted room. We wore maroon robes, just like the Italian man and Danish woman who led the event. They invited us for a round of self-introductions. All attendees were Westerners, mostly younger than the mid-thirties average. Many had read Osho's books, but the level of knowledge about him, the resort and its practices was clearly very superficial. A few admitted that they had never heard about Osho, and had showed up at the resort out of curiosity and by chance while traveling across the country. Likewise, only two newcomers claimed that they had

Figure 4.2 Sannyasins socializing outside the ashram.

come to India *exclusively* for attending the OIMR. This suggests that most visitors attend the resort within a larger itinerary that encompasses other places and interests in tourism, leisure and spirituality.

Our hosts explained some basic notions that inform daily life in the resort. They made very few, tangential references to Osho, unless a participant asked directly about him. Their presentation was informal and improvised, as they sat on cushioned mats just like the group. By a flipchart with photos of people from various ages and ethnicities, the male host elaborated on a 'human cycle of growth' through which the individual is gradually molded by dominant institutions: parents, religion, school, friends, society and nation. In line with Osho's social philosophy, the Italian man explained:

> We become obedient and responsible citizens. We are taught to follow basic rules, and to behave in certain ways: we become Italians, who are expected to be expressive, like me [laughter], Japanese (obedient), British (polite), etc. We become Christians, Jews; a man, a woman, a mother, a father, a worker – everyone is shaped by conditionings that society imposes on us and expects us to fulfill. And if we don't do that, we are criticized, ostracized, and even punished. The child – this individual – becomes an "I", a social persona imposed on us when we were just a defenseless child. As time passes by, this person grows up, becomes more and more stressed, more and more unhappy. And you feel bad because you are disconnected from the natural force of life, which is the life energy to be yourself. The result of this continuous repression – of not being allowed to be yourself – is aggression, violence, madness, unhappiness . . .
>
> So, it is against this situation that this commune – now we call it "resort" – has come about. Meditation is a very good way to become more aware of these conditionings and repressions. Here in the commune, we are all working for the creation, as we like to say, of a new human being, a person who tries to break free from these conditionings as much as possible. Our goal here is to deprogram you, to allow you to develop a new path, which is your own. This is why we work on practicing meditation and also on doing different types of workshops that include therapy.

The couple then demonstrated the main body techniques practiced in the resort, generically known as 'active meditations.' They comprised the 'Osho Dynamic,' 'Osho Kundalini' and, in a sense, the 'White Robe Brotherhood,' among others. A typical session begins with an emphasis on the body – hyperventilation, gibberish or spontaneous dance – evolving into gentler stages – slow movements, silent stillness and relaxation. The hosts emphasized that their demonstrations were just superficial illustrations, and that each person should follow and 'connect with' their own 'inner feelings' in order to 'express' them genuinely during a practice. At an anthropological level, nonetheless, their performance contributed to homogenize behavior, as social imitation is a basic learning mechanism, and an aspect that marks the culture of the resort, as will be later discussed. In any case, the Italian host added, 'This place is a big laboratory for human interaction. Try to talk to a stranger, experiment with new situations, express yourself.'

Osho dynamic meditation

Most visitors (whether sannyasin or not) planned to practice Dynamic Meditation at 6:00, but found it challenging to get up so early and then carry on with multiple activities until 22:00 or 23:00: 'This is also my vacation,' they said in excuse. My Australian room-mates (a college student and a nurse) asked me to wake them up for the early meditation, because they wanted to 'shape some discipline,' but turned out to be more successful with socializing at the bars and restaurants of Koregaon Park. Every hour, a few hundred people gathered at the Buddha Hall to practice Osho's various 'active meditations.' It comprised a spacious marbled patio covered with a huge canvas in a circus-like formation, surrounded by see-through mosquito nets, and four large loudspeaker sets strategically located. As people entered, they sat silently or lay down on the marble, facing the empty pagoda altar from where Osho used to speak.

A man wearing a black robe reached for the microphone and, speaking English with a German accent, briefly explained the five phases of the one-hour Dynamic Meditation. He started the music CD. A chaotic percussion set in, and the crowd began to violently breathe while flapping their arms for ten minutes. With a gong, the music shifted and the participants burst into a cathartic performance. By digital beats, the leader enthused, 'follow your body! Give your body total freedom . . . EXPLODE! Go totally mad.' For those standing outside, the view could be excitingly scary: the crowd burst into screaming, laughing, crying, gesticulating, jerking, groaning and roaring, with no interpersonal interaction – a mental asylum gone wild. After ten minutes, the music shifted into a stable martial-like rhythm. People now quick-jumped on the spot, with raised arms, uttering 'HU-HU-HU . . .' as feet hammered the ground. (This movement, sannyasins say, awakens 'basic instinctive energies'.) The rhythm accelerated, demanding extra effort, but it abruptly ceased with a 'STOP!' command. The crowd froze silently for fifteen minutes. With eyes closed, one sensed the body: the pounding heartbeat, the rolling sweat, the fast breathing, the inner heat, 'energy' sensations and flashbacks. Finally, by a melodic flute, the crowd gently danced, celebrating the coming day. The black-robe person watched the group at all times.

Upon this behavioral description, practitioners provided quite different explanations. For most, Dynamic Meditation was a physically strenuous practice. Many claimed to feel 'lighter' emotionally and 'energetically.' Some newcomers claimed that it was a transformative experience, because, for the first time in their lives, they were allowed to embody visceral emotions, acting them out noisily in a collective setting. Others referred to Tantra-like body 'energies' that enhanced their spiritual power, improving their meditation practice toward enlightenment. While some provided intricate details about their experiences, others claimed that it was impossible to elaborate on the matter. In a word, people seemed to largely ignore or to freely interpret Osho's technical prescriptions regarding body practices (Osho 1988). In fact, many sannyasins bluntly rejected conceptual instructions, claiming that it was all a matter of 'personal experience.' However, if interpretations varied widely, behavior tended to be surprisingly uniform in the resort.

Therapy workshops – encounter groups

Administered by a department named 'Multiversity,' therapy workshops are the main revenue source for the OIMR. Though meditation stands as the prime goal in Osho's spiritual philosophy, therapy is nonetheless an important component, usually a precondition, in shaping the 'new human being.' In the form of group workshops, these events center on practices informed by Reichian and humanistic psychologies, emphasizing the development of personal potentialities by means of intensive bodily work, emotional purging and recollection. Peak experiences and transpersonal insights are often sought and reported during this type of event (Palmer and Bird 1999; Krishnananda 1996, 1999; Bird and Pandya 1993; Amrito 1984).

A board at the plaza announced about 20 new workshops each week. These events reflected the universe of psychospiritual, humanistic and transpersonal psychologies which sannyasins embrace: body therapies integrating Reich and Tantra; massage therapies; various 'encounter groups' for self-discovery; workshops on painting, dance and creative writing; Gurdjieff sacred dance; 'advanced' meditations on Zen and Sufi; and therapy apprenticeship. Most events were basic workshops lasting three or four days, at a cost of around US$300. There were always a few dozen therapists, instructors and assistants at the resort. Originally from Westernized countries (Germany, UK, the Netherlands, Italy, the US, Brazil, Israel, etc.), they visited Pune periodically, and constituted the core of a diasporic community of sannyasins. Within a communal system, they never charged for their services, and just collaborated, networked, learned and socialized with colleague therapists and other sannyasins.

As many workshop participants did not speak fluent English (the resort's lingua-franca), the registration desk placed requests for voluntary translation on a board. I saw one for Spanish in a three-day workshop titled 'Opening to Self-Love.' I volunteered, as it was representative of a type of expressive therapy prevalent at the resort, with several points in common with psychodramatic techniques such as Biodance (described in the chapters on Ibiza). The therapist in charge of the event briefly interviewed me. She was American, in her late-forties, from a Jewish background.

In a mutual interview, therapists screened those who were interested in attending a workshop. They eventually denied access to someone deemed immature (a point to be examined further). In addition to answering questions about its goals and procedures, they asked the applicants the basic questions: 'Why do you want to join this group?' and 'Have you ever done workshops like this before?'. They also urged candidates to attend Dynamic, Kundalini and White Robe meditation sessions during the event (time schedules never overlapped), as a way to intensify psychological momentum. Studies have noted that Osho's images, references and ideas facilitate processes of disidentification and transference generally verified during therapeutic work (Palmer and Bird 1999; Bird and Pandya 1993).

'Opening to Self-Love' comprised intensive sessions during three mornings, three afternoons and one evening, in addition to three active meditation sessions each day. The group of about 20 people gathered at the plaza, and I was introduced to the man who requested translation. He was a wealthy veterinarian from Argentina, in his late forties and recently divorced. All participants were from Western/ized countries, with a sex ratio 60 percent female (as in most workshops). Five assistants supported the 'leader.' We were taken to one of the pyramidal buildings. The room was air-conditioned and comfortable, with bright windows viewing rich jungle gardens. There was no furniture other than a special sound system, and the floor was covered with thickly cushioned mattresses, pillows and piles of folded sheets all around.

The black-robed therapist said that we were beginning 'a deep work of self-discovery and awareness, with the intention of learning how to better love ourselves.' She urged everyone to come to those basic meditation sessions: 'They will allow you to keep an inner space while you work within, with awareness and peace.' She also recommended that participants should stay together during breaks and evening, 'to hold the energy together.' In a round of self-introductions, people spoke about their motivations and expectations. They mentioned a will to discover more about themselves and to become a better person. Many wanted to get rid of traits that they disliked, such as lack of self-esteem, shyness or anxiety.

She then played speech fragments by Osho claiming that 'in society, you are taken to love others but not yourself.' During two days, the group performed multiple exercises, such as spontaneous dance, pelvic movements, deep breathing, touching, trauma recall, cathartic expression and verbal recollection (sharing). These exercises varied in interactivity, as some were practiced individually, others in random or chosen couples, and others in smaller or larger groups. Physical contact (full-bodied hugs, caressing, massage) was very common, regardless of gender, but despite the emotional charge and intimate involvement, they were, at the end, very impersonal exercises. The therapist reminded participants that they

ought to become aware of emotional nodes, related to traumas and conditionings, usually originating in childhood. She also emphasized that each
person should 'connect with' these emotions, particularly those related to
forgotten memories. The basic premise – as in all cathartic workshops –
is that the modern subject is forged through the internalization of authoritarian utterances, primarily carried out by parents, and the end result is
perceived as repressive or traumatic.

The group was encouraged to enter cathartic states, 'expressing hidden
emotions.' These emotions were predominantly negative and painful. (Some
newcomers questioned, 'Does it have to be always negative? ... '.) Even
though emotional confrontation was common, physical violence was never
employed in any of the workshops I attended or asked about. Catharsis
was mostly induced by a combination of body movements, artificially
induced breathing patterns, monotonous music (New Age or Techno),
and, more importantly, the therapist's own commands, leading the group
into spirals of tension and release.

The importance of confession must be underlined. After each practice,
the group sat in a circle and individual experiences were shared. In this
confessional moment, they claimed to have become more aware about
emotional nodes that constrained their personalities and that they felt
empowered by being able to exteriorize them. Confession is thus as
important as the experience itself, because it reassures desired results and
constructs a certain type of understanding that persuades the self that it
has been satisfactorily transformed.

After two days of emotionally painful exercises, the workshop entered
a more enjoyable stage, centering on exercises that cultivate the ability to
feel pleasure and affection towards oneself, to be personally assertive and
socially expressive. These exercises comprised activities such as writing love
letters to oneself, meditating about one's heart, making eye contact to
project and receive love in random couples, auto-erotic dancing, dramatic
declarations of inner power, collective dancing, and, again, recollection by
sharing.

Drawing from a developmental perspective, it can be said that the group
was led to regress emotionally, prior to engaging in more affirmative traits.
As a general narrative, it evolved from the purging of destructive emotions,
toward the cultivation of an 'inner space.' Also known as the 'inner child,'
this notion refers to an 'untouched, warm and essential part of the subject'
that lies beyond social masks, and is developed through catharsis and
awareness (Krishnanada 1996, 1999).

This regressive-progressive journey required a protective environment
where participants could feel safe. Despite the encouragement for expressing traumatic or violent emotions, it was a principle that abuse was not
allowed, and the therapist made sure that participants listened to each
other respectfully. In fact, during the confessional moment, aggressive
comments about someone else's experience reports were dealt with on the

spot. By means of direct questions, the therapist skillfully led the person to undermine their own position, as emotional flaws emerged from underneath spurious rationalizations. Sharing was thus the predominant genre, but freedom of expression was carefully monitored according to the therapist's goals.

One incident illustrates the sentimental and ethnocentric nature of sannyasin therapies. Participants were required to mimic childhood situations in which their parents abused them emotionally (or were interpreted as such). The group then exploded into screaming in multiple languages simultaneously, as if each person was reprimanding and even offending an invisible child. As a translator, I sat against the wall and watched the impressive scene of familial inferno. Afterward, during the sharing period, a German woman enthused about 'how incredible it [was] to see the global experience of anger in all different languages.' The therapist asked if anyone wished to comment, and I raised my hand and tried to make a point that such experience was not global, but quite Western, as I asked, 'Where are the Indians, Africans and all the rest?'. The therapist cut me short and blushingly said, 'This is not the moment for this type of comment. We are now sharing experiences. Anyone else?' My comment was inappropriate. That was not a space for rational debate, but rather for emotional empathy. However, for research purposes, I had inadvertently hit into a vexing issue that haunted the OIMR: the limits of Western ideologies of self-formation being transposed to individuals of other cultural backgrounds, particularly Indians – a topic that will be resumed later.

A few notes about the efficacy of expressive therapies on participants are pertinent. Most people reported some form of psychological gain at the end of the workshops I attended or asked about: they claimed to feel more relaxed, confident and sociable (Basnet 2002; Palmer and Bird 1999; Bird and Pandya 1993). Yet, in private, other participants were more skeptical. They claimed that workshops were generally positive, but that some individuals, particularly newcomers, exaggerated their performances, expectations and perceived benefits. Psychological benefits also derived from the often-ignored social function that such gatherings enable, creating opportunities for social interaction. In fact, those who did not attend these groups tended to remain isolated in the vastness of the resort. In any case, although many workshop participants did not follow Osho in any measure, everyone agreed that therapy was an accessory to meditation, the ultimate practice for spiritual development.

Finally, not every expressive workshop was emotionally dramatic. Some focused on the physicality of the body rather than on its emotional components. 'The Art of Touch' was an introduction to massage techniques, in which I also participated as a translator. As usual, the maroon-robed group was taken to a comfortable room located behind the boutique. The 'group leader' was a young Italian man, massage therapist and chiropractor. In contrast with cathartic groups, the atmosphere was quite relaxed. The course was entirely practical, involving a series of exercises informed by basic explanations. In chiropractic systems, the body is therapeutically read in a singular manner: its surface (skin or eye-iris) contains discreet signals that reveal the health of the internal organs. Likewise, by manipulating certain parts of the body (feet, hands or abdomen), a healing effect is expected in apparently unrelated organs and systems. Another notion professes that the body is a depository of unconscious memories about the self, which can be triggered by means of touch and specific breathing rhythms, potentially enabling immediate insights that may alter behavioral patterns. Likewise, skin sensitivity can be enhanced to a point in which a blindfolded person can identify the hands of an exercise partner mixed within the group.

Sannyasin trajectories: transformation and mobility

Sannyasins fly global distances to sort out their angst or relax at the resort. This section briefly examines typical biographies, with a focus on their motivations and representations about their own self, the resort and society. Shafik illustrates the situation of a significant proportion of visitors in the early 2000s. In his late-forties, he was a well-established veterinarian in Argentina, divorced, and apparently in a 'mid-life crisis.' He had been attending an Osho center near his hometown for about two years before coming to Pune, which was his first international travel (other than a summer vacation in neighboring Brazil). He was spending all his three weeks in Pune.

> I came to Pune to think about my life, to consider new perspectives, to open new horizons. I reached a critical moment in my life, with a recent divorce and a business termination. I looked back and realized that my life has been quite boring and shallow. So I came here to regain a new freedom, and see how things in my life can unfold when I return home.

During a workshop break, he indicated a group of participants which he thought were South American. With a large smile, the tallest man replied in impeccable Spanish, 'No, I am from Austria, but I do enjoy the company of Latinos. Hi, I am Dimitri.' The other man and a teenager chuckled. Sudipo was translating to Livia, and both were from Brazil. In contrast with many participants of cathartic therapies, they remained amicable and seemingly relaxed after the sessions. From a middle-class background, Livia planned to study journalism at college. She lived with her father in uptown Rio de Janeiro. Her mother was a psychologist who had moved to Pune two years before and rented an apartment near the ashram. Livia was staying for a month and claimed that she wanted to attend the ashram as much as possible. Her style was light and friendly, playing the guitar around the resort in the company of her new sannyasin friends.

Sudipo had been living in Pune for almost two years when we first met. In his mid-forties, he was recently divorced, and, like Shafik, he was re-evaluating his life which stood in a 'transition phase,' in his own terms. But Sudipo had been more radical than Shafik, for he quit his career as a corporate accountant in Rio de Janeiro and moved to Pune where he was studying alternative therapies, developing himself as a spiritual healer. Job compensations and personal savings allowed him to live relatively well in Pune, and his fashionable Bullet Enfield motorcycle was an indication. He explained:

> I came to India for a break in my life. I decided to finish everything in my previous life, which was just a big mess. Only my daughter whom I love very much remains from that time. I came to Pune to stop, to meditate, to learn new things, and to open new perspectives in my life, for my future. So I am now focusing on my spiritual side. I want to develop it, and see what happens next.

Like many expatriates residing in Pune, Sudipo frequented other more traditional centers of alternative healing and spirituality, usually involving yoga and *vedic* diets. Pune expatriate residents did not attend the OIMR on a daily basis, because it turned out to be expensive, and, Sudipo added with a jocose punch line: 'you know what, it is a pain in the neck to be in this ashram every day.' Nonetheless, he developed contacts with sannyasin therapists and was able to join workshops as an assistant. Sudipo was thus able to learn a good deal, in addition to saving the money on workshop fees and the ashram entrance.

In comparison with all the Westerners I came across in India, Dimitri stood out for his peculiar lifestyle, occupation and biography. In his late thirties, he was a freelance tour guide leading groups anywhere in the world. He was not a sannyasin but had been regularly visiting the OIMR since 2000. He basically came to Pune in order to attend workshops, to practice Osho's active meditations and to interact with 'Asian girlfriends,' as he put it. Despite his active interest in workshops, Dimitri was not a 'groupie' (a serial practitioner obsessed with therapies). He was relatively experienced in therapies and cultivated a pragmatic approach to self-development. According to him, therapy groups had a limit in their possibility to foster one's own self. During pre-screening interviews, he openly admitted to therapists that he was looking for 'powerful workshops' (rather than 'soft exercises,' 'such as, writing love letters to myself over a pink pillow . . . '). Dimitri also let them know that he could 'make an effort' to attend Dynamic Meditation at 6:00, but that he would not attend the evening White Robe Brotherhood, which he despised as a strange cultic practice. 'I'd rather be in my nice apartment having a drink with a friend,' he would bluntly say. Sannyasin therapists admired such explicit frankness.

In order to enjoy a lifestyle which he appreciated, Dimitri spent about US$50 (about Rs. 2,500) per day in Pune, a small fortune in the Indian context. Most travelers sought to spend something in the range of US$5–20 per day. His average daily budget allowed for about US$30 being spent on OIMR workshops and private therapy sessions, US$10 on his apartment rent, and another US$10 on food, transportation, gym, etc. In comparison to other rooms temporarily or permanently inhabited by Western sannyasins, his place was exceptionally modern and decorated, containing brand new furniture and decor, cable TV, telephone, air-conditioner and a bar. He explained:

> I am not rich really. But I am always traveling because of my work, and I am already 37. I decided to have a better quality of life regardless of where I am. So, I am trying to have something here that may be equivalent to the West. This is why I am spending this amount of money, which is not that much really.

He provided a clear example of how expressive expatriates integrate labor, mobility and personal (spiritual) interests. Dimitri often traveled to India and Eastern Asia during breaks in his work. An agency in Austria and the US contacted him to guide groups anywhere in the world he could possibly be assigned to. Due to the nature of the job, Dimitri was highly skilled in managing his trips, while being able to take long 'vacations' of four to six months each year, which, in turn, allowed him to hone the multicultural abilities that were necessary in his work as a global tour guide.[5] With the decline of labor in the neo-liberal age, Dimitri found an occupational niche that suited (or shaped) his personal interests in travel and self-development, thus turning such macro-instabilities that affect millions of workers in his favor.

In this connection, Dimitri displayed singular interpersonal skills. Despite his reservations about certain ethnic dispositions which verged on stereotypical assumptions, he was nonetheless able to interact with peoples from all walks of life. In addition, he spoke multiple European languages fluently. Although relatively tall, his phenotypic traces (half-Serbian, half-Germanic) enabled him to blend in variegated situations. (Once, I witnessed him convincing an Italian woman that he was Cuban.) At a younger age, he used to travel through the Mediterranean, South America and Asia, socializing with marginal types, such as gypsies and prostitutes. In fact, he was the only person I met during fieldwork who was sexually active with traditional Indian women and Eastern Asian sannyasins. As he found white women to be mostly uninteresting, his sexual interests seemed to reflect an orientalist imaginary that eroticizes non-Western women as objects of the Western male desire. (The white female desire will be discussed in Chapter 5.)

On the other hand, hypermobility also limited his ability to develop stable relationships. Although sannyasin therapies validate emotional intimacy, Dimitri admitted that he had not been able or willing to develop his 'affairs' beyond a certain point, and usually he 'lose[s] interest.' He claimed to be open to 'settling down' and did not consider that his work was a limitation. Nonetheless, it can be suggested that excessive mobility has reshaped his modes of affective attachment in a way that disabled stability and attachment as conventionally expected from romantic relationships in the Western mainstream.

Prem[6] is a young Italian sannyasin, representative of newer generations of disciples that have been initiated after Osho's death in 1990. We first met at the 'Art of Touch' workshop. In her mid-twenties, Sonia (her 'legal name,' as sannyasins put it) was an experienced travel agent in northern Italy, where she lived either with flatmates in a big urban center, or with her parents in a small tourist village. Her father was a well-connected public servant who often facilitated job opportunities for her. Sonia was capable of starting up travel agencies, and seasonally worked as a receptionist at top hotels in tourist hotspots in the Mediterranean, Central America or the Middle East. Due to the nature of her job, Prem was able to get the best information on travel, airfares and other arrangements. More than that, being a mobile travel agent was part of a lifestyle which Sonia truly enjoyed.

It seems that occupations based on hypermobility may predispose the subject to a more experimental form of spirituality, such as Sonia's, which is typically verified in the New Age: eclectic yet centered on self-cultivation. While criticizing institutionalized religion for manipulating people, Prem was very interested in magic–spiritual practices, such as Santeria (which she learned in the southern US) and Reiki, a 'lighter and more subtle form of energy healing,' as she explained. In the meanwhile, she attended sannyasin workshops in Italy, read Osho's books and listened to his audio tapes as a form of meditation because sometimes they were in Hindi, a language Sonia ignored: 'this way I can listen with my heart, not with my mind.' Rather than material gratification, she practiced magic for spiritual fulfillment – in other words, for self-cultivation ends: wellbeing, inner peace and harmony. Cosmologically, her view on life was mystical, as she recurrently affirmed that providence grants us with what is necessary according to its own unfathomable logic, which is to be accepted with surrender and gratitude.

However, she linked her spiritual development to a troubled past. In an auto-analysis, Prem mentioned a difficult childhood with a distant father and an abusive mother, followed by teenage years marked by drug abuse and unhappy homosexuality: 'That was a very confused stage in my life. I had a girlfriend, but we had not found our identity. We were lost, just experimenting in fear.' She also clubbed hard in Ibiza. Her narrative culminated with the story of an emotionally and sexually abusive boyfriend with whom she had lived. At a turning point, she returned to her parents and developed a more harmonic lifestyle, cultivating her spirituality as a 'healing' process, as she put it. From such traumatic experiences, Sonia had learned that she ought to control the destructive potential of meta-morphic experimentation.

Sannyasin therapists

Sannyasin therapists also emulate patterns of mobility and self-marginal-ization like those verified in Ibiza. Dissatisfied with predominant moral codes, they engage with alternative practices of self-development centered on expressive and meditational ideas. This sub-section presents two veteran sannyasins whose biographies reflect those of many other sannyasins and expressive expatriates. The social networks that allow them to work and travel will be examined toward the end of the chapter.

During their permanence in Pune, therapists contribute to the Multi-versity department in charge of the therapy workshops. Considering that work in the resort is voluntary, other factors must account for the expatri-ates' periodical return to Pune. At a personal level, they feel that the OIMR is a unique place for practicing meditation, to socialize with friends and to relive old bonds of solidarity that amalgamated them around Osho. At a professional level, they benefit from attending the resort in two ways. It allowed them to interact and learn with colleagues about therapy innova-tions; moreover, it contributed to their own professional promotion in the West, as their brochures and websites may refer to the OIMR in a sug-gestive manner ('years of professional experience in Pune (India),' 'lived in an ashram under an enlightened master,' 'member of the therapy division of the OIMR,' 'advanced training at the OIMR-Pune,' etc). In sum, while direct experiences with Osho become blurred memories, sannyasin therapists take advantage of the professional reputation of the OIMR in the world of alternative therapies, which ramifies into semi-mainstream markets and corporate business.

Krishnananda is a German, Harvard-trained psychiatrist who became a sannyasin therapist in the early 1970s. Born into a Jewish family, Tom Trobe (his 'legal name') grew up in Germany, England and France, and joined medical school in the late 1960s. He described his experience at Harvard as frustrating. He anticipated the type of successful yet unsatis-fying career as a conventional doctor for wealthy clients. Therefore, while practicing various forms of Asian spirituality, he dropped medical school and went to California, and then to India where he met Osho. In Pune, Trobe gained the sannyasin name Krishnananda (in a ritual to be described later). Yet, he returned to the US to complete his medical residency, before settling down in Pune in the mid-1970s. His life trajectory up to the life-transformative encounter with Osho can be summarized in his own words as follows:

Through high school and college, I never questioned the direction that was proscribed for me by my conditioning. I just followed along trying to perform as well as I could. But then things came to an abrupt halt. I was enrolled in medical school, just having graduated from Harvard and about to begin a career as a doctor. Inside, I knew that I could not go on. I quit and drove to California. I stepped off the automatic train of my conditioning. In the years that followed, I lived in communes, took psychedelic drugs, studied yoga and meditation. I departed quite dramatically from the life I had been leading until then. I began to recognize that how I had envisioned life was extremely limited. My emphasis gradually shifted from finding success to finding truth, from exploring fear instead of avoiding fear. I eventually went back to medical school and then on to a residency in psychiatry, but my motivation and the work I have done since has always come from the inner search and longing to share with others what I have found. [...] At a certain point in all my exploring with Western therapy, I began to recognize its limitations. I was hungering for something that could give me greater spiritual insights and I naturally turned my focus to Eastern spirituality and to the paths of meditation. I spent some time going to Buddhist Vipassana retreats in America but still something was missing. I had read the teachings of a spiritual master in India and heard stories of his ashram. They interested me enough to leave a budding therapy practice in Laguna Beach, California, and go to India without any plan of when I would return. After some travels, I ended up at this ashram. [...] What I found when I met this man was a depth of stillness, grace, and wisdom that was totally different from anything I had ever experienced before. [...] It is very difficult to describe in words the relationship and the feeling that a disciple has for his master. Perhaps it is enough just to say that the gratitude and love that I have for him is vaster than any feeling I have ever had for anyone or anything. Sitting before my master I have always felt that I was looking into the eyes of a man who seems to have no fear. Even more unusual is the feeling I have, looking into his eyes, that there is simply no one there. Perhaps when our fear finally disappears, we melt into existence and that is what is termed enlightenment.

(Krishnananda 1996: 4–7)

Since Osho's death in 1990, Krishnananda has been based in Sedona (Arizona, US), although he has delivered an incredible number of therapy workshops around the world. His thirty years of therapy experience have been summarized in his books (Krishnananda 2006, 1999, 1996).

Samvado was a meditation teacher at the OIMR during my fieldwork. Despite revealing some exceptional characteristics, his biography also displays the typical transition from a conventional lifestyle into the alternative world. Lively and well humored, Sam was a large tall man in his mid-seventies when I first met him. Wearing black robes, he imparted a Sufi-based meditation practice[7] in the Buddha Hall and also taught Zen philosophy in tennis lessons at the fitness center (humorously called 'Zennis' – meditation through tennis).[8]

Sam grew up in Chicago, more specifically in Hyde Park, a cosmopolitan neighborhood that hosts the university. In the 1950s, he quit a military career to become a well-connected businessman in San Francisco. As he made public, Sam was a CIA officer working as a spy behind the Iron Curtain. In the early 1970s, however, with a critical heart condition, physicians predicted one year of life, throwing Sam in a deep existential crisis. He moved to Hawaii, 'to wait for his death,' as he put it. In the meanwhile, he joined a group of enthusiastic naturalists, adepts of physical exercise, vitamins and natural diets. After several months, Sam felt very healthy.

Sam survived throughout the decades, enjoying each day as his last. Sam also mentioned a dream that changed his life. In the dream, he saw a blue bird flying over a Zen monastery in Japan. Being a wealthy globe trekker, Sam went to Japan, but all he found was an old farmhouse that, nonetheless, did occasionally host Zen seminars. Though the manager refused his stay, Sam spotted an ashtray with the blue bird he dreamed of carved on it. He returned to the US satisfied, committed to learning Zen meditation.

Around the mid-1970s, Sam first came across disciples of Osho by chance in California. 'They were doing some crazy meditation and we watched a video of Osho. I found him extremely boring . . .' Around that time, a travel pal suggested a trip to the Himalayas. In India, Sam visited Pune and met Osho. He enjoyed the commune to such an extent that he decided to move in: 'there were lots of happy people, lots of spirituality; beautiful women, gardens, sun – it was absolutely fantastic!'. He arrived in 1978. Three years later, Sam followed Osho to Oregon, US. But since he could not physically collaborate in the construction of the commune due to his heart condition, Sam returned to the emptied commune in Pune being kept by a few Indian workers, until Osho returned in 1986.[9]

Sam noted the ongoing transformations at the OIMR. He regretted that the place had lost some of its warmth. Despite his seniority, Sam was never assigned to be a member of the inner circle (directive board). 'I am too independent to accept certain things.' He represented himself as belonging to an elder generation of sannyasins who were not in favor of many changes in the ashram, but accepted their role as adapting to the new realities while doing their best to make it a better and pleasant place to be at. Sam was determined to enjoy life as joyfully as possible. When not golfing in Europe or the US, he lives in one of the few private residences inside the OIMR.

Having detailed two typical trajectories of sannyasin therapists, what is noteworthy is their gradual disappointment with conventional life (physician, businessman), made worse by a crisis (health or university issues), along with a growing engagement with oriental spiritualities in Asia (Zen in Japan, meditation) and a conversion into the sannyasin world; finally, there is a strong component of mobility integrated with a global diaspora of sannyasins. The next sub-section examines deeper categories that identify and orient these mobile subjects with Osho's sannyasin ideology of subjectivity formation. Since his death in 1990, the devotional effervescence has given way to a more sober stance, in line with the Nietzschean Buddhism outlined above. Such orientation is formally evinced in a daily ceremonial event called 'White Robe Brotherhood,' as presented next.

White Robe Brotherhood: a video-cult for enlightenment

Resort activities halt completely at 18:00 in a silent call for the White Robe Brotherhood. A crowd in white concentrates outside the Buddha Hall, holding tiny chairs and dropping thousands of sandals on long shelves. The entrance is tightly kept by a team of ashramites, who make sure that everyone is wearing exclusively white and is perfume free.[10] Such controls inadvertently function like a rite of passage by which participants feel that they are entering a liminal dimension.

The ambience is indeed quite solemn. Very quietly, people enter the canvassed dome, dribbling lying bodies, extending mats and sitting down. Everyone faces the pagoda-style altar, in various meditative stances. A small area around the pulpit is supervised by an ashramite holding a list. The space is reserved for members of the inner circle and special guests. On the right side of the hall, musicians wait on a stage congested with sound equipment and musical instruments.

A melody starts at 19:00, and in a few moments it turns into lively band music. One by one the crowd gets up and begins to dance on the spot. A few individuals here and there remain on the floor, with closed eyes, or discreetly looking around. Women dance in a gentle, slightly spaced-out fashion. Some Indian men dance in overblown moves, explicitly staring at nearby women. Yet, nobody interacts: there is no eye contact or exchange whatsoever. The collective event is quite solitaire. It is thus curious that, despite the emphasis on authentic self-expression, behavior in the Buddha Hall is extremely homogenous, obeying patterns collectively followed.

The music grows faster and louder, culminating in a chaotic climax and a drum bang. The excited crowd then freezes while shouting 'OSHO!'. After a few moments in absolute silence, the music restarts and escalates again. This cycle is repeated three times, but the fourth drumbeat is harsher. This time the crowd shouts thrice: 'OSHO! OSHO! OSHO!'. The lights go off. Everybody sits down on the cooling marble. A few minutes are spent in silence, with gentle sitar and tamboura music being played at the background.

Suddenly, a loud drumbeat strikes, as the Zen slap for 'awakening.' The video screen slides down, and the discourse title is announced through loudspeakers. The digital signal appears on screen, and some people join hands or bow heads. Sneezing and coughing are prohibited (yet, a self-defeating rule). Nobody is allowed to enter or leave the Buddha Hall during the event. Nonetheless, in two occasions I noticed people leaving the hall, but no one tried to stop them, perhaps suggesting a laxity in certain procedures.

The videos feature Osho speeches originally recorded in the Buddha Hall or Oregon. Some introductory images reveal a highly ecstatic crowd, rhythmically clapping hands, as Osho gently and quite slowly enters the hall. The camera scans the first row and eventually focuses on enraptured white women. As I detected in conversations, those images triggered highly reflexive thoughts in those who were watching the video. Some present sannyasins appear in the video but ten to twenty years younger. The event also revealed a striking difference between the past and the present. Osho had a dramatic impact in the crowd behavior (as shown in videos), whereas video watchers observed in silence.

Osho's oratory skills defied conventional rules. He talked quite slowly, with long breaks between words. His face and body were motionless, and a few hand gestures were meticulously performed. His English had a sharp Indian accent, which newcomers found quite difficult to understand. Nevertheless, or because of these characteristics, followers considered him to be a mesmerizing speaker. In a speech titled *The Way I Speak is a Little Strange*, Osho stated that, 'It is in the silences between my words that you meditate.' In order to sustain an argument, he employed metaphors, anecdotes and referred to classic intellectuals and historic characters, building his prose in non-linear fashion. Certain topics were more appealing: his critique of Christianity seemed outdated to the audience, but his comments on relationships and gender captured their attention. However, despite his intellectual formation, Osho often argued upon clearly personal preferences. But that did not seem to upset sannyasins, because Osho emphasized the self-contradictory nature of his speeches, as a license for freedom and originality. Despite the consistency of his Nietzschean Buddhism, his multiple speeches stimulated lively debates among sannyasins, propelling them, according to Osho, to think and experience life independently.

The screen is turned off about ninety minutes into his speech. The Buddha Hall becomes completely dark and silent. The sound system then plays Osho telling jokes, about Pope John Paul II and President Reagan, and many sexist and racist ones. But sannyasins considered Osho to be a loving leader. The point is to laugh as a thoughtless spiritual practice. As Osho explains, 'I have to tell jokes because, I am afraid, you are all religious people, and you tend to be serious ... And seriousness is a cancerous growth ... Laughter brings some energy from your inner source to the surface' (Osho and Neiman 2000: 152).

A drumbeat then sets the crowd into chaotic gibberish. From their seats, people absurdly shout, cry, gesticulate, sing, groan and make other strange noises. The loudspeakers are also playing the sound of an explosive crowd, adding to the pandemonium. This situation persists for about a minute. Another drumbeat, and the crowd falls into silence. People now look peaceful in a meditative stance. Osho then, slowly and softly, recites in hypnotic fashion:

> Be silent. Close your eyes. Feel your body to be completely frozen. Now look inward, gathering all your consciousness – almost like an arrow, forcing toward the center. At the center you are the buddha. That is your essential nature. Go deeper and deeper ... The deeper you go, the more will be your experience of your eternal reality. [...] [T]he whole existence will rejoice in your silence. Just be a witness – from the center – and you will have arrived at home.
>
> (Personal recollection; see also
> Osho and Neiman 2000: 275)

It is believed that gibberish releases emotional tension, cleansing the mind for proper meditation. Osho then says, 'to make it clear,' followed by another drumbeat. The audience then faints flat on the floor.[11] Lying down, with closed eyes, the crowd listens to his mystical speech:

> Relax. You are now part of an ocean of buddhas. The entire hall is now an ocean of pure consciousness. At this moment you are the most blessed people on earth. Just remember that you are only a witness. The body is not you, the mind is not you. You are just a mirror. Everything becomes divine. This evening was beautiful on its own. This very moment you are a buddha ... When you come back, bring the buddha with you. You have to live out the buddha in your day-to-day life. Collect as much fragrance and flowers as you can.
>
> (Personal recollection; ibid.: 275)

A final drumbeat is loud and dry, the final Zen slap. The audience slowly returns from the light trance, and sits. Osho then concludes, emphasizing each of his words:

> Come back, but come back as a buddha ... peacefully, gracefully. Sit for a few moments just to recollect your experience of the space that you have visited, and the splendor that you have experienced. The last word of Buddha was *sammasati*. 'Remember.' Remember that you are a buddha.
>
> (Personal recollection; ibid.: 280)

Lights are gently lit. People slowly get up and leave the Buddha Hall. Curiously, a few Eastern Asian women are always the first to rush out. In the meanwhile, many sannyasins remain in reverential positions, and a few couples are hugging on the floor. Sannyasins envisage the White Robe Brotherhood as a moment for rejoicing in sacred aloneness; nevertheless, attending it in the company of a dear one was also deemed a special experience. After supper, the Buddha Hall will host a final night event, usually a meditation demo or a music concert (dispensing with the use of robes). For the time being though, as sannyasins leave the hall with Osho's spiritual message reverberating in their hearts, all is felt as serene blissfulness.

Sannyas ritual: freedom from yourself

Serendipity was a common occurrence in the ashram. Shafik told me about a psychic reader who correctly guessed that he 'worked with animals' (he is a veterinarian). My ritual of initiation (Sannyas) was by chance scheduled to take place in 'the most powerful day of the year': January 19, the anniversary of Osho's 'leaving the body' (death, or *mahasamadhi*). Because of its centrality in the sannyasin ideology of subjectivity formation, the neo-Sannyas as a notion and ritual practice must be considered. In 1971, Osho began to initiate his followers in an improvised ritual, largely inspired by the Hindu tradition of renunciation (sannyas). While referring to a spiritual seeker who gives up all mundane connections, Osho redefined it as 'neo-Sannyas':

> The ancient meaning of sannyas is renouncing the world. I am against it. [...] I can see another meaning far more significant [...]. I mean renouncing all the conditions that the world has given to you – your religion, your caste, [...] your God, your holy book. To me, sannyas means a commitment that 'I am going to clean myself of all those things that have been imposed on me, and I will start living on my own – fresh, young, pure, unpolluted.' Sannyas is an initiation into your innocence.
>
> (Osho and Neiman 2000: 228)

Osho regularly gathered with small groups of followers in evening meetings (*darshans*). Newcomers sat on the first row. He would stare at the person, write down a name, touch their forehead and provide a brief explanation about the name – a combination of two Sanskrit words. Then, as now, sannyasins believe that the new name is connected to the unconscious of the person, which Osho was supposedly able to grasp intuitively. It expressed, developed or challenged inner potentials. During the 1970s, followers wore orange clothes and wore a bead chain (*mala*) with his picture. In the West, these youth embarrassed relatives and strangers with their sannyasin names, clothes and ideas of enlightenment in a communal life. Ironically, the obsession with such symbols resulted in a new shackle, which meditators conventionally seek to avoid. Group pressure was a strong characteristic during the cultic stage of the movement. After the disastrous experience of Oregon, Osho urged everyone to stop wearing orange and the *mala*. In 1986, he declared:

> The emphasis was only on meditation. But I found that people can change their clothes very easily, but they cannot change their minds. [. . .] Sannyas is not so cheap. It is time and you are mature enough, that beginning phase is over. If you like the orange color, perfectly good. [. . .] But it has nothing to do with religion. So now I reduce religion to its absolute essentiality. And that is meditation.
> (Osho and Neiman 2000: 230)

In the early 2000s, the Sannyas ritual took place in the Buddha Hall each week. The naming ceremony was in the charge of the 'Sannyas Department' coordinated by 'mediums' chosen by Osho in the early 1980s. They glanced at a paper form with photograph and 'connected' with the applicant's 'energy,' resulting in a suitable name, although a new option in which the person could choose their own sannyasin name was introduced in the year 2000. All candidates went through a quick interview, having to answer the questions, 'Why do you want to take Sannyas?' and 'Are you familiar with Osho's ideas and practices?'. I have never heard about any applicant being rejected in this procedure. Quite the contrary, I have come across many converts who barely knew Osho and his ideas.

'Taking Sannyas' was a delicate issue among newcomers, including those who decided *not* to participate. Many claimed not to be 'ready' spiritually for such a 'commitment,' while others added that they preferred to develop their own 'spiritual path' 'independently.' An Israeli youngster snapped, 'Because I want to be the master of myself!'. Other visitors rejected Sannyas as a sectarian practice that could enslave the individual to the ashram. Finally, some newcomers were misinformed, believing that it mandated a legal change of names in documents, or naively believed that a computer chose their names at random, as a mischievous hoax circulated.

Those who took Sannyas wished to 'better connect with [their] inner spirituality.' They also believed that a new name would facilitate their meditation practices. At a psychological level, it served as a tool for gaining distance from one's own self-identity, allowing a more reflexive perspective. In social situations, the sannyasin name could be employed playfully to tease, confuse or dissuade interlocutors. Sannyasins thus exposed the conflation between 'legal name' as 'real name' which conceals the exogenous nature of identity formation through nominalism ('you are x'). Nonetheless, in contrast with veteran sannyasins, newer generations refrained from disclosing their spiritual names publicly, thus keeping a separation between the public and the private, a barrier that countercultural movements have historically sought to undermine.

On a warm morning, an unusually large group of 74 people gathered at the center of the Buddha Hall. We sat on cushions lined in rows, alongside the ceremony staff, a photographer and a music band. Hundreds of people in maroon robes surrounded the group. Osho's *mahasamadhi* (death) anniversary was the busiest day in the ashram. Many Indians and Westerners arrived on that day. In my cohort, there were an African-Swiss nurse, a German circus acrobat, an American dancer, Australian college students and an Italian psychiatrist called Mario Crazy Horse (due to his spiritual interests in US Native Americans).

The Sannyas ritual dramatizes the sacred nature of individuality, thus resonating with Western ideologies of an autonomous self. In spirals of intensity, people danced and sang happily as the music grew faster, climaxing in the chaotic drumming and the collective scream OSHO. Some joined hands by their heart, as everybody listened to Osho's speech fragments:

> I initiate you into nothing but into freedom. Freedom from yourself. And this is the meaning of Sannyas and nothing else. Sannyas is a commitment with meditation. It is a commitment with existence. It is a romance with existence. As such, you will not take Sannyas, it is Sannyas that will take you!
>
> (Personal recollection)

The participants are called by their 'legal' names at intervals of a minute or so. They were supposed to perform some spontaneous dance before picking the 'Sannyas certificate' placed on a pillow. Most people timidly danced around the pillow, picked the paper, and returned to their spots. Others, however, danced and laughed effusively, while a few others went down on their knees, sobbed, and threw themselves dramatically on the matted floor. Often, one of the ceremonial assistants had to walk in and gently indicate that their time was up. After all the participants had been called and received their diplomas, velvet chords were released, and the audience rushed in to the central area to celebrate effusively. Some brought flowers, hugging acquaintances and asking about their new name.

Despite the effusive nature of sannyasin rituals as well as the draconian style of resort administration (to be discussed on pp. 161–4), the 'cultic hypothesis,' raised by antagonistic journalists and Christian activists, does not hold at a subjective level. For a reason, the group upholds highly individualistic values. As sannyasins claim, a charismatic community is justified in its support for the spiritual endeavors of the individual. Spiritual development essentially is a matter of personal responsibility, to be ultimately actualized through the practice of meditation. Within this framework, collective celebrations praised the relationship between meditator and existence. In fact, sannyasins discreetly diverged upon the authority of

Osho for intermediating such a relationship. While many believed that he was an enlightened master, others saw him rather as a thought-provoking teacher. In any case, in line with Buddhism, all sannyasins agreed that enlightenment is a universal possibility, to be cultivated nonetheless and achieved individually.

Culture of expression: psychic deterritorialization and institutional control

January 26, 2001. After the morning meditation, I sat by the lagoon behind the pyramids used for therapy. Alone, I watched the bathing birds, while perusing within. I was about to complete 21 days of meditation, a period which sannyasins considered to be a minor, but still considerable achievement. All of a sudden, a strange vibration in the air tampered with my ears. The birds silenced, and the lake formed some slowly sliding rings, but it all faded in a few seconds. Sannyasins then began to receive emails from worried relatives around the world. A massive earthquake had hit Gujarat, 660 km northwest of Pune, killing 20,000 people. Were it not for the internet, the catastrophe might have passed completely unnoticed. The OIMR remained operating as usual. Several sannyasins retired to pray for the victims, but the majority was too immersed in therapy and meditation. They traveled afar, confronting earthquakes within.

In informal conversations, sannyasins circulated rumors about visitors, usually first-timers, who developed some emotional disorder during a workshop or who were sanctioned by a director.[12] The subtle impression was that this paradise was not as harmonious as the magazine *Osho Times* intended to convey. Visitors were pounded with the idea that they ought to express their feelings and opinions, as a proof of inner authenticity. However, expression was conditioned by a system of expectations, rewards and sanctions that delimited the scope of permitted behavior, with very little margin for dissent. As previously seen, even within the therapeutic setting, self-expression was monitored and even shaped according to the therapist's intentions.

In other words, a basic contradiction marked daily life in the OIMR, between the ideological pressure for self-expression and the institutional control of centrifugal behavior. In the following sub-sections, I discuss incidents that unravel such contradiction. As a remark, I chose more explicitly extreme cases as a methodological recourse for exposing invisible notions and mechanisms of control in the resort.

Some of these incidents can be related to psychological processes, which I define as 'psychic deterritorialization.' Integrating the clinical philosophy of Deleuze and Guattari (Deleuze and Guattari 1980; see also Braidotti 1994; Kaplan 1987) with incipient studies of consular psychiatry (Hays 2001; Airault 2000; Wrigley and Revill 2000; Hacking 1998; Quirot 1993; Verdoux *et al.* 1993), this notion provides an insight into the processes of derealization and depersonalization that affect Western travelers cruising exotic lands. As a hypothesis raised by a consular psychiatrist, without the protection of homeland symbolism (which holds the self together), the subject becomes exposed to unconscious pressures that may be more acutely manifested during special ritual sites, such as therapy workshops, Romantic traveling and psychedelic parties, especially when carried out in remote lands. These effects have been referred to as 'the India syndrome' (Airault 2000: 19).

Dance party

The entertainment team organized weekly dance parties at the resort's plaza. As sannyasins are fun lovers, the resort direction determined a time limit at 23:30. After days in maroon robes, about 200 people joined the party, wearing their own conventional clothes, exposing tastes and person-alities in multiple colors. DJs were often coincidently sannyasin therapists, playing a mix of soft house and world music. Because visitors were under-going cathartic therapies during the day, DJs were instructed not to play Techno trance, a potent style of electronic dance music deemed to be mentally disturbing (nonetheless prevalent in underground parties pro-moted by rebellious sannyasins in the outskirts of Pune and in Goa [D'Andrea 2006]). The cappuccino bar exceptionally sold spirited drinks and there were designated spaces in the garden for smoking, but almost nobody drank or smoked.

Yet, most people danced with enthusiasm and very expressively, in con-trast to what could have been expected from a modern crowd of substance-free individuals. Younger visitors concentrated on the dance floor, while more veteran sannyasins chatted by the cappuccino bar. A few individuals danced in an apparently exaggerated manner, as if in a pastiche of trance – they were usually Far Eastern women or Indian men. Most sannyasins were good dancers by any basic criteria. Two Indian DJs admitted a bit disdainfully, 'It is much easier to play for sannyasins. You can play any-thing, and they will go wild ...' As a regular visitor who attended the resort each year, Dimitri observed:

> Many of these people come from a small town, say, in Germany or Taiwan where everybody controls them; they cannot do much with their lives. Their boring lives in small offices and homes doing always the same thing, always the same routine. Ah, that is sad. But then, they come to Pune, and see all this beauty, all this freedom. Oh man, of course they will go nuts!

Sannyasins seek to overcome patterns of a civilization predicated on the control of nature, both environmental and psychic. Particularly in the Western(ized) world, affection is sequestered to comply with systemic requirements of efficiency and production, and becomes delimited to the private sphere or to self-effacing spaces of collective entertainment, sports and pop art, which, in turn, enhance social control and consumptive capital. In the case of sannyasins, expressive expatriates and New Agers more generally, rather than charging against the status quo, they have chosen to engage with hedonistic, aesthetic and spiritual practices in order to reform their selves, to legitimate an independent lifestyle, and consequently to influence their proximate environments. In this context, it must be asked what role the OIMR plays in their lives: is it just an institutional escape-valve that contributes to sustain the civilizatory modes that it claims to question, or does it promote truly emancipatory experiments that foster alternative ways of living and self?

Promoting and controlling self-expression

As a consequence of Osho's critique of civilization as repressive, the notion of 'expression' gained a central role among sannyasins, often more emphatically so than the notion of 'witnessing,' the core category of his spiritual philosophy. More than a therapeutic procedure, being expressive was highly valued and pervasively expected. Therapists urged and sometimes coerced participants to be assertive (or leave the group). As a source of jokes and anxieties, visitors often reported the awkward situation in which they 'did not have anything to express' during a cathartic exercise and wondered, 'Do I have a problem?'. Spontaneity, flamboyance and even some bluntness were seen as desirable traits. In tandem, formal politeness was seen suspiciously as a symptom of repressed personality. 'Politeness is a repression from your parents,' I once heard during an argument. On a different occasion, Git Prem (a German expatriate from Ibiza) introduced me to an acquaintance in Pune who plainly refused to shake my extended hand. Finally, a temporary flatmate, whom I had never spoken to, angrily demanded that I kept the toilet seat up (rather than down). As such, 'being in touch with oneself' could trigger episodes of sentimentalism or hostility, which were, at least in theory, accepted by sannyasins. Their interactions tended to be candid yet intempestive, either affectionate or aggressive, resulting in that minor confrontations over minor issues marked much of their ordinary life in Pune.

As a consequence of such ideological pressure, exerted in a bubble-like environment in a remote country, most visitors reported some form of emotional hardship during their stay. This was particularly noticeable during midweek afternoons, when cathartic workshops were peaking. Observing the number of distressed faces wandering in the resort, Dimitri, who regularly attended the workshops, noted:

> You see all these people in the ashram. They look unhappy and miserable. It didn't have to be like that, but that is what they need to go through for a while. And all these fights . . . They behave like assholes

here because they cannot be like that at home. So, this is a relatively safe environment to behave like that, without suffering serious consequences.

In this sense, in order to be peaceful at home, one ought to be aggressive in Pune. Because of this intense emotional work, visitors developed unusual forms of behavior, reasoning and sociability. This could be inferred from answers given to trivial statements. For example, I invited someone for a coffee and got a response in gravitas: 'No, today I am connecting with myself.' Or, I told a volunteer at a registration desk that I was not interested in attending workshops, and heard, 'What are you escaping from? . . .'. Also, visitors often developed acute self-distrust, intensely questioning themselves, 'Are these thoughts mine or my parents'?'.

In various degrees, such unusual statements usually came from participants of high-impact workshops, but excessive meditation in the Buddha Hall triggered similar effects. Some individuals claimed to have developed paranormal abilities, and even implied that they had achieved some form of spiritual awakening. In concordance with this analysis of psychic deterritorialization, a study notes that, 'too much meditation may interfere with logical thought process, because the whole technique is geared to take one beyond reason and thinking' (Basnet 2002: 59).

As an example of such transformations, a young woman from Los Angeles (US) was visiting the ashram for the first time. Apparently sociable and sensible, she was a dance student in college, spending her vacation in India. She gave up traveling across the country as planned in order to spend all her time at the resort. While attending a sequence of therapy workshops, her behavior altered in strange ways. Wearing the 'silence' badge, she moved slowly, with eyes looking somehow mesmerized. She took Sannyas, broke up with her boyfriend over the internet and extended her stay in Pune for an extra month, to attend more therapy groups.

Eccentric behavior was accepted insofar as it did not challenge order and authority in the resort. Those running the organization tended to overreact against any form of unaligned or recalcitrant behavior. For example, a disagreement over a garment (robe) detail could lead to the expulsion of a resistant visitor. Yet, more worrisome is the treatment that the resort dispenses to mentally derailed visitors. A young Spanish man told a workshop-mate during a break that he had been brought to Pune by a 'cosmic conspiracy' orchestrated by resort directors – a very unlikely claim. A day later, while staring at a noticeboard, he froze in a catatonic state. The gatemen took him to a psychiatrist downtown and left him there alone. During the appointment, he recovered his mental faculties, as if returning from a trance state. The physician said that there was nothing to worry about, prescribed light tranquilizers, and charged Rs. 400 (US$9) for the consultation. The young man refused to pay and angrily returned to the resort, but was not allowed in. His meditation pass had been taken. Next morning, he met with two supervisors – an Indian and a German man. According to him, they demanded that he should pay the medical fee and rudely reprimanded him: 'Your disobedience will not be tolerated. You have to follow the rules here.' Regular ashramites could justify such measures as necessary for keeping the organization in order. Yet, Indian writer Gita Mehta also noted, in the early 1970s, that mentally derailed sannyasins were excluded from the place, either hospitalized or sent back to their native homeland. She asked a senior Indian woman, 'a matriarch of the ashram,' how the organization proceeded with such cases:

> Some of our devotees get these mad ideas. Then, we have to do something. [. . .] We put them in the hospital, give them pills. Sometimes they get better and come back to us. That is very beautiful. [. . .] Those who don't get better, we sedate them, put them on a plane and send them back to their countries.
>
> (Mehta 1990 [1979]: 38–9)

Consular psychiatrists have suggested that long-term travel through mythic lands (India, Israel, Greece, Paris, etc.) may trigger mild or acute episodes of personal derailment, which usually effaces as soon as the subject returns home (Airault 2000; Hacking 1998). During my fieldwork in Pune and Goa, I witnessed cases of emotionally troubled sannyasins, travelers and expatriates which corroborate those studies. Western subjects staying in India for extended periods – particularly if it is their first visit – can undergo psychic deterritorialization. As consular psychiatrists suggest, the absence of cultural references in alien lands can cause cognitive disorientation, loosening of subjective boundaries and certainties (Airault 2000). The syndrome varies in form, intensity and duration, depending on the person's biographic background and travel experience, as well as on the nature of the place being visited. The visited space must have a radical mythological significance in order to have an impact upon the traveler. This topic will be resumed in Chapter 5. Yet, it is important to note that, in the Pune case, the resort is a specific yet quite powerful instance that may actualize and amplify the potential for psychic deterritorialization in the context of a Romantic 'spiritual quest' in India.

In conclusion, despite its remarketing as a trendy meditation resort, the organization still employed control mechanisms typically found in total institutions (Carter 1990; Gordon 1987). The meditation resort paradoxically *promoted* and *controlled* idiosyncrasy. It incited individuals to express their inner selves, sometimes resulting in the temporary derailment of structured personalities (psychic deterritorialization). Yet, when these episodes spun out of control of the therapeutic setting, the organization imposed harsh discipline. With no room for 'civilized' dialogue (toward compromise and service improvement), the resolution involved admonishing, pathologizing or expelling the recalcitrant, who could choose to acquiesce or leave the resort.

Orientalism and therapeutic apartheid

When AIDS emerged in the early 1980s, Osho requested that all sannyasins should be tested in the commune, which then was located in Oregon (US). Although forms of transmission and protection have been identified, testing has remained since then, and it is a condition for entering the resort or any other Osho center around the world. More recently, a few influential sannyasins have suggested its discontinuation, but therapists remarked that visitors feel more at ease in workshop settings when physical contact with strangers is common. Moreover, AIDS emerged as a public issue in India by the mid-2000s, and two HIV-positive cases were detected monthly at the Welcome Center. Therefore, for the time being, the inner circle maintained the procedure.

The idea of an 'AIDS-free zone' had contradictory effects. It symbolically reinforced a space of liminality in which sannyasins felt detached from the mundane world outside. Yet, HIV testing also fed rumors about sexual promiscuity among sannyasins. It is true that many visitors welcomed the possibility of sexual encounters; nonetheless, in relation to its countercultural past, the community was considerably conservative in terms of sexual conduct. As a result, lingering rumors and misrepresentations created some embarrassing situations, the analysis of which exposes the nature and limits of countercultural ideologies and practices of self-formation.

Indians comprised the largest national group of sannyasins at the OIMR during the 2000s. However, they were largely absent from therapy workshops. It was commonplace in the resort that Indians are socialized in a culture with very different conditionings. Sannyasin therapists claimed that cathartic workshops did not work well with Indians and could even traumatize them. It was pointed out that they did not react like Westerners, that they stood blasé during cathartic practices and even laughed at erotogenic ones. Osho himself reinforced the orientalist stereotype: 'Westerners have problems on how to relate, whereas Easterners have problems on how to be silent – except Japanese or those who grew up in the West' (Osho and Neiman 2000: 238).

Nonetheless, rather than accept these statements at face value, it is necessary to examine the political and ideological foundations that sustain such therapeutic apartheid. Orientalism refers to cultural ideas that not only describe but also control subjects of other cultures (Said 1978). The point, then, is to unpack the problematic nature of Western practices of self-development in sites that are densely multicultural.

To wit, sannyasin therapists worried when Indian men applied to participate in workshops. At screening interviews, they required Indians to attend, first, other more basic workshops which emphasized spiritual and mental attributes over physical ones. It is true that therapists eventually excluded applicants regardless of nationality; however, Indian men were apparently the only group that was profiled in terms of nationality and gender. Furthermore, the policy of reduced prices for Indian residents was delimited to three workshops ('Meditative Therapy,' 'Vipassana' and 'Opening to the Heart'), thus also obstructing the participation of most Indians, at the economic level, from the outset.

Another factor underlying the therapeutic apartheid stemmed from recurrent complaints made by women, both Western and Indian, that Indian men stalked them persistently. Many Indian men represented Western women, particularly sannyasin ones, as being more sexually available than their Indian counterparts. Therapists thus inspected their motivations for wanting to join workshops centered on issues of the body, sensuality and sexuality, such as Tantra and Reichian therapies. It was not that Western men were disinterested in sex, but that the difference lay in which courtship strategies were deemed appropriate and which were not. To wit, some Indian men were fully integrated in the multinational populace of the resort. Yet, they had to adapt to Western tastes and dispositions, reframing these in hybrid ways. They displayed Hellenic-shaped bodies, fashionable haircuts and clothing, embodied some Eurocentric dispositions (more reserved, blasé, individualistic), and courted women in a manner rendered acceptable (romantic, discreet, gradual, respectful, etc.). Under these post-colonial conditions, their Indianness became an attractive asset.

Indian women rarely participated in therapy workshops, but were more easily admitted once the therapist verified that they understood standard procedures, such as touching, sensual movements, confrontation, emotional sharing, etc. Daughters or wives of sannyasins, they were mainly from an educated middle-class background (Basnet 2002) and did not seem as interested in therapy workshops as Indian men were. They tended to experience the 'ashram' as a space of 'freedom' and 'love' in an apparently platonic fashion. Elderly Indian women, for example, stood aloof to Osho's countercultural tirades and joyfully revered him as a holy saint. For younger women, the OIMR provided a space where they could break away from rigorous gender and familial expectations (Goldman 1999; Palmer 1994).

By isolating gender as a variable of analysis, it becomes clear that the issue at stake is not sex, but rather subjectivity: the constitution of the self, its desire and interiority. As mentioned above, sannyasins claim that Indians also suffer repression; however, they also ascertain that sannyasin therapies are ineffective to Indian nationals. It could be speculated that, as India modernizes, cathartic therapies will become efficacious for the stressed city dwellers of that nation. But the answer is not that simple. Personal dispositions are complex sedimentations of long-standing historical, religious and cultural processes of socialization and conditioning, which do not mechanically adapt to rapid economic and technological changes. In any case, the fact remained that, unlike Westerners in general, Indians rarely lashed out against their parents or social institutions. Furthermore, they tended not to interpret their stay at the resort by means of psycho-countercultural categories, such as 'repression,' 'expression' and 'healing.' For the time being, rather than a human laboratory (as suggested at the start-up session), Indians experienced the resort as a playful garden.

Charisma and rationalization: sex, counterculture and tourism

Having images and tales of the 1970s as subliminal references, newcomers often expected to find a sort of 'flower power' community amalgamated by bonds of solidarity, eroticism and self-transcendence. Communal work, free love, radical therapy and permissive spirituality were features of a politics of self-liberation that sannyasins once fully embraced. However, at the turn of the millennium, the OIMR was anything but a hippie community. The death of Osho, the AIDS epidemic and the rise of global capitalism – along with the submergence of countercultural movements – provide the general backdrop against which the resort culture and organization are transformed. Nonetheless, matters of relationship remained as the central concern for sannyasins, against which they constantly measured their self-identity, reflexively vacillating between mundane engagement and mystical detachment. In other words, and resounding strikingly with Foucault's philosophy of the subject, 'sexuality' and 'spirituality' are the two main poles by which sannyasins seek to reshape their self interiorities, identities and dispositions. This final ethnographic section reassesses those wider transformations, by focusing on their entwinements at the level of subjectivity formation.

Sex before and after counterculture, AIDS and tourism

The press relations department regularly affixed news articles on a mural by the buffet restaurant, covering typical issues, such as the resort ongoing modernization, visiting celebrities, or artistic events promoted by sannyasins in Pune. One of these articles claimed that the resort was 'becoming more mainstream' and that visitors were having 'less sex,' meaning, a decreasing number of sexual experiences, partners and even involuntary abstinence. In a site once renowned for being erotically charged, many younger sannyasins noted, with a certain regret, that mating possibilities were not as abundant as they had initially supposed. The differences can be inferred by means of videos, books and interviews. A veteran Italian in her late forties spoke about the 'commune' when Osho was still alive:

It was lovely. Everyone was so happy. Some people would stand by the gates handing out flowers to everyone that passed by. Everyone knew and hugged everybody . . . And everybody was also having lots of relationships, and sex of course!

This was a typical statement by veteran sannyasins. In their recollections, it is the 'flower power' or 'free love' scenarios that prevail, in consonance with videos and diaries from the 1970s and 1980s (Shunyo 1999; Maneesha 1987; Devaraj 1986). The past of the 'commune' is represented as a time of intense joy, spirituality and effervescence. Seeking to grow as human and spiritual beings, sannyasins gathered in a community of affection established around a beloved master. In this context, sensual pleasures were welcomed as a way of auto-discovery and personal liberation (Palmer 1994). However, a few other sannyasins also noted the coercive pressure that the movement exerted upon communards. According to a German painter who has been to both Pune and Oregon in the 1980s:

In those times, you were either in or out. You had no choice. People would come to your room, wake you up at five because it was time to work, or because we wanted to try a new therapy or do meditation. Nowadays, you can stay here and do nothing. You can stay all day in the swimming pool, and nobody will bother you. But in Oregon, you had to participate and contribute, or you were out.

In this context, it is important to identify what corporeal and affective engagements index mechanisms of subjectivity formation operating vis-à-vis biopower/sexuality regimes. I then inquired about the role of sexual and romantic relationships during that period. He did not seem uncomfortable with my question, but replied after some thoughtful consideration. Again, he referred to the unique intersection of cultic, hedonist and reflexive elements that constituted the collective experiment:

There was much more sex in those times; but often as abuse. We had so much sex that many times you would have it even if you didn't feel like doing it. It was a sort of pressure of the whole group. And also, you know, when you are young, all you want is girls and sex. Look around. There are so many beautiful women in the ashram. But, then, after having all 'that,' in excess, you begin to discover other things in life 'Ah! There is spirituality too, cool!' . . . So, it is all more mainstream now . . . But you can still find some spots of nice alternative people here and there, within the masses.

His claims about erotic fulfillment reproduce Osho's argument that authentic spirituality is unlikely by repressing one's mundane appetites.[13]

Yet, without recourse to the binomial 'counterculture-mainstream,' Indians also detected the modernization in place. I asked an astrologer from Mumbai, who has been attending the resort since 1988, to identify the main differences across time. His answer seemed dismissive of the current stage:

> It is less spiritual now, and everything is more pleasant. In those times, everybody was against the ashram, not only internationally but Pune people as well. They did rallies outside, protesting against the ashram because couples were holding hands in the street and that was offensive. Internationally, you would not get a visa if you said that you were coming to Pune. Only brave people came here. But, nowadays, everything is easy.

In order to further explore his argument, I questioned by noting an apparent paradox: if the resort is more pleasant now, then how come sannyasins were happier back then (under Osho). He scratched his chin, and explained:

> Yes, there were lots of parties, celebration and relationships – there was much more of all that. But it was also more spiritual. Everything was more spiritual, including sex. Osho was alive, and he had powerful energies. But his energies are gone. This place is empty. Now everything is flat, and people are just pretending. They are having artificial experiences of enlightenment.

Sannyasins recurrently refer to 'energy' when talking about the cultural atmosphere of the resort, either toward excitement or routinization. The notion conveys how they intuitively measure and compare the liveliness of the environment. In general, veteran sannyasins claimed that the organization was 'cooling,' as a consequence of its growing professionalization along with more impersonal interactions. Others regretted that Osho's pictures have been discreetly removed from main public spaces.[14] In sum, the more the resort gentrifies, the more its 'energies' fade.

Translocal connections: Ibiza and Goa

The notion of 'energy' was also employed in relation to the nationalities present at the resort. In general, Indians and Americans (both North and Latin) were seen as having 'more energy,' due to their alleged effusiveness, optimism and sensuality, respectively ascribed. Conversely, Western Europeans displayed a 'cooler energy,' for their dispositions were supposedly blasé and self-contained. Germans, in particular, were deemed responsible for keeping the organization 'in line,' both in its positive and negative connotations. An American therapist commented, 'Germans occupy key-positions in the ashram. They are very focused on what they do, and once they get into the system, they just climb it very quickly.' In their turn, Israelis were simultaneously seen as lively and troublesome, notably younger travelers recently dismissed from the military. A significant proportion of sannyasin therapists are from a Jewish background, yet, in this therapy culture, Judaism is often seen as one of the hardest conditionings to break through, since it amalgamates religious, national and ethnic bonds. Young Israelis made ambivalent statements about their relation to a collective identity (either Jewish or Israeli), attempting to conciliate it with more individualistic drives. Finally, Eastern Asians suffered the positive stereotype of bringing a 'harmonious energy' to the resort, although more privately they could state that such serenity is a façade concealing inner chaos.

Sannyasins thus displayed an ambivalent attitude toward nationality, at times denying it, at others embodying it. In more personal interactions, stereotypes both positive and negative abounded: 'She is a tough German therapist,' 'I am becoming less Latino,' 'Russians are weird,' 'Israelis are troglodytes,' to name a few. Perhaps the most frequently heard question in the resort is, 'Where are you/they from?,' as if the myth of origin, which sannyasins so hardly criticized, were at the end accepted as determinative of who the subject is – including fully socialized veterans. It was as though, despite all the rhetoric about de-conditioning and cosmopolitanism, such stereotypes became self-fulfilling prophecies. To wit, even therapists adopted nationality as a criterion for assessing workshop participants and candidates, not to mention the therapeutic apartheid tacitly imposed on Indian men. All of these examples indicate that categorizations in ethnic-national lines correlate with subliminal mechanisms of group inclusion and exclusion.

These multiple interactions when extended over space and time constituted social networks whose nature, duration and extension varied enormously. While some can be traced back to the 1970s, others faded as soon as travelers returned home. Likewise, some networks were restricted to Indian regions populated by countercultural travelers, notably across the 'alternative triangle of India' which comprises Goa, Pune and Manali. A variety of other smaller networks of friends and/or therapists extended internationally. Below are summarized some of the main social webs interrelating sannyasins across Pune at the local, regional and transnational levels.

Many Indians attended the resort not only attracted by Osho's transgressive philosophy, but also by their interests in Western culture, particularly in terms of economic and erotic possibilities. Those who lived in town developed profitable businesses delivering a range of ancillary services for foreigners: accommodation, transportation, internet, trading, sightseeing, etc. Through the years, some of them counted various experiences with foreign women, and a few even got married. Dhyan, a bike mechanic and native of Pune, has been attending the ashram for over ten years. Many of his 'best clients' were foreign sannyasins. 'I learned a lot with them, especially with the Germans because they are very demanding and professional on everything.' He married a German sannyasin. Though sannyasins scorned marriage as a social institution, they could formalize a union for some legal advantage, such as residential visas. More generally, it was relatively very common to see couples of sannyasins from different national and ethnic backgrounds, even though Indian women were rarely seen with foreign men.

Taking on the biographies of therapists outlined above, this group of sannyasins also engendered their own informal networks of personal and professional interest. In the past, they had followed Osho and assumed Pune as their main residence. Yet, after his death, they became more mobile and dispersed globally (Goldman 1999). Though usually based in one country (their native or a partner's), they often deliver therapy workshops within a cluster of nations, and more prestigious professionals even engage in annual global tours. In their case, international work is a necessity since local markets, even in mega cities, are seldom large enough. In this connection, better transportation and communication technologies has enormously facilitated their displacement, while practices of self-development have entered the mainstream under variegated labels, formats and purposes, enabling these therapists to make a living. In tandem, Osho centers have multiplied around the world, becoming nodes of support and diffusion of Osho's work at a grassroots level.

Standing about 500 km apart, Pune and Goa are interlinked by ongoing flows of sannyasins, trance freaks, backpackers and tourists, traveling on buses, vans, trains, airplanes and superbikes. A large segment of these travelers are young Israelis, estimated at about 20,000 per year (*Jerusalem Post* 2004). In Goa, well-off sannyasins stay in the gentrified area of Calangute beach, whereas younger backpackers and New Agers head toward the more prosaic beaches of Arambol and Palolem. In the meanwhile, trance freaks and rebellious sannyasins gather in northern Goa, around Anjuna beach. As Chapter 5 will examine, Goa is a tourist coastal state that also hosts, at its margins, the main nodal formation of techno-trance music in the world.

At a transnational level, Ibiza and Pune are interconnected in a unique manner. Not only did I meet a significant number of sannyasins in Ibiza, but I also came across Ibiza expatriates in both Pune and Goa. The first of these encounters occurred beside the Buddha Hall, with Dan, a French hippie trader of exotic clothes at Las Dálias. I also came across Git Prem, a German sannyasin therapist who was moving to Taiwan to assist in the construction of a new Osho center. I also met Victor (*Bar M* worker) walking on the streets of Koregaon Park. He had just taken Sannyas, but seemed to be more interested in travel and romance. By the resort's cappuccino bar, a Brazilian sannyasin overheard me and claimed to be a friend of Nadi, the Biodance instructor in Ibiza. And, by the resort gates, I came across Cristina, the Ibicencan teenager who practiced Biodance. In a 'trance party' in Pune, a young Indian man noticed my t-shirt with the logo of a famous nightclub in Ibiza (*Space*), and claimed that he had lived on the island. Despite being drunk, he provided very precise information about persons and locations. In Goa, a longhaired hippie saw me wearing the same t-shirt, and claimed to 'love Sundays at *Space*,' a pun on the infamous party. He was a Spanish hippie trader in Las Dálias, whom I would later spot at trance parties in Ibiza. Also in Goa, I came across the sannyasin Alok (*Namaste* party promoter) and again with Victor, all by chance. Moreover, as I parked my bike in Anjuna beach (northern Goa), I struck up a conversation with two young Spanish men, who claimed to live in Ibiza. Months later, I indeed came across one of them by the dance veranda of *Space*. This list does not include many expatriates and clubbers whom I met in Ibiza who claimed to have lived in Goa, nor the many British backpackers in India who claimed to have lived in Sant Antoni (Ibiza). Finally, back to the Mediterranean island, Barbara introduced me to her new room-mate, a Spanish hairdresser she met in Pune. Barbara added that, in Pune, she came across Lourdes (*Jardin de Luz* owner) and other acquaintances from San Jordi flea market, all of them at the Osho resort. She exclaimed, 'Incredible. All Ibiza was in Pune!'

Considering the remoteness and smallness of Ibiza and Pune, it is striking that both places have been sharing the same subjects coalescing into a single globalized countercultural diaspora. It is also important to note such transnational flows in their historical and cultural contexts. Expressive expatriates have been fleeing to Ibiza in various waves since the 1930s. There they experience the island as a utopian paradise and node of an international circuit of Romantic traveling. While in India, many of these Ibiza-based expatriates have become sannyasins, following Osho to Oregon and then back to Pune. As sociologist Danielle Rozenberg states, Ibiza is an 'island of sannyasins' (Rozenberg 1990: 82).

During the 1980s, while participating in Ibiza's nightlife, they have imported various New Age techniques from the US, including the use of MDMA for therapeutic, meditational and recreational uses. In their interactions with British and German clubbers on the island, sannyasins have inadvertently contributed to the emergence of the rave movement, a culture centered on electronic dance music and digital art. Techno then rapidly flowed into the mainstream explosion of rave parties and corporate nightclubs in Western Europe, thus delineating one countercultural genealogy that runs from Pune, to Oregon, to Ibiza, to London, and to cosmopolitan segments of the global youth.

Conclusions: enlightenment guaranteed

The Osho ashram–commune–resort has suffered various transformations since its inception in the early 1970s. Nonetheless, after the death of Osho in 1990, it took a very specific direction toward gentrified modernization, and a new demographic profile is noticed: a smaller number of visitors, mostly wealthier mainstream urbanites, who have largely replaced veteran sannyasins of a countercultural bent as they also age. This process hinges on a classic question: 'What happens to a charismatic community when its spiritual leader disappears?' The scholarship on sects and cults has noted that a general decline in membership and legitimacy is likely to follow; however, the OIMR has survived Osho, despite the fading of its former rebellious effervescence. As Max Weber aptly suggests, although explosions of charisma remain possible, routine and tradition are likely to prevail as primary organizational forces. In fact, this has been the 'price to pay,' as some sannyasins say, in order to keep the work of Osho going. But the resort director, an English physician, reinterprets the past within an evolutionist purview:

> Those times are gone. We need to see the commune as an evolving place. It is like a school. Back then we were in the kindergarten; now we are in high-school; and we hope someday we will move on to a more advanced stage.

Without Osho's charisma to hold things together against internal and external challenges, the resort had to adapt quickly to the legal and cultural structures of Pune, India and the West. Any practice that could be seen as offensive to conventional tastes was ostensively banned (such as nudity, sexual promiscuity, drugs, rave parties, etc.). More widely, though inter-national travel and communication have dramatically improved, neo-liberal capitalism has imposed a new order of difficulties. With the decline of labor, wages and state protection, it is not as easy for Western sannyasins to stay in India for extended periods, as enjoyed by former generations. In the meanwhile, the rise of a new Indian middle class has propelled the growth of the proportion of these nationals at the OIMR. Yet, they bring a different set of expectations, preferences and dilemmas that will have to be addressed adequately by resort therapists and managers. The loos-ening of the therapeutic apartheid is likely to be noticed in the near future.

This chapter has thus examined main trends, practices and represen-tations by which sannyasins seek to problematize and transform the modern self. As noted in therapy settings, daily interactions and reading materials, the topic of relationship is their main source of concern and anxiety, about which they unsuccessfully seek to be disentangled from and about which Osho was required to address ad nauseam. In their view, social order obstructs personal actualization by means of institutional repression, primarily carried out through the family. Against that, sannyasin therapies seek to displace power-knowledge forms which have been internalized as 'conditionings.' The therapist then employs devices of symbolic manipulation (claims), visceral provocation (catharsis) and semiotic reinterpretation (sharing) in order to entail the desired transformation of the self. By combining therapy and meditation, sannyasins claim that it is possible to neutralize such power-knowledge forms, thus reconfiguring the self, at least to a certain extent.

Nonetheless, in addition to identifying how sannyasin practices resonate with the expressive and spiritual needs and dispositions of Ibiza expatriates, this study has exposed some of the cultural limits of these practices of self-formation, by noting two conundrums that invisibly haunt the resort. While claiming that power is repressive, the overemphasis on topics of repression, expression and confession misses the point that power also *produces* certain experiences and understandings about the self (Foucault 1976). In this regard, catharsis is not only a 'release' of 'repressed' materials, but also a productive device, skillfully employed by the therapist, for restructuring self-identities, according to specific goals.

The absence of Indians from cathartic therapies suggests that categories of 'repression/expression' are specific to Western modes of subjectivity, if not the very nodal cause of the existential dilemma that they seek to overcome. The Western self is a product of a singular religious, political and scientific configuration, which historically crystallized in notions that determine the nature of the modern subject: 'guilt,' 'interiority,' 'repression,' 'confession' and 'self-mastery,' all of which have coalesced to forge the Western self as a hyper-individualized entity, under the authoritarian orientation of Judeo-Christian monotheism (Weber 1992 [1905]). Quite differently, the Indian self has been shaped under the polytheistic and ritualized orientations of a colorful and hierarchic civilization (Dumont 1980), thus differently responding to unsuitable practices and categories imposed by Westerners. In other words, as different selves are constituted within different sets of institutions and ideologies, the efficacy of a therapy, healing system or self-technique depends on its ability to address deeper categories of subjectivity formation that are sustained or problematized in a given society.

As a step further, after 'repression' has been exorcized through therapy and meditation, the subject is then seen in a reflexive space of relative freedom in which she is forced to construct herself responsibly (Giddens 1992, Foucault 1984f). In other words, after repression is 'lifted,' the subject is confronted with the ethical question of how to live properly (Foucault 1984c). In social terms, with the decline of morality in high modern civilization, one response has been the development of an aesthetics of the self, by which the subject seeks to balance divergent life-values (religion, economy, politics, science, war, eroticism, etc.), while continually reassessing the risks and consequences of her acts and thoughts upon herself, others and future generations (Lash 1994; Taylor 1991; Foucault 1984c).

However, although relatively freer to cultivate their 'inner Buddhahood,' sannyasins, expressive expatriates and New Agers – modern Westerners in general – will remain entrapped in the institutional-ideological regime that they seek to transcend insofar as they overemphasize the ideas of 'repression,' 'expression' and 'self' indefinitely. Like the German film described on p. 132, what more and more sannyasins want is 'enlightenment guaranteed.' Others, however, will dissent from the resort's rampant post-charismatic commercialization, and carry on with experiments of subjectivity (de)formation in Goa – the topic of Chapter 5. Whereas sannyasins dangerously celebrate solipsistic individualism, a *postmodern* self requires a kind of reflexive sensibility that considers the self in relation to a substantive care with the other, polis and ecology (Hadot and Davidson 1995).

5   Techno trance tribalism in Goa
The elementary forms of nomadic spirituality

'This noisy barbarous amusement we do condemn and prohibit.'
Catholic Diocesan Decree against
Hindu festivals in Goa, 1777

Introduction: the psychedelic contact zone

In Romantic imaginaries, the journey to the East is a mythic ritual in which the traveler transforms herself in the process of discovering the Other, more fundamentally expressing the wish to overcome the spiritual malaises of modern civilization. The further and the longer a trip is, the more charisma it grants to the traveler. Along with the status to be enjoyed back at home, the traveler invigorates herself, even at the price of an existential exile, since such a prolonged absence fosters utter individuation. In other words, rather than a mere spatial displacement for entertainment, traveling is framed as a veritable practice of self-formation.

Figure 5.1 'Three renouncers' – a Techno trance DJ and two Hindu sadhus.

In the late 1960s, a handful of beatniks and hippies meandering across Central Asia entered India and almost incidentally reached Goa, a former Portuguese enclave on the west coast of India. By the Arabian Sea, they gathered on the secluded beaches of Anjuna and Vagator villages. Precarious roads led to the place, linking the state capital Panaji to Mapusa (a town in the northern district), and then to Anjuna. As more Westerners traveled through Southern Asia on 'magic buses,' the New Year's Eve in Goa worked as the meeting-point for the countercultural diaspora (Sharma 2004; Odzer 1995). Ironically, while fleeing the West, they have benefited from Goans' Christian–Portuguese legacy, somehow imaged as accepting of their individualist dispositions (Axelrod and Fuerch 1998).

After a dormant 1980s, the 'Goa scene' re-emerged in the early 1990s when post-hippie, post-punk 'freaks' developed a potent variation of electronic dance music, blasting overnight in 'full-moon parties.' The music genre was named 'Goa trance' – also known as 'Techno trance' or 'psy trance', due to its allegedly mind-altering effects, particularly when combined with the intake of psychedelic drugs. Since then, a few thousand Westerners have gathered in northern Goa each year, to attend the 'party season,' a series of spontaneous, usually illegal dance events known as 'trance parties.'

Conventional patterns of leisure behavior, such as collective effusiveness and laxity, are not seen in trance parties – quite the contrary. The prevalent mood among trance freaks tends to be introspective and almost ceremonial, as if indexing something of a sacred nature (St John 2004). Veteran trance DJ Goa Gil once declared: 'A Goa party is not a disco under a coconut tree: it is spiritual initiation' (Goa Gil n.a.). As it will be examined, Techno trance combines leisure and religiosity in a ritual assemblage that recodes the modern self in its cognitive, affective and identity modes. In addition to the bellicose stance as a response to neo-liberal pressures, the seriousness of freaks at trance parties dramatizes the dangerous effects of psychedelic experience upon the self, therefore justifying the sacred sphere of protectiveness.

Trance music historically derives from a wider cultural movement of electronic dance music that emerged in the late 1980s, at the confluence of new digital technologies, globalized exchanges and neo-liberal exploitation. The resulting nebula of digitalized genres and party scenes – which I refer under the umbrella term 'Techno' – is ritually sustained by variegated forms of 'rave,' a multimedia dance event of an effervescent nature that reshapes self-identities in consonance with destabilizing effects of globalization upon tradition, identities and subjectivities (St John 2004; Collin 1997; Jameson 1991). Scholarship has discussed the political, religious and erotic implications of Techno, whose intrinsically polysemous and hybrid nature precludes any simple generalizations (St John 2003; Borneman and Senders 2000; Ingham *et al.* 1999; McKay 1996). Easily mistaken as a recreational practice, rave works as a 'super-sensory experience which, in concatenation of meaning, offers insights on the possibility of postmodern religion and/or alternative spirituality' (St John 2004: 40; see also Reynolds 1998: 5). While disseminating in a multiplicity of subcultural and commercial forms, Techno has historically emerged from the counter-hegemonic matrixes of gays, clubbers and hippies, simultaneously resisting and embodying the predatory effects of neo-liberal capitalism (Reynolds 1998; McKay 1996). In its more politically conscious variants, Techno constitutes the first counterculture that intersects with the digitalized, hypermobile and reflexive features of globalization.

By the turn of the millennium, while Goa persisted as the global mecca of Techno trance, 'Goa parties' have proliferated throughout the world: notably, in Western Europe, Israel, Russia, Japan, the US and Brazil. Nonetheless, the genre has never directly surfaced on the pop media, even though some of its musical elements have been cannibalized into docile forms of dance music, as well as into advertising and post-modernist action movies. As such, Techno trance has largely remained circumscribed within countercultural segments of clubbers, freaks and ravers. Lest its potentially transgressive meaning may get lost, they oppose any attempt at commercializing this music, and also dislike the presence of outsiders – particularly tourists – at trance parties.

As an important caveat, freaks are not tourists. Whereas the latter consume travel and exotic places for short periods and within tightly structured labor/leisure lifecycles, alternative subjects assume remote places as 'homes' for extended periods and within an ethos that seeks to integrate mobility and spirituality into flexible labor/leisure strategies. Moreover, while scorning the 'commodification of experience' verified in the dispositions of conventional tourists (MacCanell 1989), freaks present a pragmatic engagement with native cultures, and more closely emulate the skeptical, romantic and elitist gaze of the 'post-tourist' (Urry 2002). For all their material and cultural particularities, it is wrong to conflate them with tourists. In Deleuzian terms, tourists belong to the striatic space of dwellers, while freaks live by the lines of flight of nomads.

However, the growth of tourism has challenged the viability of the trance scene in northern Goa. While trading exotic commodities in 'hippie markets' (for tourists) and bazaars, global nomads have to cope with the unintended consequences of rapid modernization. Along with the rest of Goa, the villages of Anjuna and Vagator upgrade hostels and restaurants in order to attend to a growing number of visitors. Price inflation, littering, state surveillance and impersonal relations seem to undermine the material and symbolic conditions that enable the experimental edge of the trance scene. Thus, whereas Indian businessmen run nightclubs and 'hippie parties' for masses of Indian and European tourists, Techno freaks must search for more secluded locations deemed suitable for their psychedelic rituals. At the onset of the twenty-first century, it was evident that the praised, bucolic aura of Goa was fading against the ongoing modernization of the region.

By investigating the social organization and rituals of the Goa trance scene, I seek to understand the identity and subjectivity formation of Techno freaks as well as of the world of expressive expatriation overall. Trance parties dramatize the impact of globalization upon expatriate subjectivities, which shatter and reshape self-identities through practices of hypermobility, marginality and metamorphosis (Chapter 1). In other words, the Techno trance scene exposes the elementary forms of a 'nomadic spirituality' which propels and sustains this world, as an instance of the postidentitarian predicament of globalization. Furthermore, such analysis must consider the trance scene as a social formation that engages with local and translocal forces, configuring a 'contact zone.'[1] The global counterculture has to negotiate its conditions of territorialization with agents, forces and institutions located in semi-peripheral locations.

In this chapter, I first introduce the Goa trance scene in relation to its connections to Pune, as it claims to oppose the spiritual tourism embodied in the commodification of the Osho resort; and also in relation to contexts of Goan economy and society which nest the global trance scene locally. Second, the chapter analyzes the social organization of the 'party scene' in northern Goa, with a focus on the economic conditions of event production and promotion. In addition, I identify the basic criteria of belonging in a code that delimits various degrees of proximity to the scene. Third, the chapter discusses the cultural dimension of Techno trance by means of an analysis of ritual and symbolism. I identify a Durkheimian-like binary temporality that sustains the trance scene in tribal fashion, along with Deleuzian notions that circumvent the excess that marks the experience of 'raving' in order to address it, even if indirectly so, at the level of subjective and collective interiorities. Finally, toward a more general discussion, the chapter considers the impact of traveling upon the self, as my fieldwork confronts incipient studies on the psychiatry of travel (Hays 2001; Airault 2000; Wrigley and Revill 2000; Hacking 1998; Quirot 1993; Verdoux *et al.* 1993). While positively engaging with this scholarship, I also expose the power-knowledge implications of consular psychiatry which, at the intersection of state and science, reproduces the normative criteria of modern subjectivity in a global age of high volatility.

More widely, I propose that expressive expatriates constitute a cultural site of experiences and meanings that anticipate some of the predicaments of cultural globalization. As instances of neo-nomadism, they have been experimenting with rootlessness, mobility and cosmopolitanism long before these tropes became celebrated by academia and the press as cultural conditions of contemporary life. As such, I suggest that behavioral patterns, social tropes and cultural effects presently identified among these global nomads will be more socially diffused in the wake of cultural globalization, even if in milder, less visible forms.

The Pune-Goa connection: rebel sannyasins

Still in Pune, an Indian sannyasin told me about a 'trance party' to take place in the city outskirts. As usual, the event was announced through restricted word-of-mouth. It was located on the foothill of a plush veranda restaurant overseeing a greenish river coiling through misty pitfalls (see Figure 5.2). Along with psychedelic music and kaleidoscopic decoration, the picture acquired surreal overtones. The DJ table stood between two loudspeaker sets facing the dance floor, framed by fluorescent drapes which reflected UV lights with a phantasmagoric glow. The crowd comprised a mix of sannyasins, Techno freaks, backpackers and young Indian men.

I spotted the main organizer, Parva (his sannyasin name). Apparently in his mid-thirties, he was self-fashioned as a rough biker, unshaven and wearing a leather vest and silver earring. Originally from England, Parva had been living in India since 1990, spending winters in Goa and summers in Pune. He made his living as a bike mechanic and paraglide instructor. Foreign tourists would pay him Rs. 1,200 for a thirty-minute paraglide jump (or US$25, the monthly salary of many Indian workers).

He has been attending Techno parties since they began in the early 1990s.[2] He promoted two parties, 'accidentally', as he says. 'People just

Figure 5.2 End of a trance party in Pune, winter 2000.

asked me where my party was, while I had nothing in sight, really.' As joint-ventures between expatriates and natives, these secret events were usually illegal, due to their highly improvisational and ephemeral nature. Nonetheless, people from the upper strata were regularly seen attending, as Parva's comment illustrates: 'The daughter of this businessman came in a Rolls-Royce with golden radiator, can you believe it?!'

As an Osho sannyasin, Parva scorned the direction of the 'meditation resort' in Pune. After the death of Osho, the new direction assumed a model of institutional adaptation and gentrification that upset a segment of sannyasins that cultivated a more countercultural orientation. Divergences escalated to a point when in 1994 the resort direction called police to arrest sannyasins under charges of drug consumption (*Indian Express* 2004). Reflecting the critique of many, Parva's comments about the resort were acidic:

> They say that we drain their energies with our trance parties. But we are much more sannyasins than they are! I have more sannyas on the tip of my finger than all of them together. I am an Osho sannyasin, they are just 'ashram sannyasins.'

He was, in fact, just one in a diaspora of sannyasins who departed from the OIMR to various degrees. Living across Pune and Goa, they frequented hangout bars, but rarely went to the resort, while looking down on 'ashram sannyasins.' The resort direction repudiated those who demonstrated any interest in psychedelic parties, shamanic experiments or bohemian activity. In their turn, rebel sannyasins repudiated the organization for its upmarketing orientation (as outlined in Chapter 4). They imagined Osho as an open-minded leader who welcomed novel experiments – such as Techno parties – and tolerated deviant behavior even when he disagreed with it.

While ashramites admonished any cheerful references to Goa (I was once jocosely reprimanded not to wear my Goa soccer jersey inside the resort), both Techno freaks and sannyasins developed a symbiotic relation in interconnecting Pune and Goa. At any moment there was a flow of Westerners traveling by bus, train, taxi, motorcycles and airplane between both places. My first trip to Goa coincided with the arrival of Rick[3] in Pune. An American engineer with Indian parents, I first met him in the Chicago club scene a few years before. He came to attend a family wedding in Mumbai, but said he was more interested in knowing the Goa trance scene. He was a fan of rave music – 'despite being from the mainstream,' as he often repeated in ambivalent regret. We met in Pune and took the overnight bus, on which we interacted with two other American backpackers who evinced a clear discomfort with local climate and hygiene conditions.

Goa, tourism and 'hippies'

Goa is a unique state of India. Located on the western coast, about 600 km south of Mumbai, it is India's smallest state with a coastline of 105 km, stretching 55 km inland, totaling an area of 5,702 sq km. Formerly a Portuguese colony, since its annexation by India in 1961 Goa has been suffering intense modernization. With a 1.34 million population, the state has the highest national per-capita income, and also ranks very high in measures for infrastructure, urbanization, health, literacy and civil rights (*The Economist* 2004; Goa Directorate of Planning Statistics and Evaluation 2000).

Geographically, Goa is made up of low river basins along 80 km of palm-fringed beaches. Plateaus of 30 to 100 m high extend into the hilly area by the eastern border. Average temperatures range from 24°C to 32°C, typical of tropical monsoon climate. A dry warm season lasts from November to March, and the hot months of April and May are followed by a cooling yet highly humid rainy season which lasts from June to October. With rich vegetation and fauna, the Goan landscape is populated with coconut trees, palms and banyans, as well as monkeys, reptiles and various bird species. In urban peripheries, a considerable number of stray dogs can be noticed.

Tourism is one of Goa's main industries in terms of revenues, labor employment and amplifier effect (to be discussed below). In addition, the state also counts on agriculture (rice, coconut, cashew nut and sugarcane), fishing, mining (iron ore and bauxite exported to Japan, China and Germany), some manufacture (chemicals and consumer products), and a considerable level of external remittances from émigrés working in Persian Gulf countries. Throughout the 1990s, the rise of a new middle class has increased levels of consumption, though state-led industrialization has been hampered by its limited infrastructure. In the meanwhile, a growing number of international charter flights has sparked debates over a project for a new airport in the state (*Financial Express* 2003).

Demographically, Goa features a 1.34 million population (about 40 percent non-Goan), enjoying above-average rates for life quality in the Indian context (*The Economist* 2004; Goa Directorate of Planning Statistics and Evaluation 2000, 2002). Despite fashioning itself as a distinctively Christian-influenced Indian state, only 27 percent of the population professes the religion (mostly Catholics). The remainder is 68 percent Hindu and 5% Muslim. The Hindu majority predominates in the larger hinterland (known as the 'New Conquest'), whereas the Christian minority prevails in the main urban centers of the coastal area known as 'Old Conquest.' The Christian minority is overrepresented in bureaucracy, press and university, as well as in its influential transnational diaspora (to wit, the first 'non-resident Indian' passport was granted to a foreigner of Goan ancestry).

Politico-administratively, Goa state comprises two districts subdivided into eleven sub-districts (*talukas*). In addition to the capital Panaji, the state population is highly dispersed over 44 towns (Margao, Vasco and Mapusa as the main urban centers) and about 360 villages. These communities elect a number of local counselors who designate 40 members who will constitute the Legislative Assembly, which, in turn, appoints the Chief Minister of the state. Employing about 49,000 civil servants, the state bureaucracy is an influential actor. Party politics tends to reflect wider national arrangements, with the secular Congress Party setting the tone of political negotiations locally, with dissidents congregating at the Hindu nationalist BJP or the regionalist MGP (deSouza 2000). After independence in 1961, Goa became Union Territory under direct control from New Delhi. However, amid popular unrest and nationalist maneuvers, Goa was declared a State in 1987. Konkani is the national language, functioning as a crucial marker of Goan identity, though in the past dismissed by some as a 'dialect of Marathi.' English nonetheless predominates in the press, business, university and tourism.

It is not for nothing that Goa is often referred to as 'the Ibiza of Asia' and 'the Cannes of Asia.' In the mid 2000s, the state was defined as one of the world's top five 'hotspots' of tourism, according to European tour operators. In addition, Goa became the permanent site for the International Film Festival of India, until then an annual itinerant event, thus promising to attract even more vacationing politicians and Bollywood celebrities.

Tourism is the leading industry and largest employer of Goa, generating annual revenues in the order of Rs. 15 billion (US$320 million, or 8.8 percent of total tourism revenues of India) (*Navhind Times* 2004; *Times of India* 2004d). With over 2 million tourists visiting Goa each year during the early 2000s, about 320,000 were foreigners, mostly from UK, Russia, Germany, Scandinavia, Gulf States and Southeast Asia. Due to climatic conditions, the tourist season overlaps with the trance party scene, during the warm dry period from November to April, before the monsoon season.

Goans skillfully explore a distinct image, simultaneously Indian and Western. In addition to a visible Portuguese legacy, Goa self-fashions itself by comparison with the Mediterranean. In their interactions with tourists, Goans emphasize their Portuguese–Christian heritage, noted in colonial architecture, religion, gastronomy, carnival, vintage clothing (over sari), civil law (praised by Neru as the most advanced of India), as well as in people's first and family names. Perhaps as a consequence, since colonial times, Western visitors have been reporting that the Goan ethos is quite familiar to them.

The prolonged presence of 'hippies' and 'rave parties' (terms commonly used in the local press) have reinforced a belief that Goa is a liberal place, as Indian visitors repeat. This is a topic of heated debate among Goans. While state authorities prioritize investments in upscale resorts (*Times of*

India 2004c), a strident anti-tourism lobby, summoning elements from the Church, urban NGOs and the press, has defended a rather conservative approach to the sector. Both state and lobby publicly blame 'hippies' for the problems of prostitution, pederasty and school absenteeism that affect Goa (Afonso 1989). However, several studies provide a different picture, agreeing with my own observations in the field. Due to their isolation and resource concentration, high-end resorts have proven to be socially conflictive and environmentally detrimental. On the other hand, low-budget tourism provides a more direct and deconcentrated injection of income into local communities that would otherwise be excluded from the economy (Stabler 1997; Wilson 1997a, 1997b; Hausler 1995). Northern villagers are aware of the risks involved with tourism of a leisure type. But rather than resenting hippies, northern villagers cultivated organic, often amicable relations with them. These foreigners may have inadvertently triggered a type of modernization which fostered (or made visible) social problems. However, despite high levels of drug consumption, freaks were never involved in crimes against Goans. In fact, northern villagers worried about the political decisions seasonally made at the capital, Panaji, curbing, according to varying circumstances, the seasonal party scene, which is the main income source in many northern villages.

A mosaic of diverse peoples interacted closely in that region: villagers, trance freaks, backpackers, Israeli ex-soldiers, Japanese hippies, Osho sannyasins, Nepalese workers, Goa businessmen, beach vendors from Karnataka, Kashmiri traders, European charter tourists, drug dealers, junkies, sadhus, etc. Though populated by petty criminals and many other marginal types, the socio-economic order in northern Goa was rather determined by shady deals struck among businessmen, bureaucrats and politicians. Local communities then secondarily enjoyed the relatively stable and profitable environment. As freaks pointed out, even though the 'scene' is potentially dangerous (due to drugs, strangers, corruption and lawlessness), the situation in the region was exceptionally peaceful. This picture evokes the notion of 'contact zone,' defined as a space of exchanges and inequalities comprising a highly heteroclite mix of peoples that interact in a precarious equilibrium. In fact, economic inequality, labor exploitation and cultural stereotypes marked the interactions among Goans, Westerners and immigrants, almost always favoring local businessmen with the connivance of state authorities.

I focus, nonetheless, on those interactions whose analysis can reveal why and how India operates as a charismatic magnet for Western subjects of the counterculture. Low cost of living is an indispensable condition, as many point out at a first glance, but it does not explain why India has been favored over other countries which would better suit this economic rationale. I thus examine local arrangements of power insofar as they shed light on understanding forms of coercion *in the West* which lead these renegades to flee to Asia. As I seek to explore, India matters because it is conducive to a dialogic process whereby the Western self attempts to reshape itself critically and experimentally. By traveling to places of symbolic power, trance freaks try to eschew and recode the institutional and ideological effects of the nation-state (the regulatory regime of the administration of collective and subjective bodies). In this picture, by deploying mobility as a tactic of repositioning through space and identity (while resonating with emerging conditions of globalization, as seen in Chapter 1), the self and its body become a site of struggles wherein countercultural formations seek to engender alternative experiences of the self.

A note about the terms 'hippie' and 'freak' is pertinent. Although sharing a countercultural horizon, they embody distinct subcultural dispositions that refer to different historical circumstances. Whereas the 1960s hippie exodus amalgamated the cultural rebellion against affluent technocratic societies (Roszak 1995), the 1990s rave diaspora stemmed from the economic harshness of neo-liberalism along with the embracing of new digital technologies applied to art (Reynolds 1998; McKay 1996). 'In the 1960s the young dropped out, in the 1980s they are dropped out' (McKay 1996: 52). Though transportation and communication have improved dramatically since the 1960s, the decline of labor and welfare in the current capitalist period has hampered traveling opportunities among the youth.

More closely, hippies and freaks also differ significantly in terms of practices, values and representations. Unlike hippies, freaks do not practice nudism or free sex, nor see these as components of a liberation politics. While AIDS likely had a cooling effect in experiments of inter-corporeal hedonism, Techno trance embodies certain militaristic proclivities that contribute to an ascetic body politics seen among freaks. In contrast with hippies' Luddite orientation, freaks are more pragmatic in adopting new technologies (sound systems, internet, biking), praised for their power to derail the self. Both generations have indulged in drugs, but the meanings have differed significantly. Hippies saw psychedelics as an uplifting way to socialize and to explore alternative perceptions of reality. Contemporary freaks consume drugs more privately, as a challenge to their tough structured ego, unleashing a silent battle within. Influenced by the punks of the late 1970s, they have assumed a penchant for shock, despair and nihilism, and, even though many freaks are ecologically minded, the overall orientation is skeptical about positive social transformations. In contrast with hippies' 'flower power,' they disdain expressions of affection and abhor devotional forms of religiosity. With little interest in oriental spiritualities, freaks favor fragmented hybridizations of East and West, away from the New Age cult of self-development. In conclusion, whereas hippies once heralded utopia, freaks now impersonate the somber possibilities of neo-liberal globalization. As it will be of importance in this chapter, in contrast with hippies who favored daytime and night-time activities alike, freaks prefer the nightlife thrill, cultivating its Gothic undertones as the new spirit of the underground. Roughly put, freaks are a contemporary hybrid of hippie and punk.

Day Life: the social organization of the trance scene in northern Goa

Early morning, the overnight bus from Pune dropped us in Mapusa, the main town in northern Goa. Rick, the two backpackers and I took a taxi toward Anjuna village. On the road, the driver told me that his name is Anthony and he is Christian. For mutual bemusement, I introduced myself as Nataraj (my Osho sannyasin name, a Hindu dancing deity). He smiled. Familiar with Western displays of eccentricity, Goans also seek to differentiate themselves from the rest of India.

Still in the taxi, one of the young women became suddenly distressed, demanding that we be taken to the guesthouse which, after all, we had all agreed to go to, no matter how much we reassured her. Upon arrival at *Manali Guest House*, she seemed relieved. Embarrassed, she apologized and told me that she did not know why she behaved that way. This episode could have been ignored, if such anomalous behavior were not recurrently manifested by Western travelers. It was a caveat for situations to come, which I assess as a process of psychic deterritorialization, to be discussed later in the chapter.

After checking in, Rick and I sought to check the 'party scene' on the beach. Those expecting an Ibiza-like daytime frenzy would be disappointed. A few tourists lay on the sand, with surrounding cows eager for the fruits

Figure 5.3 The foreign core of the Anjuna hippie market.

that vendors insistently pushed on them. By the sea, two white men played racquetball wearing tiny thongs. The rustic landscape comprised the beach, with green vegetation up the hills and a few straw restaurant shacks. The weather was hot, and the dark sea unattractive. A shack owner complained that 'the party season was weak' because of hash police repression in the previous year. Whether or not these were accurate remarks, the beach was indeed quiet and empty, in contrast with the massive hippie crowds featured in photos from the early 1970s. Rick relied on me for any minor decision, basically behaving like a pampered tourist. Via email, he arranged to meet a couple of friends at the *German Bakery*, a hangout for expatriates and wealthier freaks.

The village of Anjuna hosted about twenty hostelry facilities, mostly family-run guesthouses built in the premises across their own houses. There were a few upgraded hostels with modern amenities, such as swimming pool, sauna, cable TV, etc. Many villagers rented rooms inside their residences. Accommodations were usually clean, although hygiene in public spaces (streets and restaurants) could be an issue for unaccustomed visitors. In a stark example of the effects of unplanned urbanization, while internet centers were seen at every corner, many restaurants lacked running water and open 'pig toilets' could still be seen around the millennium.

I first stayed at *Manali Guest House*, a well-equipped establishment located at the center of the village. It is a family-run business, which also included an internet room, bar, a second-hand book store, currency exchange, travel office, rental motorbikes and a taxi van. The Manali family lived in the house beside the six-room guesthouse, in addition to thin tinfoil rooms built on top of their house. They were one of the wealthiest families in the village, but apparently few people liked them. According to a traveler guidebook, *Manali* was 'a good-value [. . .] but not the friendliest in town.' Due to its relative high prices (over Rs. 200 per room, about US\$4), its clientele was not regular freaks, but backpackers peripheral to the party scene.

Hardcore freaks and other veteran expatriates stayed in cheaper areas, such as the inland areas of Chapora and Assagao where houses were rented for the season or the year. A modest two-room house could be rented for Rs. 50,000 (US\$1,100) per year. Larger colonial houses were shared by large groups of younger freaks, resulting in rents as low as US\$20 per month per person. Such collective arrangements, however, were frequently disturbed by harangues over privacy, noise, romance and drugs, whose chronic abuse resulted in more quarrels.

Of historical relevance, *Joe Banana's* restaurant was the first hippie hangout in the early 1970s. It is a central reference in Cleo Odzer's biography (Odzer 1995), and some of the expatriates that I met in Ibiza, such as Rochelle, were familiar with the place and former eccentric punters. Located in south Anjuna, *Joe Banana's* was owned by Joe's son Tony Almeida. Joe opened the restaurant in the late 1960s, after returning from

Kenya where he had worked as a factory mechanic. Their establishment became very popular among hippies because they were one of the few families to speak fluent English. Hippies had *chai* and pancakes while socializing, or came to ask for accommodation, or other errands and favors. As Tony recalled, 'There were no guesthouses back then, just some houses and huts. The nearest police station was in Mapusa, and they never cared about what was going on here.' He also enthused about the 'unbelievable' amount of drugs being transacted and consumed in the region – basically, hashish, marijuana, heroin, cocaine, etc. His comments were not isolated:

> People were much crazier, more druggie, with more junkies. But they also had more presence. They had more personality. They were more alive, much more than today. Young people today do drugs too, but they are more quiet.

Like Manali, Tony has economically prospered. With the growth of tourism, the core of the freak scene moved north, and his restaurant was no longer a main reference. Nonetheless, Tony built five houses, which he rents to German and English expatriates who pay him US$1,000 (Rs. 45,000) per year per house. After six months (the maximum visa period), they lend their houses to friends or relatives. Tony closes the restaurant in late April, ordering maintenance before the rainy season arrives in June. Noisy refrigerators are turned off until October, allowing his family 'to rest peacefully,' as he notes.

Biographic silence and transnational (dis)connections

Through curvy palm-lined roads, we reached the *German Bakery*, a patio bar and restaurant, renowned for its 'organic' pastries. Hindi music, rock or trip-hop made the musical background. The place was regularly attended by young backpackers, wealthier freaks and other expatriate regulars of Goa. In a laid-back atmosphere, they walked around on barefoot, lay down on cushions and shared hashish smoke. The bakery was owned by a German sannyasin who had managed Pune's homonymous coffee shop in the 1980s. The concept was very similar to the alternative bars in Ibiza, such as *Las Dálias* and *Khumaras* (Chapters 2 and 3). In fact, I sometimes came across Ibiza's *Las Dálias* hippie traders at Goa's *German Bakery* totally by chance.

Rick introduced me to Meena and Surya, whom he had met in the Chicago nightclub scene (names altered, see Note 3). They were diasporic Indians from upper middle-class families with branches in northern India, New York City and Malaysia. The couple met at a medical school in Bangalore and developed close connections with trance freaks in Goa and New York. Although countercultural in spirit, Meena and Surya were about to take up medical residences in the US, where she grew up:

America sucks your soul in, and you become a slave of the system. All we want is to have our medical residency there, make some money, and then move somewhere else, to live with real freedom, enjoy life, and maybe set up some NGO to help local people in India or Malaysia.

Expressive expatriates criticize Western civilization in general, but America epitomizes the worst of materialism, control and impersonal relations. Meena and Surya accepted their medical residences in the US as a challenge to be confronted within their cosmopolitan diasporic dispositions, as a temporary situation to be tolerated in the world of opportunities.

The couple was very curious about Ibiza, but did not ask me any personal questions. In the meanwhile, they smoked hashish-tobacco cigarettes, which Rick tried for the first time. We ate and arranged to meet at a trance bar in Vagator later that night. As we left the *German Bakery*, I noticed that Rick was still very intoxicated and he accepted my suggestion to take a ride on my motorcycle.

On the road, he questioned me in an unusually aggressive manner. 'You did not tell them that you are spying. You are betraying my friends. I know that I am from the mainstream but your work will destroy the scene!' I quickly realized that Rick had become very impressed with the remarks I made in Chicago and Pune about fieldwork difficulties faced by researchers and journalists in the trance scene in Goa. Those impressions were now greatly amplified in a state of drug-induced paranoia. In addition to the golden rule of never arguing with people on drugs, I reassured him that I would introduce my work to his friends that night.

At *Nine Bar*, Meena and Surya were glad to know that I was researching the trance scene, to such an extent that I had to ask Meena to be more discreet when introducing me to her acquaintances, some of whom were indeed hostile to newcomers. Other freaks began to identify me as a 'Techno magazine writer,' or as a 'student of tourism,' usually accepting my presence with some performed disinterest. It was thus ironical that the only explicit manifestation of hostility toward my research came from someone who repeatedly declared to be an 'outsider.'

More generally, despite the audio-visual richness of Techno culture, verbal communication among freaks was quite limited. There were instances of lively discussion in bars and restaurants, but overall, the few-words habitus prevailed. Outgoingness, curiosity and talkativeness – often found among backpackers – were sanctioned by freaks with looks of disapproval, evasive answers or blunt silence. In fact, direct questions about one's past or occupation were very rarely asked. Conversations revolved more desultorily around issues of travel, party and drugs. Freaks almost never spoke about their past, and they despised elaborated rationalizations: 'It is better to live without opinions,' an Israeli trance freak (and geriatric nurse in Germany) once told me. The contact zone was thus populated by selves that were eccentric yet opaque.

On a surface level, such biographic silence stems from an environment marked by marginality and dissatisfaction. Everybody suspected, knew about, or was involved with some sort of illegal activity, particularly drug dealing and consumption. Others were involved with the smuggling of exotic goods, often involving a series of minor bribes. Many travelers were also fleeing from petty crimes or existential dramas in the West: separation, abuse, boredom, despair, as well as smugglers, prostitutes and other outlaws on vacation. Another segment of trance freaks did not want to contradict their countercultural bearing by disclosing their privileged social position, sustained by family or welfare allowances from rich countries. Finally, drug abuse, intense spiritual practices and the traveling mood itself contributed to undermine a logocentric – reasoned and articulated – narrative about oneself as a coherent individual.[4]

A more basic condition underlies these variegated motivations and stances. A countercultural disposition to break up with modern regimes of subjectivity formation opposes history as the product of the sovereign state in its drive to control its domains and subjects (Deleuze and Guattari 1980). Therefore, the acceptance of linear history corresponds to the *subjection* to dominant apparatuses which countercultural agency seeks to overcome. In this sense, the more countercultural the subject, the less biographic it becomes, asymptotically disappearing from historical record (Manning 1998; Green 1986). In other words, these expatriates do not want to be recognized by their pasts, constructed under social conditions imposed on them, but rather in relation to a drive for autonomy by which they feel free to fashion their own self-identity, as purified New Agers or transgressive trance freaks.

At a methodological level, the politicized silence of freaks constituted a challenge to conventional methods of data collection. Compiling their biographies likely contradicts the modes of self-representation that they seek to adopt. I was thus caught in an aporia between a subculture that opposed logocentric reason, and academic protocols regulating systematic representation. It became clear that, as a solution, I should disregard the ethnocentric assumptions underlying the axiological 'I,' while keeping the 'individual' as a unit of analysis (Dumont 1983). Biographic silence could be circumvented at least partially, by engaging the natives in their own modes of representation and positioning. Rather than try to make my interlocutor produce statements about a past they sought to ignore, I rather addressed their current relation to the trance scene. Occupational and chronological data would then emerge, and be culturally meaningful, if considered in relation to the actual engagements that the subject assumed while reshaping itself.

Jean was a DJ who has been living in Goa since the mid 1990s. Originally from a middle-class family in France, he first came in the 1980s in his early twenties. He rented a house in the countryside of Bardez (with a monthly rent of Rs. 1,000 (US$22)). It had a spacious living room with beach mats, pillows and a hammock, placed around his DJ equipment (a sound system with mixer, portable CD/mini-disc player, amplifier and two powerful loudspeaker sets). Among the minimalist furniture in the living room (a few chairs, cushions, beach-mats and a hammock), the only high-tech luxury seemed to be a cable TV broadcasting French programs. In his bedroom, there were a small bed, a table and a small closet. The kitchen was virtually empty, with a few bananas, cookies and a gallon of drinkable water, besides a mini-refrigerator. The bathroom was a pig toilet in the backyard. Despite such simplicity, Jean was content with his home. His only complaint was the permanent risk of thieves who had already broken into his house three times, stealing his sound mixers while he was away. Jean explained that local gangs target foreign DJs because of their good sound equipment and updated music collections.

He did not apply for a residence visa because, although staying in India for extended periods, he regularly traveled to France and other typical sites of the global trance scene. During the party season, he played in trance bars and parties. Jean often spent the rainy season in Goa, staying most of the time indoors, reading science fiction, watching TV, socializing with expatriates and Goans, and playing trance music. Drawing on his lifestyle, the following examples serve to illustrate how spatial and spiritual mobility becomes constitutive of trance communities and subjectivities.

I attended a trance party that Jean and friends organized at the hilltop of Spaghetti beach.[5] It was the early hours of April 12, 2001. In an unusual music shift, Jean played an odd track, slower and funkier than the trance typically played. A few days later we met by chance at a restaurant. He spoke English with a sharp French accent, peppered with expressions of the contact zone: 'I am wired, very wired. I haven't slept in three days. I can stay with no sleep, no problem, but I have to eat.' After ordering his meal, I asked about that singular track, 'Ah,' he smiled, 'that song was in honor of Yuri Gagarin, because April 12 was the day he landed on Earth.' He then explained: 'I read astronomy and science fiction for hours and hours,' and remarked, 'but only in the rainy season . . .' References to astronomy and ufology abounded in the trance scene as well as in rave culture more generally, and trance DJs expressed such fantastic imaginaries more fully. To wit, the walls of Jean's living room featured drawings of extraterrestrial creatures in psychedelic landscapes containing the 'om' symbol, behind a blue ceramic statue of Shiva.

The spatial and symbolic volatility of trance freaks was also reflected on the level of affective relationships. With the end of the party season in May, Jean departed to Paris where he would stay with friends and family until September, then leave for Madagascar in order to visit his girlfriend, and then return to Goa in November. A year later, I asked him about his partner. He seemed confused, 'What girlfriend? Ah, now she in Reunion Islands, but I don't know about her,' he said, shrugging his shoulders. 'She was supposed to come but didn't say anything, so I don't care. I thought you were talking about the Singaporean girl.' Years later Jean migrated to Thailand, where he seemed to have settled down with a girlfriend and two children. Nonetheless, he still participated in the local trance scene, while also traveling to Goa and France regularly. Due to their continuous engagements with mobility (both spatial and personal), affective relationships among freaks, sannyasins and backpackers tended to be unstable and volatile, often represented and sustained through notions of absolute trust, stoic individualism and abandon. The resulting personality often was simultaneously melancholic and indifferent.

How freaks are able to sustain economically this transnationally mobile and relatively labor-free lifestyle is an obvious question. Their strategy involved keeping living costs very low, particularly in South Asian countries (such as rents varying from Rs. 1,000 to 5,000 per month, or about US$20 to 100). In addition, their income combined variegated sources activated in contingent ways, and several possibilities will be described here. In the case of a trance DJ, Jean, for example, could count on the eventual support of his parents who lived in France. He also earned money by playing at rave festivals in Western Europe and sporadically traded second-hand sound equipment. Last, he occasionally traded drugs, with hefty profits. But, because this was not his main activity or concern, it would be misleading to dub him a 'drug dealer,' besides the fact that the trance scene did not recognize him as such.[6]

Drug dealing was a highly profitable if risky endeavor. It was seen as the easiest way to gain freedom from work, insofar as the individual was able to forge relations of trust in the scene. For example, Jean was approached by an acquaintance who asked if he could arrange 300 pills of MDMA for a group of Japanese tourists. Quite easily, Jean quickly obtained the substance, and was paid Rs. 600 for each pill that cost him Rs. 400, thus amassing a one-transaction profit of Rs. 60,000 (US$1,300) – had Jean had more time his profit would have been higher. Similarly, freaks could smuggle ketamine (a liquid hallucinogen) in deodorant bottles that were hidden in their luggage in flights back to Europe or Israel. One liter of the substance was purchased in Goa for US$400 and sold in the West for US$6,000. In comparison with other drugs, the transportation of ketamine (a veterinary anesthetic) was considered low risk, because its legal status in several countries is undefined. In India, its possession is not a crime, merely requiring a veterinarian's prescription. In sum, with a few days dedicated to a creative scam, a freak could live well – accordingly to their needs, values and standards – for about a year or even two. Nonetheless, this type of adventurous trading seemed to have become more discreet and modest over time, particularly when compared with the daring endeavors of transnational hippies in the early 1970s, as noted by some veterans and biographical accounts (Odzer 1995).

The integration of labor into a counter-hegemonic lifestyle varied significantly among freaks. Many worked in bars, hotels, farms and travel agencies in Western countries over half of the year, saving as much money as possible. A few owned workshops in Bali, Nepal or Thailand, manufacturing and exporting exotic goods such as clothing, gems and woodcraft, to be sold at highly inflated prices in tourist and decoration outlets in the West (*New York Times* 2004). Other expatriates developed alternative careers as handcrafters, hippie traders, DJs and therapists, enabling them to be more fully integrated with global countercultural formations in India and elsewhere. They can purchase exotic goods in Mumbai, New Delhi or Rajastan, sending their commodities to Western countries but in separate parcels. Several others worked at the weekly Anjuna flea market during the tourist season in Goa.

The 'Anjuna hippie market' took place on a large terrain beside the beach, each Wednesday of the tourist months, from late October to early April. The huge Kasbah comprised hundreds of tents, mostly run by Indians from various regions, surrounding a much smaller number of Western hippie traders concentrated at the core of the market. In the meanwhile, throngs of taxis brought tourists in and out. A variety of products were on offer, such as handcrafts, gems, clothes (hippie, ethnic and conventional), party wear, pirate CDs of trance music, spices, incense, drapes, mats, etc. There was also a bar compound, which included rows of tables aligned under large canvases. The hippie traders socialized in the 'foreign area,' which displayed their artisan products, while some also offered massage and divinatory arts (tarot, numerology and Maya astrology). All traders paid a small fee to the landowner in order to set up their booth. The event began in the early 1970s, as a small gathering of hippies who tried to sell unwanted belongings, either to travel more lightly or to get cash for purchasing drugs. Throughout the 1990s, the market grew manifold, attracting an ever growing number of domestic and foreign tourists along with Indian vendors who now ran over 95 percent of the stalls of the 'hippie market.'

In contrast with freaks who worked in service jobs in the West, these hippie traders have been able to integrate mobility as a component of their economic strategies and alternative lifestyles, as the following examples illustrate. Originally from Western Europe (names and locations concealed), Joanne sold party clothes at the market. She first came to Goa as a backpacker in the mid-1990s and came across the trance scene by chance. There she met her partner Pietro, another expatriate who redistributed Himalayan hashish in the local scene. They rented a large yet rustic house in the region and traveled to their European homelands during the monsoon. Their only child spoke four languages, including Konkani. Some Goans estimate that about 30 white children spoke the Goan language fluently.

Renate sold bikinis which she imported from Bali or Brazil. Her phenotype blended Germanic and Rastafarian elements, as she was in fact half Dutch and half Caribbean. Her four-year-old child stood beside her, playing with a backgammon board. The father was an Israeli musician.

Renate had plans to go to Brazil, a growingly attractive 'hotspot' in the global trance scene. Otherwise, as recurrently seen among international couples, their traveling patterns encompassed a triangulation involving Goa (or other paradoxical paradise such as Ibiza or Bali) and the partners' homelands, visited on an almost yearly basis.

Bojan was a handcrafter and trance DJ. He produced leather items (bags, belts and sandals) which he sold at the Anjuna market, while also offering readings of Maya astrology, a complex divinatory system that has become popular among New Agers throughout the 2000s (see Barbara in Chapter 2, p. 55). Originally from Slovenia, Bojan first visited India in 1976. Back then, he worked as a computer technician in a bank in now-defunct Yugoslavia:

> One day I was looking [at] the terminal screen, and got a flash that if I stayed in that work, I would soon become green like the screen. So, in one week I was on the road back to India, all by land and on my bike, with a plastic bag as my luggage.

The war in Yugoslavia catalyzed his decision to migrate to India in 1991. Also a sannyasin, he first stayed in Pune, 'but I decided to come to Goa, after seeing all the hypocrisy in the ashram,' referring to the draconian purges promoted by the resort management following Osho's death (see Chapter 4, and section above on Pune).

These expatriates have abandoned the homeland marked either by structured conditions of ordinary life and work, or by no less stressful pressures of neo-liberal instability. They migrated to semi-peripheral locations in order to shape an alternative lifestyle by which values of autonomy, pleasure and expression can be at least partially actualized. In addition, mobility is integrated into their life strategies, in an attempt to evade modern regimes of labor, citizenship and morality. As such, the following quote by Bojan discloses how alternative expatriates rationalize their decision to come to India:

> Goa is a melting point for East and West, and already India is the only country in the world that is female, round, and the karma yoga is instantaneous. Most of the West is macho robotics, man-made world where feelings are secondary. It makes them candidates for ulcer, cancer and other consuming illnesses. India is still a country where people smile at you in the street. They look in your eyes, which is like catching a glimpse of the soul, and everything is possible. It is the total opposite of the Western squareness.

Similarly to responses heard in Ibiza, expressive expatriates in Goa also assessed modern life negatively, while praising alien lands and their natives in Romantic fashion. As a generalization verified within New Age spiritualities, gender notions also reflect their re-evaluation of the ideal life. The exoticized Other embodies positive attributes that are deemed feminine: they are 'affective,' 'holistic,' 'nurturing,' 'intuitive,' etc., providing a nemesis of Westerners who, over the course (and 'curse') of civilization, have lost their humanness, wholesomeness and mystery. Such valuations are crystallizations of a dialogic process that constitutes self-identities. With reference to such perceptions of absence in the modern spirit, Renate suggested that: 'People come to India because it is a mirror of yourself. You realize things about yourself that you wouldn't at home.' These native formulations are veritable instances of longstanding historicities of orientalist Romanticism (Pratt 1992; Said 1978; Bruford 1975).

However, while idealizing pristine qualities attributed to the native, Westerners often ignored material and motivational differences. Though questioning the imperialism of tourists, trance freaks seemed to overlook their own economic superiority in relation to most of the Indian population they interacted with, no matter how frugally freaks may live while in India. Such discrepancy placed expressive expatriates in an ambiguous position of exploration and exploitation, affirming a type of cosmopolitanism which ironically sought to remain aloof to both East and West. In this connection, they often missed the fact that natives also had their own ulterior motivations and aspirations, sometimes significantly unchanged by their interactions with aliens. In their narcissistic appreciation of the Other, Westerners remained blind to the economic, sexual and symbolic interests of natives who, as a matter of fact, rarely complained about such romantic misrepresentations; quite the contrary, some skillfully sought to take advantage of them (Mehta 1990).

The economy of trance parties: drugs and agonism

Bojan was regularly invited to play as a guest DJ at underground bars and trance parties. Unlike most trance freaks, he did not travel as much, usually spending the monsoon seasons in Goa, or only going to Europe when offered a seasonal gig as a DJ in beach bars on the eastern Mediterranean. He played at larger rave parties in Bangalore, which provided him enough money to cover his yearly rent in Assagao (a sub-district near Anjuna). He owned a classic super-bike Bullet Enfield, but, as often happens in the scene, he suffered a bike accident and almost had his leg amputated in 2003. With no health insurance, the trance community quickly raised funds for his surgery and treatment, while the hospital crew reduced their fees when they realized that Bojan was not a tourist but a long-term resident. This accident thus reveals forms of solidarity and acknowledgment that underlie the scene in Goa.

In our conversations, his answers were strongly critical about the modern West, although tempered with a mystical outlook on life in general. Once, we talked about a trance festival to occur in Kenya (Africa) around a

moon eclipse. While likely attracting a few thousands freaks internationally, I noted that a trip like that requires a certain amount of money that
would prevent many freaks from attending the event. He pondered:

> Yes, it is a bit exclusivist, but the energy keeps flowing. You may not
> go to one of these gatherings, but you go to the next one. There must
> always be a group of people to keep it going. Anyway, no matter
> how limited you are in money, if you tune in with the energy, you
> will find a way to be there. [After brief silence, he added:] Money is
> the energy of the heart. It flows and circulates. The system controls
> or tries to control it, but you have to know how to deal with it, and
> move within it.

In fact, the party scene was enmeshed in a web of local interests and
international circumstances that defines the season accordingly. The
number of 'large' parties (from 100 to 1,000 people) could vary (from 10
to 30) from year to year. While seeking to avoid the strict commercialization of trance parties, freaks had to negotiate with villagers, businessmen
and police, in order to secure some party activity. Trance parties occur
without an official permit. Since the licensing procedure is extremely
morose, freaks turned to stealth techniques along with the bribing of police
officers. Due to the abundance of drugs, trance parties were an easy target
for police, whose action was prompted by a mix of official and ulterior
motivations. On the other hand, local communities generally favored the
party scene, hoping to see a large number of freaks, backpackers and other
young tourists. On a larger scale, international war and terrorism often
had a negative impact on mainstream tourism, but freaks claim that such
problems do not interfere with their travel decisions. In this situation,
northern Goans become more dependent on the hardcore community of
trance freaks, who could then enjoy even lower prices and weaker police
raids. In sum, depending on the arrangement of local forces and international circumstances, the 'party season' could be deemed 'good' (in folk
parlance), meaning multiple parties with an excess of foreign travelers,
or 'bad,' meaning marked by tough state intervention and hindrances
to travel.

Freaks and Goans had quite different interests in trance parties. The
former were amateurs who excitingly revered such events as almost sacred
rituals, and professed to be against their commercialization. However,
they had to accommodate the economic interests of Goans and other
mighty Indians in the scene. Initially, there were large bar-restaurant entrepreneurs who wanted to increase profit margins by means of special
permits, which restricted competition from other bars. With the assistance of expatriate artists, they upgraded 'trance bars' in Gothic style.
In addition to being spaces of socialization among freaks, these venues

provided some relief when trance parties became scarcer. During the New Year's Eve, main tourist resorts organized 'raves' that attracted thousands of Indian males. They had to wait in long lines, and pay a hefty entrance fee (Rs. 500 (US$10)), whereas foreign 'hippies' were immediately allowed in for free. This was an attempt to render such events more 'authentic'; after all, 'hippies' are a tourist attraction for Indian tourists. However, unlike uninformed backpackers, the larger freak populace avoided such gatherings until morning time, arriving only after the tourist mass had left.

A large segment of the village population made their living on the party scene. Local youth teams profited from providing sound systems and bar service at trance parties. In addition, they were brokers in informally negotiating the possibility of parties with police officers, usually involving the recourse to bribery using funds provided by Western promoters. Without their intermediation, trance parties were virtually impossible. Furthermore, a 'chai economy' developed around the party venue. *Sari* ladies spread beach-mats on which they sold candies, cigarettes and *chai* (tea) brewed on the spot. Due to the exoticism they added to the psychedelic scenario, freaks enjoyed their presence. Finally, other villagers provided indispensable ancillary services, such as rental bikes, internet connection and drugs, in addition to bars and restaurants, as well as hostels, grocery stores, bike mechanics, etc. In sum, even though the party scene was populated by mostly low-budget travelers, it actually generated a considerable amount of revenues that were directly appropriated by the local population (Stabler 1997; Wilson 1997a, 1997b; Hausler 1995).

In contrast, Western party promoters did not seek economic gain; quite the contrary, they often lost money in the activity. Against common belief, they did not promote parties for selling drugs. Certainly, drug consumption was very high and promoters saw it as a way of creating a 'nice atmosphere.' In their quotidian life, some of them eventually transacted drugs as a one-off easy deal, but this was not a consistent practice employed for promoting or funding parties. Though British and Russian gangs sought to control drug trade in charter tourism areas, they never interfered with the party scene itself, lest they upset Goans' direct interests. As a result, drug dealing was carried out by a variety of individuals who discreetly but freely pushed hashish, acid, ecstasy, heroin and ketamine at trance parties.

An average trance party required a budget of about Rs. 35,000 (US$750). Western party promoters raised the money, which was equally spent on renting the sound system and on bribing (*baksheesh*) police officers. They sought to collect donations from friends and acquaintances of the scene, in addition to their own money. Often, a small fee of Rs. 50 (US$1) was charged as an entrance fee, and extra donations were requested during the event: in the morning hours, a box would be passed around, as the DJ interrupted the music, inciting the crowd to contribute. By all means, promoters were glad to break even; if not, they paid any difference with their own resources. They were aficionados who organized parties because they wanted to play and to be acknowledged as scene DJs. A team of party promoters involved a small group of friends. Veteran freaks operated in more multinational networks, whereas younger promoters grouped themselves by nationality (usually Israelis). Each team sought to promote one, seldom two parties each season, or face the risk of party saturation. DJs who contributed with more money or were more popular in the scene were allowed to play longer gigs and received more invitations. According to DJs, playing trance music is a quasi-addictive activity that produces mind-altering effects. They do seem transformed as they play for hours in a row, hardly speaking to anyone, other than smoking hashish.

In conclusion, though embedded in the political economy of northern Goa, the trance party scene must be understood as propelled by a logic of agonistic competition and charisma among DJs and their followers. They sought to charge the scene, by throwing larger, longer and 'wilder' parties, outdoing previous events, and gaining prestige as outstanding promoters and DJs. Their aliases and track titles indexed scientific and religious jargon, which expressed and fed an imaginary of magic, technology and tribalism denoting the general orientation of the scene (a topic to be resumed later in this chapter).

Codes of belonging in the trance scene: problematizing the Western self

Westerners related to the trance scene at various levels of involvement. Furthest of all were charter tourists, unaware of any countercultural formations in India. Mostly from the UK, Germany and Russia, they stayed on Baga and Calangute beaches, about 5 km south of Anjuna, or towards the south of the state, in the more isolated, all-inclusive resorts of Salcete. In relatively cheap two-week vacations, they confined themselves to the hotel swimming pool, hopping to nearby bars and restaurants, besides some conventional sightseeing, and a visit to the 'hippie market.' A taxi driver eventually persuaded young couples to attend a 'hippie party' at a trance bar in Vagator, but seemed uncomfortable with the monotonous trance music in such proto-barbarian environments. Inebriated friends nonetheless would quickly hit the dance floor.

Another type stems from the influx of backpackers traveling across India, arriving in Goa to check the party scene. Mostly from Western Europe and Israel, they soon took one of the following trajectories. Those from an apparently structured or middle-class background tended to favor daytime activities (beach, restaurant and sightseeing). They found techno music aggressive or tedious, and complained about the unfriendliness of freaks. Dissatisfied, they departed after a few days, heading south or north (after or before the monsoon, respectively). In contrast, another segment fully embraced the party scene. They rearranged their traveling schedules to fit the party scene and a conversion process quickly ensued. Drawn from a working-class background or from troubled families – or often both – many were familiar with marginal subcultures of punks, bikers, squatters, ravers and clubbers, including experiences with drugs and other law infractions. Above all, they revealed utter dissatisfaction with their lives back in the homeland. In contrast with pampered first-timers, they never complained about India's precariousness; quite the contrary, they seemed to rejoice in self-imposed hardships. Rather than choose clean accommodation, they preferred to pay a few cents less to sleep on dirty mats in derelict huts, water wells surrounded by sick animals, among other precarious conditions. These preferences, however, were not determined by economic calculation, but must be seen as fodder for identity challenges and heroic tales that they would tell back at home (Newman 2001b; Kaur 1999).

In terms of social class, behavior and mentality, these travelers looked very much like the bohemian workers who seasonally stay in Ibiza (see Chapter 3), except that the former do not work in India. They also indulged in hedonist experiences, centered on parties, drugs and (to a lesser extent) sex. The low cost of living gave them an unusual purchasing power, although a penny-saving disposition soon prevailed in relation to any rupee overcharged by natives. Also similarly to their Ibiza counterparts, they held nationalistic preferences, reinforced by their gregariousness. But the continuous exposure to transcultural situations, involving an incredible variety of social types, could gradually loosen their ethnocentric certainties. In the opposite direction, they could begin to favor interactions with alien peoples, and even reject their compatriots for a while. As a result, a few of the travelers emulated centrifugal trajectories characteristically seen among expressive expatriates.

Finally, the core of the trance scene comprised a multinational populace of freaks, DJs, party promoters, Goan insiders and other expatriates, as exposed throughout this chapter. The local scene operated as a node interconnecting a multitude of mobile freaks in India and even globally. They shared information about travel experiences and typical itineraries, as well as about trance scenes in other parts of the world and incoming parties locally. In Goa, they often rode potent motorcycles, as the classical means of transportation across a regional circuit of trance parties which overflows Goa.

However, there were many expressive expatriates who, although closely related to trance freaks, favored a calmer ('shanti') and more bucolic lifestyle, away from the hedonistic excess. Many were involved with yoga, alternative therapies and New Age spiritualities, and did not want to beset notions of 'inner balance' and 'purity.' Others just enjoyed a simpler life centered on reading and thinking about one's life by a peaceful beach.

Elderly hippies eventually attended trance parties, enthusing about how the countercultural 'spirit' has remained or changed.

The trance scene broke down in a myriad of subgroups, whose logic of organization resembled clan formations. Affinities developed or faded upon differences in taste and exchanges of music and drugs, as well as sex and affection. Nationality has been the most basic criterion of organization, associated with stereotypical expectations, along with linguistic barriers, since English was spoken at various degrees of fluency. Israelis comprised the largest national group, followed by Japanese, British, Italians, Germans, Scandinavians, and a rapidly growing number of Russians. Stereotypical generalizations over national origin frequently derived from ordinary yet superficial interactions which constitute the contact zone, such as: 'Israelis are stubborn, troublemakers,' 'Indians behave like children,' 'German freaks are chaotic,' etc.

On the other hand, veteran freaks could interact in a more cosmopolitan fashion. In order to navigate the contact zone, they put aside or manipulated such stereotypical representations to their advantage, and established more genuine relationships with both natives and expatriates. It must be noted that national preferences, as some freaks aptly noted, were justified in pragmatic rather than ethnocentric terms:

> It is a question of language. When you get tired of speaking English, you join people of your country, with whom you have other things in common. But then you get tired of that too, and want to hang out with other people.

As a tentative generalization, it can be suggested that more adult expatriates with extensive traveling and countercultural experiences tended to be, at least pragmatically, more cosmopolitan than younger first-timers who traveled in compact groups.

Gender patterns were also imprinted on the trance scene. The most common group type comprised four to six people, apparently led by a male who makes decisions, exhibits scene knowledge, and dexterously prepares drugs for his companions. Alternatively, there were a smaller number of female groups, around four young women, who motorcycled to parties, socialized and protected each other against male intruders. Some of them had boyfriends who, nonetheless, stayed at hotel rooms due to chronic fatigue induced by drug abuse (heroin and hashish).

In terms of mating patterns, interethnic or international couples were common, though Indian women were rarely seen with foreign men. Strikingly resonating with Nora's observations about the 'curse' that Ibiza casts in separating stable couples upon arrival, the same phenomenon was apparent among foreign couples traveling in India. It was usually the woman who took the initiative for separation. She either joined a party 'sisterhood,' or sought a more individualized path, traveling alone or in the company of an erotic partner and guide, often a native man. In contrast with feminist studies claiming that women are passive objects of travel culture, the cases of female sannyasins, Techno freaks and backpackers in India indicate that women are playing a more active role in defining their own self and agency (Craik 1997). They instantiate the notion of *feminotopia*, understood as 'idealized worlds of female authority, empowerment, and pleasure,' as 'women travelers sought first and foremost to collect and possess themselves' (Pratt 1992: 160, 167).

Their decisions originate from situations of discomfort and inequality. They report dissatisfaction with their boyfriends, jobs and moralities in the homeland, as negative motivations that propel them to go to India. Yet, romance in the post-colonial setting is often marked by cultural, ethnic and economic differences, which, nonetheless, charge the erotogenic nature of the relationship. However, the situation of traveling expatriates in India corroborates studies of colonial travel and gender:

> Whether love turns out to be requited or not, whether the colonized lover is female or male, outcomes seem to be roughly the same: the lovers are separated, the European is reabsorbed by Europe, and the non-European dies an early death.
>
> (Pratt 1992: 97)

Similarly, a review on tourism and gender studies has noted that: 'Once back home, most women abandoned the tourist's desire to escape the usual disciplines and norms of everyday life by indulging in hedonism, fantasy and unrestrained sexual encounters during the course of a holiday' (Craik 1997: 132).

What the scholarship intersecting tourism and gender has missed, nonetheless, is that a residue of women and men will refuse to return to the same life conditions that await them in the metropole. As noted throughout this book, they reassess modern urban life negatively, as characterized by disciplinary and predictable routines that seem meaningless, and even more unappealing under the derailing effects of neo-liberal capitalism. As previous chapters indicate, after 'paradise' is experienced, an existential challenge must be confronted: either a return to the routines of conventional life, or a radical decision for trying the hopes of expressive cosmopolitanism. In this case, they will have to overcome the difficulties of a new life, until they are able to integrate their personal interests into alternative labor strategies. Whether or not resuming former life routines in a post-traditional world of uneasy conditions, 'we have no choice but to make choices' (Giddens 1994: 187).

Although participation in the trance scene was fluid and uncontrolled, a code of belonging clearly defined who was an insider and who was not. Through empirical observations, it is possible to identify the underlying premises that define belonging, as exposed next. In innumerable situations, I noticed freaks leaving the dance floor, somehow annoyed with the arrival of effusive teenagers and tourists, usually Indian males. It has been suggested that freaks are elitist and even racist (Saldanha 2004); nonetheless, such accusation misses the point. Although freaks often adhered to ethno-nationalist references, racism is not intrinsic to any ideological component of trance culture.

In fact, Indians occupy various positions in the scene, some of which are materially and symbolically privileged, varying from inside members, to material brokers, to romanticized icons, to annoying tourists and other outsiders. First, there are the local gangs of Goan youth who provide and control the party infrastructure. Some of them also enjoy trance music, and become active DJs. Second, the scene is also inhabited by diasporic Indians as trance insiders, locally and globally. As a good example, in addition to being regulars in the New York trance scene, Meena and Surya introduced me to some of their friends who were key DJs and promoters in the Goa scene. Curiously, they complained about university colleagues who came from Bangalore, but whom they identified as annoying outsiders. Third, besides *sari* ladies who provided the *chai* economy, Hindu renouncers (*sadhus*) rather pertained to a symbolic register that is constitutive of the countercultural opposition to civilization. With an exotic complexion, they introduced the *chillum* (cylindrical pipe) for hashish smoking and the hallucinogenic datura tea to hippies back in the 1960s. Despite the incommensurable gap between Western dropouts and Hindu *sadhus*, both nonetheless share an otherworldly orientation, cultivated not through intellectual speculation, but rather through the cultivation of ecstatic experiences involving drugs and meditation.

Finally, a note on the unique insertion of some socially marginalized subjects is elucidative. Jojo was regularly seen at trance bars and parties, dancing and also interacting in English and Hindi. Fit and young, he wore glasses, ragged clothes and torn flip-flops. Originally from northern India, he worked in menial jobs for food, some money and a sleeping place. He lived like a vagabond, with all his belongings in a blue bag. Free and dispossessed, his lifestyle seemed to fascinate young foreigners, including female teens, who interacted with him quite amicably. In the West, Jojo would most likely have been ostracized by the same travelers who otherwise admired him. In the trance scene, his apparently free and carefree condition was an interesting addition to the wildness of types inhabiting the psychedelic contact zone.

In conclusion, belonging in the trance scene is defined by the sharing of a countercultural problematic (or a relatively convincing performance of it). The usages and meanings that freaks confer to the practices of travel, dance and drugs differ significantly from those verified in conventional leisure sites associated with entertainment and tourism industries. To them, a trance party is not a merely recreational activity but rather entails a transgressive spirituality of the self. Countercultural belonging refers to a cultural space for the cultivation of forms of subjectivity and sociality that eschew the discipline of state, utility and reason. The hedonistic and effervescent nature of a trance party will be analyzed later in this chapter. Though it is important to note that national, ethnic and class references play a role in their ordinary interactions, they are not the defining features of such counter-hegemonic apparatus of subjectivity formation. The problematization of the self and sociality explains why freaks scorn tourists and authorities, regardless of nationality and race: outsiders ignore the nature of such countercultural experiments and meanings.

New Age in Goa: the 'circle of light'

Bojan told me about the 'circle of light,' a spiritual practice involving crystals and group meditation. These sessions took place at Pipi's house every Friday afternoon. When I arrived, several motorcycles were parked by her house, a spacious colonial house located a few kilometers from Anjuna village. About 30 people socialized at the backyard, all foreigners, with a slight majority of females, ages varying from twenties to fifties. Dozens of gems were symmetrically displayed around a large pink quartz, beside metal bowls and lit incenses.

Pipi and Luigi led the weekly event. She was an English–Australian expatriate residing in Goa, but periodically traveled to Australia, the UK or Brazil, in order to visit relatives or to trade gems, which she negotiated for decorative or healing purposes. Pipi was a veteran of the alternative world, jocosely known as 'Pipi of Woodstock,' due to the rock festival she attended in New York in 1969. In the early 2000s, she rarely attended trance parties. In her house there was a showroom displaying hundreds of gems and crystals, which she sold to wealthy tourists in the area of

Figure 5.4 Crystal healing practice in Goa.

Calangute beach. Yet she offered private crystal healing sessions free of charge to friends and acquaintances. While some senior expatriates in India lived on pensions and funds issued from their respective homeland, it was unclear if Pipi had other income sources.

Luigi was a young Italian expatriate on the global trance scene. In Bali he owned a workshop that produced party wear, which he exported to Goa, Israel, Italy and Brazil. He periodically visited these places, attending their respective trance scenes and staying at friends' houses, exemplifying how global nomads establish social networks that allow them to holistically integrate economic, leisure and personal interests.

His spiritual interests derived from a derailing experience with hallucinogenic drugs. In a radical episode under the effects of LSD, Luigi mystically said, 'My ego disappeared in the cosmos, and I met god. It was so strong that it took me five years to reconnect with reality.' I asked if it was a 'bad trip.' 'No, it was not a bad trip, but it changed my life completely.' He learned about the 'circle of light' a little after the episode, during a stay in Australia. He explained, 'The circle of light is a healing meditation created by trance people, by hippies: people outside the system who will bring about the New Age.' According to him and Pipi, there were several communities around the world that practiced the circle of light.

He admitted nonetheless that few people in the trance scene cultivated such ideals of love, peace and harmony. 'This is why we are doing this work, to bring more consciousness to more and more people.' Similarly to Jean and Bojan, Luigi indulged in fantastic explanations of the spiritual dimension to trance parties as an otherworldly phenomenon.

> When a trance party happens, it creates a vortex of energy that spirals up into the sky, attracting our alien brothers from the Pleiades, and they come to watch us. The better the party, the more energy it concentrates. When everybody is on acid, the vibration has a higher frequency, and this brings transformation!

It is worth noting that more than half of the participants who regularly attended Pipi's circle of light were also directly involved in the trance scene, spotted at parties and bars on an almost daily basis. Before the crystal healing began, some prepared hashish pipes, which were smoked and passed around always anti-clockwise (toward the right). Others just passed them along without smoking. For freaks, smoking is not merely a form of intoxication or socialization. As they explained, it could also be like a religious rite that allows the smoker to 'slow down the mind' and enable them to better connect with the spiritual work individually and as a group.

Luigi and Pipi began the session. In order 'to balance the flow of energy,' women and men sat interspersed outlining a large circle, centered on the quartz crystal formation. They often referred to the group as 'brothers and sisters,' and characterized the circle of light as 'a work of love, something that comes from the heart.' As interestingly, in all of the sessions I attended, they emphasized the multi-locale, globalized aspect of the healing practice, which not only was carried out by other various groups around the world, but also served to heal the planet. As such, the circle of light aimed at collective as well as personal healing. The pink crystal located at the center collected our love energies, retransmitting them toward the core of planet, from where it was redistributed to heal wherever it was most necessary.

With closed eyes and holding hands, the practice began with the group chanting the sound *om* for about five minutes. Everybody then lay down, pointing their heads toward the crystal display at the center. Pipi and a few assistants walked around, placing tiny stones over each person's body – notably, the forefront, the chest, and the lower abdomen – 'centers of energy.' Some people asked for extra stones on the lungs, since air pollution and chronic hashish smoking took a toll on their respiratory systems. Next, Luigi played the Tibetan bronze bowls, gently sliding a rubber stick on their borders. As people later recalled, the long reverberating sound had a deep relaxing effect. In the meanwhile, Pipi rose from the lotus position and slowly wandered around the group.[7] She would then stand in front of each person, making wide arm movements and stroking her hands, as if sending an invisible energy or fluid. After about 20 minutes, Pipi calmly instructed the group to 'slowly return to our bodies . . .' Her dogs were mostly silently messing around the group during the ritual. She brought tea and cookies, as the group resumed chatting, while placing used stones in wooden boxes, to be washed for 'purification.' New Age healers claim that such crystals absorb people's 'negative energies.' Participants marveled at how the crystals placed on their bodies became slightly darker after the session. The group then gradually left Pipi's backyard, as the sun descended.

Those who were involved in the trance scene would soon attend *Nine Bar*, a sunset trance bar, located at the hilltop of Vagator beach. As an open-air hangout, each day it hosted different trance DJs who played until 22:00 (the time was defined by a legal permit). *Nine Bar* evolved from a dark wooden shack into a hectic venue with elaborate Gothic-like decoration and a potent sound system. The crowd of some 250 people peaked at about 21:00. When *Nine Bar* closed, they dispersed for dinner and to arrange their drugs, later resuming their nocturnal pilgrimage. They would go to other trance bars or to a free party. The cultural logic that animates the trance scene is examined next.

Night Life: nomadic spirituality in psychedelic rituals

Daytime for freaks drags slowly in India. 'The so-called "hippies" do not lead an active life. [. . .] Life is slow. Some would call it dull' (Newman

2001b: 215). They get up late and spend their time indulgently: chatting, emailing, reading, smoking hashish and listening to trance music. Others calmly prepare their merchandise (handcraft, CDs, drugs, etc) that will be sold in hippie markets and parties, or posted to their bases in the West. In the afternoon, they may ride their motorcycles to watch the sunset at the beach: yet, 'to comment on the beauty is to be gauche, trite, and most definitely a newcomer. It is a near sacred moment' (ibid.). They will later gather in restaurants and trance bars, and it is at night that action actually begins.

What must be noted is that daytime dullness is a structuring counterpart of a lifestyle that is centered on night-time excitement. Both in its ordinary life and ritual dimensions, the Techno trance scene curiously instantiates a binary model that Durkheim formulated with regard to social life in primitive societies (Durkheim [1912]). According to him, individuals experience society at two complementary stages: the 'economic,' characterized as ordinary, mundane and tedious, and the 'religious,' characterized as extraordinary, sacred and effervescent. States of collective effervescence are more intense at night, as the individual's perceptions and reason more easily give way to ecstatic experiences (pp. 244–5). The following passage by Durkheim is revealing:

> Sometimes the population is broken up into little groups who wander about independently of one another, in their various occupations; [. . .]. The dispersed condition in which the society finds itself results in making its life uniform, languishing and dull. But when a corrobbori[8] takes place, everything changes. [. . .] Once they come together, a sort of electricity is formed by their gathering, which quickly transports them to an extraordinary degree of exaltation. [. . .] The initial impulse thus proceeds, growing as it goes, as an avalanche grows in advance. [. . .] If we add to all this that the ceremonies generally take place at night in a darkness pierced here and there by the light of fires, we can easily imagine what effect such scenes ought to produce on the minds of those who participate. [. . .] Feeling himself dominated and carried away by some sort of an external power which makes him think and act differently than in normal times, he naturally has the impression of being himself no longer. [. . .] Everything is just as though he really were transported into a special world, entirely different from the one where he ordinarily lives, and into an environment filled with exceptionally intense forces that take hold of him and metamorphose him. How could such experiences as these, especially when they are repeated every day for weeks, fail to leave in him the conviction that there really exist two heterogeneous and mutually incomparable worlds? One is that where his daily life drags wearily along; but he cannot penetrate into the other without at once entering into relations with extraordinary powers that excite him to

the point of frenzy. The first is the profane world, the second, that of sacred things. So it is in the midst of these effervescent social environments and out of this effervescence itself that the religious idea seems to be born.

(Durkheim [1912]: 245–7)

This passage could well describe the social and ritual life in the Goa trance scene.[9] Also interesting is the fact that, as Durkheim focused on primitive societies, freaks evoke notions of 'tribe' and 'shamanism' to refer to their collective events. As a trance DJ once noted, 'It is like a tribal gathering with ten thousand drummers banging all night long – it is maddening.' More generally, primitive religion has been translated into Techno and New Age pastiche forms, by which freaks and neo-pagans intend to 'revive the tribal' through 'shamanic rituals,' as a way of redeeming the 'lost essence' of being human, originally integrated with community life, nature and mystery. However, the search for an original moment before interdiction is ontologically impossible, for the subject and her desire are a product of the very civilizational regimes that she seeks to overcome. The primal interdiction instituted the logocentric reason that irreversibly fabricates the atomized subject and her desire for reunion.

In order to understand the nature of countercultural categories, this section examines ritualized practices of the trance scene – notably, style as performance, and parties as rituals – observed in Goa, yet crosschecked with Ibiza and elsewhere. More specifically, it seeks to evince how the duality 'profane-sacred' plays itself at the level of subjectivity, as reported in experiential reports that derive from the subjects' engagements with such digital rituals. This binary defines the daily cycle through which the self is shattered during the night and reconstituted during the day. The trance party is therefore analyzed as a ritual assemblage that dramatizes tensions and categories that constitute global countercultures in relation to wider contexts. In substantive terms, this ritual expresses dilemmas of mobility and marginality that mark the position of trance freaks and expressive expatriates in highly globalized environments. In this analysis of style and ritual, I identify a 'nomadic spirituality' that operates as a powerful category – both existential and analytical – that informs and dramatizes the impact of globalization upon the self, as theorized in Chapter 1.

Mobility and expression

They ride potent motorcycles down the narrow roads of the Goan countryside. These are one-lane roads closely framed by palm trees, and dangerously shared by reckless trucks, buses and stray animals. The rustic Bullet Enfield is the favorite machine in the scene, with its ominous bar protecting

Figure 5.5 Techno bike Amazon.

the biker's legs. Easily available for rent, many regulars prefer to buy it (from Rs. 20,000 to Rs. 150,000 or about US$500 to US$3,000) and keep it in some mechanic's yard when they travel overseas. According to freaks, to drive an Enfield on Indian roads is a liberating experience, as the sensorial stimulation of open mobility disrupts ordinary notions of time and space. The smooth swinging, the monotonous droning, the slapping breeze, the blurred environs of green, the coiling side lanes, are all stimuli that trace a deterritorializing escape-line, corresponding to mild states of mind alteration, particularly during the after-effects of a narcotic episode, enhancing the hypnotic effects of open mobility, silent euphoria and transcendence. The Enfield, in sum, embodies the power of technology to erase the ego, not as much as in the case of a fatal accident, but rather in rejecting 'subjection' to criteria of discipline, utility and control.

Mobile technologies contain the potential for new gender forms, as female freaks dexterously ride such superbikes. Their facial expressions are serious, aggravated by dark sunglasses and the semi-military fashion, configuring a veritable Techno Amazon. Studies have noted that women tend to embody more explicitly the identity traits of a subcultural style (Pini 2001; McRobbie 1994b). To wit, their clothing is functional yet intimidating: tank tops, boots and GI trousers under multi-pocket skirts. Dreadlocks, Mohawks and cornrow hairstyles symbolize the spirit of resistance against the white men's civilization. In long and intense – 'wild' – parties, some freaks paint warrior-like traces on their skin, fashioning themselves as *psychedelic guerillas*. Bodies, too, portray subcultural meaning. While fit, young and fashion-conscious, freak women often expose a dissonant abdominal fat. Even though their work and dance activities may account for body asymmetries, in reality this fat rather opposes the aesthetic valuation of the apollonian body which is epitomized in the hypertrophied muscle, strong yet *subordinate* to the will of reason.

Trance parties occur in secluded open-air areas: against a cliff or a hilltop facing the ocean, or in the woods. Music starts after midnight, most people arriving around 2:00, with more hardcore freaks gradually arriving by sunrise. It extends into daytime and often carries on for a few days uninterruptedly. The end is unknown even for promoters, as the machinic event unravels contingent to multiple factors, such as the possibility of police raids, the endurance of the crowd and equipment, as well as on-site negotiations among promoters, suppliers and brokers. The event is announced by word-of-mouth a few days before, but the exact location is only disclosed when the venue is finally ready, at the last minute. This measure seeks to evade outsiders, while building up excitement in the party crowd. Nonetheless, some backpackers and tourists will invariably show up, particularly at the beginning. More generally, secrecy is only tacitly performed, since villagers and even police authorities know of its location, as the scene knows that informal agreements involving fiduciary advantage are inevitable in Goa.

Looking for the venue, the digital stomping is the first signal of proximity. Next, a sea of motorcycles can be seen parked on irregular terrain. At a closer look, a compact crowd bounces within an audio-visual apparatus that includes a thundering sound system, dark lights, psychedelic drapes and banners. The party crowd subdivides in a myriad of groups and types: mostly freaks, but also backpackers, *chai* ladies, taxi-bikers, village children and a few tourists. A *sadhu* may eventually show up, begging for money or smoking hashish with veteran freaks. The general picture is orientalist, hi-tech and tribal.

Many smoke a blend of hashish and tobacco, either in hand-rolled cigarettes or from a cylindrical ceramic pipe (*chillum*). In small groups, the smoker crouches, holds the *chillum* upward and inhales the smoke, while someone stands in front with a lighter on. Curiously, while such duo position visually connotes oral sex, *sadhus* refer to the *chillum* as the *Shiva lingam* – the phallus of god. By sucking god's penis, the dizzying and mind-splitting effects of hashish indicate that the smoker has 'got in touch with Shankar Shiva.' While passing the pipe around, the smoker utters (gagging, or holding the breath as much as possible): '*bom Shiva*,' '*bom Shankar*,' or '*bom!*' – a hail to Shankar, the 'stoned Shiva.' As *sadhus* have taught, the pipe is always passed anti-clockwise. The person grabs it with the right hand or otherwise raises the object to the forehead as a purification rite. The smoker exhales an impressively thick white cloud and silently gets up. No comments about faintness are allowed, as the smoker has to be strong: in times of global neo-liberal predation, the Techno freak must be tough like a nomadic warrior.

In this spirit, public demonstrations of affection are virtually absent. There is no touching, hugging, holding hands or kissing in the scene.

Visual forms of communication (eye contact, flirtation or smile) are limited, although bursts of laughter eventually mark an animated conversation. In the private sphere, the ascetic ethos is slightly relaxed, but as a young expatriate observed, 'I go to their houses and ask myself if they are really couples . . .' Insiders dismiss these notes, claiming that there are flirtatious and erotic exchanges amid freaks, albeit very discreetly – '*like in the army*,' Surya noted. Even so, despite the abundant display of flesh, the prevailing attitude is never flirtatious or provocative, but rather quite asexual. As we will see, dance is never interactive or seductive. In fact, some freaks noted that drug abuse and poor diets hampered their libidinal drives, particularly in the hot weather. And AIDS has certainly played a restrictive role, more generally. However, other Techno subcultures, such as club and rave, have displayed a quite different, if not opposite, affective-sexual ethos (D'Andrea 2005, see Chapter 3; Collin 1997). These differences suggest that slight but consistent differences in musical genre and drug abuse, along with local conditions of state surveillance and spatiality, translate into sharper differences in terms of subcultural ideology and disposition (see differences among freaks, hippies, bohemian workers and underground clubbers described in this book).

However, such toughness and asexuality do not mean that a body politics is absent from the trance scene. Temporarily removed from the tight surveillance controls that dominate in metropolitan societies, these traveling subjects can gather in a community of hedonistic spirituality. The trance party is a ritual practice in which power and reason are confronted through the limit-experience of 'trancing' ('raving'). Rather than merely performing resistance against the system (as subcultural studies have proposed and been criticized for), the effects of digital rituals upon the self must be properly scrutinized for its implications in the analysis of cultural globalization.

The Techno trance assemblage: aesthetics of power and limit-experience

Because the forging of the self is actualized at the experiential level, the analysis of subjectivity formation must consider experiences which are enacted in sacralizing rituals. As a dramatic instance, a limit-experience evinces the possible ways by which the body, power and identity intersect at the realm of traumatic or sublime. It transgresses the boundaries of coherent subjectivity, 'tearing the subject from itself' at the limit of living, intensity and impossibility (Jay 1993; Foucault 1978). Yet, in a second stage, recollection is necessary in a space outside: 'an experience is, of course, something one has alone; but it cannot have its full impact unless the individual manages to escape from pure subjectivity in a way that others can at least cross paths with or retrace it' (Foucault 1978: 40).

Figure 5.6 A trance party near Anjuna beach. Overnight events extend into morning time and are often uninterrupted for a few days.

The sharing of such events creates bonds of solidarity among individuals and allows them to make sense of their lives in the encompassing world.

Limit-experiences are often induced by means of altering devices, understood in Weberian terms as 'intoxicating elements of orgiastic sensuality': music, dance, drugs and touch, among other techniques (Weber 1913). Non-ordinary ways of perceiving reality thus entailed can be disruptive of identities at multiple levels. At a political level, the phenomenological retooling may result in a situation in which the dominant authority loses its legitimacy to control subjective and collective bodies. However, as it is impossible to eradicate such transgressive practices absolutely, they become marginalized in a process that reinforces exclusionary moralities. The ritual exploration of limit-experiences is then confined to secret societies, as the trance scene illustrates.

Trance parties have been designed to engender a magic aura that remits participants into a cosmic temporality. Some events are scheduled to happen at auspicious moments connected to astronomical events, such as a full moon, an eclipse or a seasonal equinox. The audio-visual paraphernalia is spatially displayed with the aim of disorienting sensorial perceptions – dark and loud, with unusual lighting and smoke (Corsten 1998a). UV lights produce a phantasmagoric glow on white clothes, eyes and teeth, and intensify the effects of kaleidoscopic drapes featuring oriental and extraterrestrial landscapes. Blasting at high volume, the music is complex yet repetitive. Its bass waves reverberate upon the skin and through the body mass, giving the impression of molecular dissolution. People dance in the crowd but individually, facing the DJ deck located between loudspeaker turrets. The DJ silently ('telepathically') interacts with the crowd by means of musical buildups and plateaus of intensity.

On the table, typical belongings of a trance DJ can be seen: lit incense, oriental statuettes, cases of CDs and DAT tapes, and music catalogues (listing track titles, beats-per-minute (BPM) speed and idiosyncratic marks).

The crowd spontaneously alternates between dancing and watching (or smoking). Hundreds of bodies bounce in synchrony with relentless digital beats. Body movements are structured on a monotonous two-step march on the spot, matching the music at its strongest rhythm, whereas arms hang loose. This footstep performs and reflects physical tiredness and mind alteration, as a result of the long hours of dance and drug abuse. With the morning light, uncanny eye movements are noticed: zigzagging according to the music beats, with breaks matching the body (at about twice per second). The eye-stare is regressive, primitive, almost animal. New Agers too report metamorphic experiences of becoming a bird or reptile, particularly in neo-shamanic sites involving the ceremonial ingestion of a hallucinogenic sacrament. Rave and New Age shamanism are radical instances of the conceptualization of a postidentitarian self known as 'becoming animal' (Deleuze and Guattari 1980).

The trance party unravels as a dynamic machine that gradually absorbs the dancers, by making them feel as members of a pulsating organism. The dance event is 'not a mere context, but the text itself, the primary unit of observation and analysis' (Ronstrom 1999: 136). Such assemblages of bodies–technologies–ideology then fully unleash the ecstatic experience of 'trancing' (also known as 'raving'). Marked by an excess that is ungraspable in logocentric reason, raving correlates with a collective state of transpersonalism, which dramatizes the impact of hypermobility and digitalization upon the subject (Jameson 1991).

Technology and multimedia art are thus hybridized in a proto-religion (Corsten 1998a; Reynolds 1998), in which the DJ plays the role of a *digital shaman*, responsible for creating and maintaining a collective state of ecstatic communion. Rather unconsciously, the DJ emulates traditional shamanic techniques, improvising on a sequence of music tracks which follow a seamless beat-matching pattern. The queuing of chosen tracks is decided on the spot, as the DJ tries to intuit and influence the reactions of both dancing and standing crowds. By 'taking the crowd in a journey,' the DJ seeks to engender an atmosphere in which ordinary notions of time, space and self are dissolved. The crowd thus indulges in abandon and togetherness, and the event becomes a seemingly timeless experience, a 'temporary autonomous zone' (Bey 1991) magically disconnected from mundane reality. The DJ functions, in sum, as a witch doctor, managing magic in order to heal spirits and control events (Mauss 1904). Ravers report experiences of self-transcendence and redemption triggered in such orgiastic gatherings. In other words, and paraphrasing Foucault's account on knowledge regimes of the body (1976), the DJ operates like a master of *ars erotica*, prolonging pleasures within a crowd that understands itself as a fellowship of initiates.

To that end, Techno trance music is spiral or rather fractal. Its composition is complexly multi-rhythmic, featuring the introduction and removal of variations of sound, with loops and breakdowns, establishing itself in a chromatic process of continuous variation (Deleuze and Guattari 1980). The genre often displays epic refrains, including samples of orchestral music (Romantic, Baroque) or ethnic instruments (didgeridoo, sitars), as well as speech fragments of religious and scientific figures (Timothy Leary, Martin Luther King, sadhus, neuroscientists, etc). Onomatopoeic sounds are identified as 'spiritual,' 'plastic' or 'supernatural.' While 'lacking in sensuality,' trance has been described as 'New Age music with metronomic pulse-beat' (Reynolds 1998: 176).

Trance music literally embodies the ethnomusicological notion of 'structured sounds.' By persistently listening to the endless pounding, listeners report no longer to hear music, but a meta-music of absurd sounds. *Chai* ladies, taxi drivers and other outsiders refer to Techno trance as 'crazy music' that only 'crazy people' can appreciate. In fact, music producers of Techno, ambient or New Age genres seek to engineer tracks that not only mimic but also trigger altered mental states, thus configuring a 'science of psychedelic sounds' (Reynolds 1998) whose effects seem to be greatly amplified when combined with drugs or body techniques, such as massage and meditation. As such, outsiders claim that electronic dance music can only be appreciated under the influence of drugs. Based on a comparison of multiple reports, it seems that, even though trance freaks can enjoy the music with no recourse to drugs, someone unfamiliar with hallucinogens not only takes longer to appreciate Techno trance, but is usually unable to perceive certain nuances of sound tapestry. Upon trying drugs, the newcomer reports that they are able to notice minor variations of sound, more richly and creatively.

Raving is inflected not only by subcultural inclinations and musicological effects, but also by the type of consumed drug, which impinges a specific pharmacological mark on the experience. The hallucinogenic experience (with LSD or ketamine) takes the form of a *psychedelic asceticism*, characterized by mental states of hyper imagination and mystical transcendence. Differently, the entactogenic 'ecstasy' (MDMA) engenders an *oceanic eroticism*, sensed as orgasmic sensations and overflowing immanence. In both cases, there is an overwhelming sensation that the individual is merging into the crowd, in a process of de-subjectification (deterritorializing asignification), involving potential rewards and dangers – sacred madness. Whether or not drugs are necessary, participants tend to agree that the basic intoxicant is the music, which overtakes the subject and makes it dance.

A good track is described as 'very powerful' as it 'takes you on a journey,' usually referring to compositions that feature a more violent, fast and complex rhythmic structure topped by a visceral refrain. Similarly, a memorable party is often depicted as 'full power' and it 'blows your mind.'

The raving experience is similarly described as a 'deep trip' in which you 'lose your mind.' Not by coincidence, DJs define their task as being 'to take the crowd on a journey.' In consonance with the mobility motive, a 'nice trip' is wished to someone ingesting a hallucinogen. 'Spaceships' and 'intergalactic voyages' are trivial metaphors of the psychedelic 'journey' into transpersonal dimensions, whereas the word hallucinogen is rooted in the Ancient Greek *alyein*, which means, 'to wander,' referring to the distracted gaze of trancing shamans. All of these examples are symptomatic of non-ordinary experiences of the self, integrating power and mobility into musical representations of affective, visceral effect.

Techno therefore relates to power, both as an intrinsic quality of the music, and as a device that shatters the self. Because of its aesthetic, cultural and psychological connections with the force of power, Techno instantiates Deleuze's conceptualization of contemporary art, as 'not a question of reproducing or inventing forms, but of *harnessing forces*' (Deleuze, in Bogue 1996: 257). Accordingly, electronic music sets forth a 'physics of affection' that unravels upon nature and force, favoring a logic of sensation over perception. As such, rather than linear, narrative and verbally demarcated, Techno art is rather recursive, immanent and deterritorializing.

The rave assemblage thus both expresses and entails the struggle between power and form that tears the raving subject apart. By decoding the subject, the rave assemblage transforms the dance floor into a field of *psychic zones*. The dancer then senses the struggle: chaotic forces that seek to break loose through the spiraling refrain, while the shifting structure of rhythms hold the system together. This symphony of systolic-diastolic forces thus traces a line of flight that remits the self in variable directions. As intensity sets in, iterable sounds transform Techno into a meta-music that derails one's perception and understanding of oneself, its body, time and reality. Sensoriality is the first region of the self to be affected: vision alters, hearing enhances, skin sensitizes. Ordinary reason is then distorted with the relativization of one's mental and affective references, in a surge of insights and memories that saturate and implode ordinary reason. The bounded ego collapses. Sounds and lights acquire tangible textures, engulfing the dancer in the protective space of a cosmic womb, entailing self-transcendence, ecstatic epiphany and pleasurable death. Raving is an experience in which the dancer becomes the dance. It is orgiastic and ascetic, private and collective, inside and outside – it is a dismantling organism, a Body without Organs.

Within such economies of excess, a trance party never climaxes but remains looping and spiraling in plateaus of intensity (Deleuze and Guattari 1980). The iterability (repetition-cum-difference) of Techno also expresses the neurotic short circuit that clashes boredom and excitement, reconfigured in chromatic aesthetic forms. A good DJ operates on intensity and retention, building up orgasmic tension and seldom releasing it. A rave party must remain at the edge of experimentation: the Body without Organs of Techno, unfolding as a nomadic desiring-machine, setting the lines of flight that move towards and through the realm of personal transcendence at the extraordinary.

The impact of this limit-experience on ordinary life and self-identity cannot be underestimated. It is not that raving triggers an affection that vanishes itself, but rather that an overwhelming emotion shatters personal references, challenging coherent being not only during but also after the experience. As participants often report, this is a limit-experience that can unravel either as a spiritual epiphany or mental illness (Airault 2000; Foucault 1978). This is why trance parties are enveloped in an aura of sacredness, referring to tacit rules of behavior and reverence that seek to protect the subject from the destructive potential of raving. This in part explains why freaks are protective of their events against outsiders.

By examining trance ritual and style, I detected a 'nomadic spirituality' as a core category that intersects global and countercultural processes both empirically and analytically. On one level, it refers to the cultivation of alternative experiences of the self, as a crucial element in the formation of a counter-hegemonic apparatus that eschews the market, state, science and morality. At another level, it refers to the cultural predicament of globalization which transforms self-identities reflexively (Giddens 1991). As such, Techno tribalism should not be seen as revivals of pre-modern life, since social complexity and atomic individuality render the retrieval of an original self as naive and farcical. Quite differently, Techno tribalism provides ritual grounds for a meaningful narrative that accounts for the rise of hypermobile lifestyles, as instantiated by trance freaks. The collective effervescence that characterizes these global countercultural rituals must be considered within these parameters: through the group – as a necessary condition – but because of the subject (Heelas 1996; Maffesoli 1988).

Psychic deterritorialization: madness in India

Trance parties are just one instance, even if a highly dramatic one, of 'nomadic spirituality.' In circumstances with no relation to drug experiences, other Western travelers develop unusual idiosyncratic traits. Intense meditation and therapy practices in spiritual centers also contribute to shake their cognitive and affective structures (Chapter 4). Conversely, charter tourists remain immune, not only because of the shortness and artificiality of their stay in India, but also because of their leisure interests, not at all aimed at challenging their self-identities beyond the ethylic binge by the sun. In considering the case of distressed travelers in India, the point is to address how travel experiences, under specific meaning orientations, undermine ethno-nationalist premises, existential certainties and even the mental capabilities of Western subjects moving across exotic lands, particularly India.

This phenomenon, which I term 'psychic deterritorialization,' has fluctuated through history. Ian Hacking refers to specific arrangements of cultural expectations, medical taxonomies and institutional controls as 'cultural niches' that precipitate the emergence and disappearance of specific forms of mental illness (Hacking 1998). As such, in modern history, the first appearance of 'travel madness' in the eyes of public authorities occurred in late nineteenth-century France, where it was diagnosed as a psychiatric condition named 'dromomania': an irresistible compulsion to move long distances, triggered by migraine seizures, amnesia and kleptomania. Quite curiously, Hacking notes that most dromomaniacs were lower middle-class men, citizens under structured conditions who were neither too poor to wander freely like tramps, nor resourceful enough to afford a grand tour like the bourgeois. Roughly put, in order to travel they had to disrupt social and psychic structures. More widely, Hacking considers its emergence in genealogical terms, as an unintended consequence of a context characterized by state surveillance, the glamorization of tourism, medical theory debates, and the advent of the bicycle as a fascinating artifact of privatized mobility. Hacking notes that, due to changes in scientific models (resulting from medical feuds rather than from epistemological gains), dromomania virtually disappeared as a medical category and, mysteriously, as an empirical phenomenon.

However, such disappearance refers to invisibility and inattention, and not to inexistence. Quite to the contrary, I maintain that mobility remains as a force that potentially derails self-identities. Studies on counterculture and consular medicine corroborate my fieldwork: psychic deterritorialization can occur through practices of hypermobility, and, I argue, increasingly so in the rise of globalization processes. The last and most visible wave of self-derailing travel in recent history refers to the hippie invasion of India in the early 1970s:

> The diplomat had calculated that of the quarter of million French people on the Indian subcontinent, a good eighty percent were in pursuit of mind expansion or obscure salvation. [. . .] Considering the difficulties of remaining intact in Asia, most embassies have [. . .] allotted doctors or psychiatrists, often both, whose only function is to deal with the casualities of the great pilgrimage.
>
> (Mehta 1990 [1979]: 21)

While countercultures have explicitly engaged with travel experimentation, it must be now considered under the impact of globalization as an aggravating factor, since the acceleration of flows of peoples and images has taken an unprecedented scale. As a general hypothesis, under growing conditions of globalization marked by processes of hypermobility, digitalization and multiculturalism, the phenomenon of psychic deterritorialization will become more socially pervasive, variously affecting other segments that become exposed to such global pressures. In this light, the study of Western travelers in India provides an interesting case upon which to examine the interrelations between mobility and subjectivity, particularly as it occurs within the larger streams of globalization.

Upon arrival in India, a few travelers may keep their passports at consulates. While being a measure of precaution, metaphorically it denotes that they are leaving their 'identities' behind (Airault 2000). As a psychiatrist based in the consulate of France in Mumbai during the early 1990s, Regis Airault cared about the mental health of consular workers, and in more urgent cases would rescue and even repatriate long-haul travelers who became mentally ill in the country. The surprising number of cases he treated led him to document such phenomenon in the book *Fous de l'Inde: Delires d'Occidentaux et Sentiment Oceanique* (Airault 2000). It is worth noting that most of the cases he refers to took place in Goa and Pune. According to him, India acts as an amplifier of minor idiosyncratic symptoms (p. 53), which may escalate to mentally dysfunctional levels. A colleague even asks: '*L'Inde rend-elles fou, ou les fous vont-ils en Inde?*' ('Is it India that makes them crazy, or is it that crazy people come to India?' p. 13).

Before critically examining his interpretive model, it is important to identify the relations of causality between travel and mental illness. Airault affirms that the orientalist trip can be either 'pathological' or 'pathogenic.' A trip is pathological when traveling is motivated by a 'delusional idea' that occurs at home, an emotional stress that stems from life hardships (often a separation or chronic sub/unemployment). In a few cases, there is some previous connection to drug abuse or psychiatric proclivities (such as paranoia or manic depression). In any of these cases, it is a discomfort with external or psychological situations that motivates the subject to travel. In contrast, the 'pathogenic trip' results from the very impact of mobility upon the self, particularly in exotic lands:

> The trip itself is the cause of an acute psychic unbalance in people thus far 'normal' (with a relative psychic balance): their perturbation emerges during their displacements across India. In this case, traveling triggers a crisis that is marked by the general failure of the mental regulation of the traveler.
>
> (Airault 2000: 25)

My empirical research corroborates his claim that only a few travelers derail completely; most of them go through 'a minor vacillation of identity,' which only temporarily weakens their personal certainties (Airault 2000: 52). Over the course of weeks following the initial shock (as summarized in Chapter 4), the traveler gradually develops some unusual behavioral traits, which tend to be either euphoric or anxious and melancholic. They may report insightful experiences during meditation, while others even suggest that they have found some sort of 'spiritual enlightenment.' A few travelers may refuse Westerners and 'go native,' usually ignorant of local languages, cultural codes and power relations (Mehta 1990). Rather than a relaxing vacation, others manifest persistent anxiety, which may escalate to panic attacks. In more dramatic cases, it may involve a mild nervous breakdown or a mental collapse. Such difficulties are more pronounced in first-time travelers from a highly structured, middle-class background.

Veteran travelers, nevertheless, seem to have become immune to such crises, though they also recall embarrassing episodes from former trips. They gradually gain a familiarity with native peoples and local expatriates with whom they develop stable relationships, often associated with economic agreements or spiritual learning. At least, they have been able to adapt their own 'dysfunctional' idiosyncrasies as a lifestyle that is accepted by other expatriates and amused natives. In this connection, these veteran travelers say that going to India feels like 'returning home' (Begrich and Muehlebach 1998) or 'returning to the mother's womb' (Airault 2000: 57):

> The Indian experience invites for an exploration of origins. It triggers the most archaic dimension of our thought, which is the source of the process of symbolization. It activates our buried relation with our parents, resonating a sense of harmony as well as of ancient anxiety: phantasms of corrosion, separation and annihilation. In India you become nothing, or almost that.
>
> (Airault 2000: 57)

However, it is not any trip that entails a crisis of subjectivity. Airault somehow agrees with a colleague who claimed that 'India can make you crazy' (p. 25); nevertheless, he remarks that this phenomenon similarly occurs in other places and to other peoples (such as Japanese youth in Paris, or Christian tourists in Israel). Expatriates recently arrived in Ibiza may develop such incoherent traits, likely due to an imaginary of freedom that connects the person to the island in a carefree fashion. It thus seems that specific places hold a 'mythic power' that unleashes certain emotional-semiotic reactions which can overwhelm the self. In other words, the 'pathogenic travel' does not happen at random:

> These unbalances do not simply derive from climate, mystical environ and drugs, but to the fact that our reality depends on the symbolic universe that determines us and on the phantasms[10] that animates us. If we are exposed to a different universe for a long time, our reality is undone and is replaced by the country that occupies a mythic position in relation to the homeland.
>
> (Airault 2000: 101)

Although insightful and empirically grounded, the analytical model set forth by Airault stumbles on three critical issues: orientalism, globalization and biopower. First, while describing how exotic myths transform the traveler's psyche, Airault projects and reifies Western representations that romanticize India as 'timeless,' 'adolescent,' 'motherly' and 'death-wise.' The author thus feeds an imaginary whose self-derailing effects he seeks to dispel as a consular doctor. Second, the study does not consider how processes of globalization may be directly affecting identity and subjectivity forms (Povinelli and Chauncey 1999; Giddens 1991). Finally, Airault ignores the deeper imbrications of his position as a consular psychiatrist in relation to Techno and New Age formations in India. While countercultures question the institutional foundations of mental illness in advanced societies, Airault dismisses these counter-hegemonic experiments as 'delusional' and 'immature,' stuck in the enjoyment of an eternal present. As such, from a critical perspective, by medicalizing the modern subject, the doctor ends up reinforcing the institutional-ideological regimes that engender 'mental disease.' The consular psychiatrist is a *sui generis* incarnation of the biopower of state and science which produces the centrifugal traveler that Airault will paradoxically rescue and 'bring back to reality.'

Having explicated the exclusionary modes of consular psychiatry, the fact remains that Western travelers in their quest for authenticity in exotic lands will vacillate, derail and collapse – in a word, deterritorialize. In the previous section, I employed the Deleuzian view on modern aesthetics in order to address the subjective effects of the rave assemblage in patterns that I have termed 'nomadic spirituality.' We must now consider psychiatric categorizations as a way of evincing the nature of psychic deterritorialization.

As the journey extends, the subject may start to question the veracity of perceived aspects of reality, its 'suchness,' and whether or not it is being properly interpreted by the self. Known as 'derealization,' this mental process is typically expressed in thoughts such as, 'That is surreal. It seems that what I am seeing is not quite real. Is that really happening or is it just my imagination?' The intensity of unstructured interactions in exotic environments, as well as the prolonged exposure to psychedelic parties, cathartic therapies or meditation marathons may combine in ways that engender sensations of strangeness as an experience of detachment from the external world. Yet, derealization is a mild aspect of the neurotic, if compared with the more sinister possibility of the paranoid:

> As the journey extends for various weeks, the traveler may be caught up in an insidious feeling of depersonalization. A part of oneself has become strange, and seems to have been absorbed by 'Mother India.' It is no longer a shock, but a progressive subsiding of our mental skills. Very different from ours, the symbolic universe where we immerse in India undermines the foundations of our identity and

completely disrupts our references. Slowly, we sink in the pitfalls of a profound existential doubt over our role in this world and our views of life and death.

(Airault 2000: 77)

Beyond derealization, the traveler now suffers its own depersonalization. The self is no longer an entity unconsciously taken for granted, and even the body is oddly perceived, immersed in a state of hyperreality. Natural lights seem to shine differently and the appearance of things acquires a dreamy overtone. Within oneself, unusual questions arise, such as 'Am I here because I want, or did something (or someone) conspire to bring me here?'; 'I don't recognize my thoughts as mine. It feels like I am not really myself'; or 'My body feels strange. I am losing touch with myself.' Untrammeled reflexivity thus undermines one's sense of identity and time linearity, necessarily affecting the ability to monitor ordinary agency in daily life. This loss of 'ontological security' is coupled with a rise in existential anxiety (Giddens 1991). The resulting behavior has been noted throughout this book: the subject develops mystical or paranoid dispositions; they may become excessively expansive, talkative or reckless. In tandem, basic routines such as sleeping, eating and hygiene can be severely disturbed. Quite curiously, if India amplifies symptoms of derailment, it also tolerates the eccentricity of foreign travelers as somehow amusing (Mehta 1990).

But deterritorialization cannot persist for too long, or the free lines of flight may turn into the destructive lines of death (Deleuze and Guattari 1980: 423). The derailed traveler thus tends to regain their contact with the external world known as 'reality.' In most cases, psychic deterritorialization is mild or episodic, and the subject regains the ordinary faculties while still in India. A few others, however, will plunge into deeper chaos, requiring the intervention of friends and natives, and in the last instance, of a consular agent. In the worst circumstance, the traveler is flown back to their homeland. Curiously, as they lose their 'identities,' passports also disappear in about half of the cases (Airault 2000: 186).

Repatriation is more than a consular procedure; it is also a healing process. As an institutional and symbolic incarnation of the state, the consular agent 'accompanies the traveler in their inner journey [. . .] reintroducing references within a perspective of return and temporality' (Airault 2000: 184–5). At home, the patient dramatically improves as if returning from a 'malaria of the soul' – hospitalization becomes unnecessary. Mental faculties are regained, emotional pain subsides and ordinary life is normally resumed. The traveler recalls this experience of self-derailment as a positive memory rather than a personal failure. Nonetheless, Airault notes that about a fourth of these repatriated subjects will 'relapse.' As he puts it, 'India is a toxicogenic that operates like a veritable drug, creating psychic and physical dependence' (p. 190).

However, Airault does not consider those travelers who developed psychological distress *after* the trip. In this case, rather than an effect of unstructured freedom, psychic deterritorialization stems from a refusal to continue one's life coping with conventional life schemes: boredom, meaninglessness, predictability and stress. Many will force themselves to adapt to prior life conditions, often recurring to compensatory mechanisms, such as addiction, self-medication, consumerism, biographic efforts, etc. Others fail reintegration not only due to psychic conditions but to biopower imperatives: without education, documents, references or discipline, they are unable to find an economic insertion or institutional tutelage. A few others, however, will seek to develop a lifestyle that more closely relates to such experiences of liberation, pleasure and expressivity. In some cases, they may move to a semi-peripheral region or country, and start a new career, usually more 'alternative,' based on more expressive and autonomous values. They will become either bohemian workers or expressive expatriates. In response to Airault's metaphors about the toxicology of India and the immaturity of countercultures, global nomads would say that India is not the drug but rather the medicine for the soul.

Conclusion: nomadic spirituality and smooth spaces

The trance scene quickly fades in April, in face of the impending monsoon season. Most freaks return to Israel, Japan or Europe (including Ibiza). Others move on to the Himalayan foothills, Nepal, Thailand and Indonesia (Bali). In the West, they either resume conventional jobs in farms, factories, hotels, pubs and travel agencies, or carry on as hippie traders, handcrafters, artists, yoga teachers, therapists or drug dealers. They may renew their six-month passport visas in order to return to India in the following season. In the Indian Himalayas, the villages of the Parvati valley accommodate the Techno trance scene in the mountains. It is mostly attended by Israeli youth, many of whom have been recently dismissed from the military service. A few dozen freaks remain in northern Goa, relaxing in more intimate parties. Within these spatiotemporal gates and routes, 'the nomad does not move' (Deleuze and Guattari, 1980: 381): they are permanently trying to keep the smooth space of creativity and experimentation.

As seen, the trance scene is an object of diverging interests and meanings. For villagers and corrupt authorities, it is a basic source of income. In their turn, foreign tourists consume trance parties as innocuous leisure, while domestic Indian tourists see it as an amazing way to have a taste of the West in their own country. For backpackers, trance parties constitute an exciting way of forgetting existential dilemmas from the homeland. And at last, for freaks, a trance party is a quasi-sacred ritual enmeshing spirituality, technology and political claims against and beyond modernity. In this sense, Techno trance simultaneously resists and expresses tensions and the possibilities of global capitalism at the turn of the millennium.

These countercultural formations – practices and cosmology of Techno and New Age – are regulated by patterns that I designate as 'nomadic spirituality.' At one level, trance rituals dramatize the impact of hypermobility and digitalization upon subjectivities, processes that saturate the cognitive ability to make sense of a colossal global order (Jameson 1991). At another level, Techno trance regiments the subject into a counter-hegemonic apparatus that congeals hypermobility and marginality as a tactic of opposition against the dominant regimes of state and morality (biopower/sexuality). In rave parties, such regimentation is carried out by means of transpersonal devices that saturate the body, and implode ordinary modes of perception, affection and behavior. It thus engenders different experiences of the self and sociality that potentially depart with the biopower-sexuality regime (Chapter 1), even though these experiments also impregnate the scene with self-destructive and nihilistic components.

Expressive therapies, trance parties and long-haul traveling are all instances of nomadic spirituality. In many cases, the subject succumbs to the derailing effects of hypermobility and subjective experimentation, amplified by the symbolic power of exotic lands. Nonetheless, it is worth noting that the diaspora of expressive expatriation had been experimenting with rootlessness and estrangement long before these became celebrated as conditions of a now globalizing world. These alternative sites of experimentation may thus anticipate some of the emerging predicaments of cultural globalization, as theoretically outlined in Chapter 1.

Finally, as I interacted with charter tourists, backpackers, sannyasins, trance freaks, bohemian workers and expressive expatriates in India and Ibiza, I realized that their apparent individuality was not as pungent and interesting as the social, cultural and spatial conditions that gradually reconfigured their inner selves in India. Despite the rhetoric of autonomous self-determination, travel transformed most of them into caricatures of smiley tourists, openhearted meditators or rebellious freaks. But among those for whom hypermobility became a constitutive component of their metamorphic identities, it makes no sense to try to ascertain what behavior is 'authentic' or 'true.' For a reason, they have sought to defy fixity and nominalism, by engaging in often risky practices that grant them a fluidic quality (Braidotti 1994; Maffesoli 1988). In the 'contact zones' of hedonistic spirituality in India, I witnessed the fragile and volatile nature of Western egos. The axiological 'I,' noted by Louis Dumont, was becoming something else.

6 Global counter-conclusions
Flexible economies and subjectivities

Reflexive transformation is a leitmotif of Western modernity, progressing – modernists believe – toward universal happiness and enlightenment. However, such a claim of teleological progress has been disputed by countercultural movements as farcical – an Enlightenment ideal of utopia that would be better replaced by Romantic versions of infinite dys/utopias. Yet, paradoxically, these cultures of resistance have been emerging from *within* modernity itself, manifesting expressive, cosmopolitan and reflexive tropes that arise from the very modern dynamics they criticize.

Globalization complexifies this dialectic by speeding up self-reflexivity in non-teleological and unpredictable ways (Giddens 1989; Wallerstein 1989). Hypermobility and digitalism have become constitutive of counter-hegemonic practices and ideologies that depart from conventional regimes of the nation-state, morality and the market – although in a contradictory position of reproduction and co-optation. As contemporary expressions of this interplay between counterculture and globalization, Techno and New Age are thus situated at the intersection of countercultural *continuity* (since classical Romanticism) and postmodernist *rupture* (by globalization). A focused analysis of these formations may shed light on understanding the possibility of *alternative modernities*.

Within contexts of flexible capitalism (as the main economic axis of globalization), expressive expatriates have learned to explore interstitial spaces of leisure, art and wellness; informal economies, alternative business and what is left over from the welfare state. Neo-nomadic strategies include autonomous, seasonal or part-time jobs, more or less autonomous and expressive in nature, and they may also count on parental allowances, inheritance or state-based unemployment support. A combination of all of these sources can be noted most of the times, along with relatively frugal strategies of expense control. In Ibiza, Goa and Pune, typical sites for income-generation are also spaces of socialization, such as hippie (tourist) markets, sunset bars, New Age workshops, spiritual centers, night-clubs and trance parties (raves).

By territorializing in semi-peripheral locations, global countercultures have an impact on local communities. The presence of alternative expatriates and travelers in remote villages has historically provided a deconcentrated source of income for a large segment of local inhabitants, in addition to granting a queer charisma to such locations (Davis 2004; *New York Times* 2004; Saldanha 2004; Ramón-Fajarnés 2000; Cerda-Subirachs and Rodriguez-Branchat 1999; Joan I Mari 1997; Wilson 1997b; Odzer 1995; Rozenberg 1990; Paul 1937). However, these places are gradually invaded by larger waves of conventional tourists and migrants, propelled by native and global strategies of tourism development in which expressive expatriates inadvertently become objects, indicators and beneficiaries. Tourism and entertainment industries create economic opportunities for natives and expatriates to make a living, sometimes with an exceptional cumulative gain; however, this scenario often turns into a self-cannibalizing quagmire, for the ensuing commodification and overregulation of paradisiacal venues, practices and imaginaries undermine the sustainability of neo-nomadic formations. At a later stage, big hotel chains become the main economic actors of local massification or gentrification of tourism, in any case resulting in environmental degradation and social exclusion (*The Guardian* 2006; Newman 2001a; Ramón-Fajarnés 2000; Routledge 2000; Dantas 1999; Sen 1999; Rozenberg 1990). Inflation, overwork, pollution, surveillance, urbanization and overpopulation compel expressive expatriates to re-evaluate their insertion in such transformed environments.

Transnational flows of countercultural subjects, practices and ideas, and the resulting circuits and networks, are shaped in contact with a variety of agents, forces and structures at various levels (from local to global). As a classic example, the repression of rave culture in the UK in the early 1990s led to the emergence of corporate clubbing in that nation, and also provided a new impetus to the party scenes of Ibiza and Goa in the wake of electronic dance music globally. It is pertinent to note that, although tourism is a critical industry in Balearic, Mediterranean and Indian regions, only in Ibiza and Goa have exceptionally high rates of growth and modernization been verified (perhaps with Kerala as another exception) – to wit, Ibiza and Goa display some of the highest per-capita income rates of Spain and India. Throughout the 2000s, northern Goan villagers have mostly complained about the police intervention against the trance party scene for stifling their main source of subsistence. State authorities at the capital Panaji have thus to recalibrate their decisions in order to accommodate diverging interests in tourism development. Likewise, the Osho resort has emphatically adhered to the formula of institutional accommodation and rampant commercialization of spirituality and therapy. In sum, and more abstractly, the global interconnectedness which emerges from infinite flows of countercultural elements also unravels through systemic attritions and disjunctures verified among social, political and economic domains (Urry 2003; Appadurai 1996; Hannerz 1996).

At a theoretical level, the notion of neo-nomadism was developed upon two interrelated claims. First, current understandings of globalization (based on notions of network, diaspora and cosmopolitanism) are insufficient to address the critical features of complex globalization, notably, the postidentitarian effect of hypermobility. Second, having considered self-marginalized expatriates as an empirical instance of global mobility, this study has sought to develop a dialogue between nomadism and nomadology as a step toward a theory of neo-nomadism, an intellectual yet empirically instantiated device for examining the cultural implications of hypermobility.

In a Weberian sense, the neo-nomad is an ideal-type, unraveling upon the productive tension between evidence and concept. On the one hand, it refers to a minority of high-modern renegades involved in hypermobile formations that seek to evade systemic regimes of the political, economic and moral mainstream. In fact, displaying various degrees of engagement with spatial and subjective mobility, only a few of these alternative subjects remain permanently 'on the road' (as mistakenly assumed about nomads in general). Most expressive expatriates live in one or two foreign places, and intermittently travel across exotic and homeland locations in a geographic triangulation. This pattern confirms John Urry's claim about temporary rest and replenishment as a condition of mobility. 'Overall it is the moorings that enable movements. And it is the dialectic of mobility/moorings that produces social complexity' (Urry 2003: 126).

As verified in the biographic trajectories of expressive expatriates, the simultaneity of multinational backgrounds, periodical spatial displacements and transpersonal experiences is a defining feature of neo-nomadism. By integrating practices of self-shaping/shattering within a mobile lifestyle, they develop a nomadic mentality that attempts to make sense of the impact of globalization in their lives and environments. Expressive expatriates have been experimenting with strangeness, rootlessness and displacement much before these qualities became considered by the media and academia to be predicaments of contemporary life. Their familiarity with such predicaments demonstrates the richness of neo-nomadism as an analytical site that probably anticipates emerging conditions, processes and trends of cultural globalization.

Hence, sociological theories suggesting that alternative subjects are a social product of neo-liberal exclusion miss the longer countercultural historicities of Romanticism, and also fail to understand why and how these subjects make critical decisions for transforming their life trajectories. Certainly, material contexts powerfully affect the range of possible decisions, actions and dispositions. However, it is less an issue of industrialist, technocratic and neo-liberal determinations, and more about modernity itself. Away from the alienation and routine of contemporary life, expressive expatriates seek to integrate labor, leisure and spiritual practices into a meaningful life strategy which is irreducible to economic explanations. In their search for holistic charisma in a fragmented world, mobility becomes not only an economic tool for the reproduction of their lifestyle, but also a counter-hegemonic practice of subjectivity formation, predicated on tropes and experiences that depart from the modern subject of sexuality/biopower.

In this connection, it is important to note the two quite different styles of subjectivity formation that are verified within global countercultures. New Agers cultivate the self as an inner substance to be shaped within holistic ideals, whereas Techno freaks implode the ego during pounding rituals of Gothic digitalism. Such polarities, nevertheless, must not be seen as exclusive but rather as complementary orientations. At a social level, expressive expatriates ordinarily transit across Techno and New Age sites, in patterns of belonging that can be either simultaneous or oscillatory, in forms of engagement at the sphere of cultural production, consumption or often both. Techno freaks attend crystal healing practices before promoting trance parties, which they see as very spiritual. Their electronic music (both Techno trance and New Age ambient) contains motifs experienced as psychedelic and ethereal. New Agers may consume shamanic hallucinogens during a rave party, aloof to modernist distinctions between leisure and religion. Osho sannyasins consider their careers in party promotion, therapy and art as closely connected to their lifestyle values on expression, meditation and celebration. DJs are often inclined to oriental philosophies, with friends already involved with New Age practices in a global diaspora of countercultural exchanges. In sum, rather than exclusive entities, New Age and Techno become permeable styles: neo-tribes rather than subcultures (Bennett 1999; Maffesoli 1988).

More substantively, Techno and New Age are sites under which global hypermobility correlates with pragmatic, fluid and metamorphic identity forms. On a surface value, affiliation interests are represented under temporal adverbs, 'Yesterday I was into rave, today I am into Wicca, tomorrow I may try Zen.' As such, alternative subjects regularly migrate across Techno and New Age sites of experience in their quest for non-ordinary understandings about their own self and proper sociability. Nevertheless, under the dizzying variety of New Age labels and practices, there is considerable consistency, which is based on a pattern of religiosity that I have termed *nomadic spirituality*: a condition of reflexive experimentation geared toward an understanding of the self which attempts to keep itself in line with the shifting realities of global mobility, digitalism and multiculturalism, while ambivalently resonating with trends toward reflexive individualism and ephemeral consumerism (Carrete and King 2005; Brooks 2000; Lash 1994; Taylor 1991; Campbell 1989). The infinite exchanges between Techno and New Age formations are also an expression of such nomadic spirituality, coalescing in a common semiotic ground that cultivates alternative experiences of the self, encoded by post-sexuality modes and a Romantic critique of modern life. In other words, Techno and New

Age simultaneously constitute and express a global counterculture that, while being continuously co-opted by states of discipline and markets of desire, also entails the possibility of alternative identities based on meta-morphic experimentation.

Upon this ethnologic assessment, the neo-nomad is also a concept that addresses the fluidic and metamorphic (neo-tribalistic) nature of subjective affiliations and identity formation under conditions of intense global-ization. 'Nomadism: vertiginous progression toward deconstructing identity; molecularisation of the self' (Braidotti 1994: 16). The scholarship has noted the corrosive effects of globalization on the stability of identity, resulting in reflexive, fundamentalist and nihilistic responses (Appadurai 1996; Beck *et al.* 1994; Turner 1994). However, while focusing on the mapping of flows and networks, the scholarship has overlooked the (re)constitution of subjective interiorities in elective affinity with such a deterritorializing predicament (Gille and Riain 2002; Burawoy and Gille 2000; Povinelli and Chauncey 1999). At the ethical realm, the fragmented and colonized nature of modernity necessitates the ability to confront the majoritarian law and to rebalance the polytheism of values (Goldman 1988; Foucault 1984i; Weber 1918). The content of neo-nomadism is thus not made of striated substance but of provisory forms in flux:

> The nomad does not stand for homelessness, or compulsive displace-ment; it is rather a figuration for the kind of subject who has relin-quished all idea, desire, or nostalgia for fixity. This figuration expresses the desire for an identity made of transitions, successive shifts, and coordinated changes, without and against an essential unity.
>
> (Braidotti 1994: 22)

Nomadology more generally refers to the possibility (and risk) of cultural change under conditions of globalization. The postidentitarian predicament of hypermobility is imbricated with a logic of control and resistance that reshapes the nature of dissent in globalized societies (Hardt and Negri 2000; Deleuze 1995). More closely seen, neo-nomads interact with seden-tary societies in a fragile symbiosis, whether in the sunny semi-periphery or bohemian districts of the global city (Lloyd 2006; Stalnaker 2002; Stanley 1997). Despite fleeing the mainstream, expressive expatriates are soon followed by tourists, urban developers, migrants and yuppies, and a dialectic of liberation and accommodation is permanently in action, period-ically renewing itself in different spaces, sites and times, and in paradoxical consonance with the capitalist logic of consumption and reproduction.

The utopian imaginary of neo-nomads thus exerts a seductive influence upon sedentary societies, as media, advertising and leisure spaces indi-cate. In a sense, 'the more [countercultures] capture the feeling of modern alienation and anomie, the better they serve consumptive capital.' (Povinelli 2000: 521). How conventional dwellers and tourists are enticed to experiment with a neo-nomadic lifestyle is a question that requires further investigation. Yet, in the places that expressive expatriates share with sedentary peoples, it is not uncommon to witness young tourists inquiring about alternative gigs in nightclubs, hippie parties and spiritual resorts (instances of Techno and New Age), and later 'drop out' to be seen in some other node of the global countercultural circuit, whether it be for a season or for a whole lifetime ...

Notes

1 Introduction: neo-nomadism: a theory of postidentitarian mobility in the global age

1 An abridged version of this chapter was published in the journal *Mobilities* (2006, 1: 95–119).
2 By 'critical studies' I refer to a constellation of empirical and theoretical studies that includes not only the critical theory of the Frankfurt School but also the French post-structuralism of Foucault, Deleuze and Guattari, as well as critical insights from a Weberian-Nietzschean tradition. Agger 1992; Calhoum 1995; Foucault and Lotringer 1989; Fuery 2000; Halperin 1995; Horkheimer and Adorno 1972; Moraru 2001; Nealon and Irr 2002; Neuenhaus 1993; Norris 1994; Owen 1994; Poster 1989; Schrift 1995; Szakolczai 1998; Taylor 1990.
3 His place was located a few hundred meters from my field residence.
4 As a biographic note of significance, towards the end of his life, Weber had to reconsider the role of aesthetic-erotic practices in engendering a life politics. His conviction on an ethics of vocation was shaken after his brief interactions at the countercultural commune of Ascona in the Swiss Alps foothills. There he witnessed the shattering effects of unconventional forms of art and affective relationship (Green 1986).
5 'Sexuality' is a socio-cultural apparatus of practices, institutions and knowledge (*scientia sexualis*) that constitutes the modern subject. It reflects control mechanisms of the nation-state and related institutions (science, family, church, workplace, army) in controlling populations and individuals (biopower). Sexuality is constructed as a category and domain of obscure causalities, pathologies, external intervention and deciphering of the subject, to whom 'desire' is the central element in the production and control of modern selves and their interiority (Dreyfus *et al.* 1983; Foucault 1976).
6 The destabilization of identities is also discussed in queer theory studies (though paradoxically circumscribed to sexual identity). ' "Queer" acquires meaning from oppositional relation to norm. It is by definition at odds with the normal, the legitimate, the dominant. [. . .] It demarcates not a positivity but a positionality [and] describes a horizon of possibility whose scope cannot be delimited in advance.' (Halperin 1995). I propose that this conceptualization must be deployed more generally, in the analysis of global processes, such as hybridization and reflexivity, upon identity and subjectivity formation.

In this view, the notion of *queer* refers to the destabilization not only of gender identity but of any form of identity (biographic, ethical, religious, aesthetic, social, etc.), which seems to be particularly the case under conditions of globalization.

2 Expressive expatriates in Ibiza: hypermobility as countercultural practice and identity

1 This book utilizes the international system of units (SI) for measurement (metric, Celsius) and the military 24-hour code. Currency exchanges converted into the US dollar refer to the moment the figure was collected: rupee, peseta (until year 2002) and euro.

2 About 30 per cent of this figure does not reach Ibiza, being held by tour operators and airline companies in the UK, Germany, Italy, and mainland Spain (Govern de les Illes Balears 2003; interview with Ibiza Tourist Board in summer of 2003).

3 In Ibiza, geographical locations have both Spanish and Ibicencan names. In line with regionalization trends, I adopt the local terminology. As an exception, I employ 'Ibiza town' and 'Eivissa' to refer to the capital city, while keeping 'Ibiza' for referring to the island as it is internationally known. Among current adjectives ('Ibizan,' 'Ibiceño,' and 'Ibicenco'), I chose 'Ibicencan' because it is a direct English translation of the Catalan word that tends to prevail internationally.

4 The purchasing power of a US dollar in pre-euro Spain was considerably higher than in the US. I personally estimate that one dollar purchased 30 to 50 per cent more in Ibiza than in Chicago. However, when the euro currency replaced the peseta in 2002, this cost differential largely disappeared, and dramatic price inflation, in real terms, tended to push Spanish prices toward the Western European average.

5 In the field of alternative therapies in Ibiza, certification was a concern among therapists and clients. But rather than a legal requirement, it was seen as a proof of competence through apprenticeship. Above all, the reputation of a therapist was determined by her efficacy according to clients, a process reinforced by word-of-mouth.

6 Though oxymoronic, I designate as 'Spanish expatriates' those nationals who moved to Ibiza for the same countercultural motivations as those other national groups that integrate the populace of expressive expatriates.

7 I was requested to not reveal exact locations.

8 Es Vedra is an Ibicencan variation of the Latin expression 'the veteran', as for Ancient Romans the sea rock resembled an old standing soldier.

9 It is important to note the presence of several 'international schools' in Ibiza, all small and privately owned institutions. The remoteness of the island and the smallness of its population (45,000 in 1971) indicate the significant presence of expatriates in the cultural life of the island. More will be said about international schools in this chapter.

10 Biodance is a psychodramatic system for self-development by means of group exercises integrating music, expressive movement, affection and touch. Upon the countercultural premise that institutional repression cripples the body's vitality, a Biodance therapist seeks to foster a sense of holistic self through

psychodramatic exercises that work on corporeal, affective, social and transcendent aspects of subjectivity. In tandem with the overemphasis on the notion of 'experience,' wording is limited during Biodance sessions, usually during brief periods of collective sharing.

11 His perception of this type of expatriate life was strategic in the development of my research. I am grateful for his suggestions about the 'globalization of countercultures.' As we first met, Kirk readily suggested for me to investigate 'a global network of alternative lifestyle that interconnects Ibiza, Goa, Bali and Maui.' My study thereafter has been, in a considerable extent, an attempt to verify this hypothesis and possible causes and implications of the phenomena.

12 Although such generalizations often befall in a simplistic economy of stereotypes, it is striking to note how effective some assumptions are at the level of mainstream national cultures. Nora's comments can be transposed to large clubbing tastes and dispositions of English, Germans and Mediterranean peoples. This topic will be resumed in the next chapter.

13 In addition to the interview content, it is important to note the context in which it takes place. Had I been more formal in my approach to expatriates, interview opportunities and rich information would have been missed. The unusual and unexpected circumstances in which the ethnographic encounter may occur must be acknowledged as constitutive of the practice of knowledge production, particularly true in the case of fluid countercultures.

3   The hippie and club scenes in Ibiza's tourism industry

1 Sections of this chapter were published in the journal *Culture and Religion*, under the title 'The Spiritual Economy of Nightclubs and Raves: Osho Sannyasins as Party Promoters in Ibiza and Pune.' (7, 1: 61–75, March 2006).

2 In 1999 Ibiza's socialist government implemented a 'construction ban' on most natural areas of the island. Based on previous legal dispositions, the moratoria suspended all licenses for construction in non-urban areas granted before October 1990. Since its inception, the legality of the construction ban has been questioned by conservative politicians, local mayors and urban technicians who claim that it debunks acquired rights and invades a legal space that is to be regulated by a law on urban planning and by local municipalities themselves. Nonetheless, so much for legal technicalities: the electoral victory of the right-wing *Popular* party put the construction ban to an end, with the immediate relaxation of all monitoring and reinforcement mechanisms. A six-lane highway began to be built in 2006, under massive street protests from expatriates and the local population. At a wider level, it must be noticed that urban regulation and construction bans do not contest capital but rather guarantee its reproduction, by attempting to contain deleterious effects of capitalistic expansion. As such, whereas the new highway (if concluded) may actually have a negative impact on land values, capital and environment, the surplus of capital concentrated by the Ibicencan hotel industry has been reinvested in the Dominican Republic.

3 The term 'freak' will be discussed in Chapter 5. It refers to segments of white Western counterculture of the 1990s onward that hybridizes elements from hippie and punk subcultures yet in a post-subcultural neo-tribal style, rejecting dominant forms of capitalism, consumerism, conformism and intellectualism. While inheriting the appreciation for rustic lifestyles, exotic travel, psychedelia

and communal life from the hippies, they have embraced powerful technological assemblages of Techno trance music, and are skeptical of social transformation. Likewise, from punks, freaks have inherited modern pessimism, and a taste for transgressive and militaristic fashion. In a sense, a person who embraces a freak neo-tribal style stands somewhere between the hippie and the punk poles.
4 CDs became a prevalent DJing device in the early 2000s onward.
5 A new noise regulation demanded that all nightclubs should build roofs by 1990.
6 Names were altered for privacy issues.

4 Osho International Meditation Resort: subjectivity, counterculture and spiritual tourism in Pune

1 An abridged version of this chapter is being published in the *Journal of Humanistic Psychology*, under the title 'Osho International Meditation Resort: An Anthropological Analysis of Sannyasin Therapies and the Rajneesh Legacy' (47, 1: 1–26, January 2007).
2 Sannyasins reject being seen as a 'religion.' References to 'religion' and 'cult' in this chapter are neutral analytical categories utilized in the scope of the sociology and anthropology of religion.
3 This estimate is based on the number of new registrations processed daily at the Welcome Center: about 60 during the high-season (November to February), dropping to 30 and 15 during mid and low seasons. This estimate does not include tourists who see the resort in quick tours.
4 Osho later proposed 'Zorba, the Greek' as a complement to Buddha. The 'new human being' joyfully celebrates life and ascetically meditates upon it. Zorba indexes the same host of attributes found in Zarathustra.
5 Dimitri gave me feedback on a former version of this text while traveling across Armenia, Georgia and Azerbaijan in 2003.
6 Her sannyasin and legal names were modified, in order to protect privacy, and exact locations were also concealed. Prem is a very common sannyasin name. Nonetheless, I sought to make sure that evidence remains accurate and meaningful.
7 *No Dimensions* is a one-hour dance-and-whirling practice developed by a Sufi dancer under Osho's supervision. It was the 'last meditation' Osho 'created' before his death. Whirling represents life as a hurricane, a challenge that requests the cultivation of inner-centeredness at its eye.
8 In a Zen perspective, any mundane activity can be performed with aesthetic zeal, such as tea preparation or archery. The goal is in allowing the mind to be fully absorbed in the present, dropping any concerns with results and techniques, while reaching a balance between discipline and relaxation as an expression of self-mastery.
9 While in Oregon, top sannyasins asked Sam to investigate right-wing politicians who opposed Osho, as well as a bomb explosion at the hotel sannyasins bought in Portland. Sam did not find any evidence that could be used against their suspects. Likewise, Sam is skeptical about the preposterous claim that the FBI poisoned Osho while in jail (due to immigration infractions).
10 Osho was allergic to scents, but the control procedure has been kept since his death. It is claimed that perfumed scents can disturb meditation. The White Robe is the busiest event of the day, and ashram directors hold that it is something to

be kept. Nonetheless, it also operated at a ritualistic dimension of control and liminality, which enhanced the ceremonial nature of the event.

11 As videos demonstrate, the hall was so crowded during Osho lectures that thousands of collapsed bodies partially piled.

12 The 'inner circle' alone counted 21 authorities (although many were scattered around the world). In its communal legacy, distribution of authority was often unclear, and decisions did not correspond to formal lines of power, delegation and responsibility. As it seems, many communards exerted more power than would be normally necessary to accomplish organizational ends. The direction was clearly closed to any critical suggestions, a posture which ground-level staff tended to reproduce in interactions with visitors and among themselves.

13 It is interesting to note that biographic accounts about Buddha Gautama suggest that, before joining the spiritual path, he was a prince likely exposed to mundane activities (orgiastic banquets, sexual license and war games), encouraged among the young nobility of his time.

14 According to the OIMR director, that was one of Osho's decisions to be executed according to a time schedule after his death.

5 Techno trance tribalism in Goa: the elementary forms of nomadic spirituality

1 Intersecting global and colonial studies, the notion of 'contact zone' designates a space of encounters and exchanges among radically different groups, involving conditions of inequality and conflict as well as of hybridization and negotiation. See Hannerz 1989; Pratt 1992. Agreeing with Pratt: 'By using the term "contact," I aim to foreground the interactive, improvisational dimensions of colonial encounters so easily ignored or suppressed by diffusionist accounts of conquest and domination. A "contact" perspective emphasizes how subjects are constituted in and by their relations to each other [. . .] in terms of copresence, interaction, interlocking understandings and practices, often within radically asymmetrical relations of power.' (p. 7)

2 There were acoustic parties with drums and live rock music in Goa during the 1970s, until the arrival of digital sound systems in the late 1980s.

3 Most names in this chapter were altered in order to protect privacy. Any piece of information that could embarrass or endanger any subject was occluded. Nonetheless, I made sure that descriptions remained precise and meaningful.

4 The regular intake of drugs altered ordinary notions of temporal linearity, and biographic accounts were often fragmented, odd and expressionistic. LSD and hashish fostered a mystical otherworldly orientation, whereas the talkative effects of MDMA were recoded in silent interactions deemed 'telepathic.' All of these symptoms are commonly verified in cases that modern psychiatry describe as 'schizophrenic.' Finally, the sharing of such transpersonal experiences contributed to engender a collective identity that is sensed as removed from the ordinary world, erasing personal memories and teleologies, striving for an endless (but impossible) enjoyment of the present.

5 Southernmost portion of Vagator beach, once densely frequented by Italian travelers.

6 The notion of passive drug dealing better captures the sporadic nature of such activity, carried out by the active request from an acquaintance, and taking

place in a subcultural setting that trivializes drug consumption as a basic form of socialization and ritual enactment.

7 Pipi and Luigi kindly permitted me to watch and photograph one session.

8 It is a collective ritual in which women and, sometimes, outsiders may participate.

9 Durkheim was concerned with the problem of consensus (solidarity), as a basic mechanism that binds society together. In contrast, countercultures explore systemic fissures, which, in post-Durkheimian criminology, would be interpreted through notions of anomie and deviance.

10 A Phantasm is defined as 'an imaginary scenario whereby the subject experiences a desire that is unconscious but deformed by defensive mechanisms.' (Airault 2000: 140).

Bibliography

Abu-Lughod, L. 1999. *Veiled Sentiments: Honor and Poetry in a Bedouin Society*. Berkeley, CA: University of California Press.

Afonso, A. 1989. *Tourism in Goa: Socio-Economic Impact*. Institute of Social Sciences of New Delhi Manuscript Report 2.

Agger, B. 1992. *Cultural Studies as Critical Theory*. London: The Falmer Press.

Airault, R. 2000. *Fous de l'Inde: Delires d'Occidentaux et Sentiment Oceanique*. Paris: Payot.

Amitabh, S. 1982. Shree Rajneesh Ashram: A Provocative Community. *Journal of Humanistic Psychology* 22, 19–42.

Amrito, S.D. 1984. Rajneesh Therapy. *Journal of Humanistic Psychology* 24, 115–18.

Anderson, A. 1998. Cosmopolitanism, Universalism, and the Divided Legacies of Modernity. In *Cosmopolitics* (eds) P. Chea and B. Robins. Minneapolis, MN: University Minnesota Press.

Appadurai, A. 1996. *Modernity at Large: Cultural Dimensions of Globalization*. Minneapolis, MN: University of Minnesota Press.

Aveling, H. (ed.) 1999. *Osho Rajneesh and His Disciples: Some Western Perceptions*. Delhi: Motilal Banarsidass.

Axel, B. 2002. The Diasporic Imaginary. *Public Culture* 14, 411–28.

Axelrod, P. and M.A. Fuerch. 1998. Portuguese Orientalism and the Making of the Village Communities of Goa. *Ethnohistory* 45, Summer, 439–76.

Barfield, T. 1993. *The Nomadic Alternative*. Englewood Cliffs, NJ: Prentice Hall.

Basnet, C. 2002. *The Way of Neo-Sannyas: Sociological Perspective on a New Religious Movement in Nepal*. Kathmandu: Udaya Books.

Beck, U., A. Giddens and S. Lash. 1994. *Reflexive Modernization: Politics, Tradition and Aesthetics in the Modern Social Order*. Cambridge, Oxford: Polity Press in association with Blackwell.

Becker, J. 1999. Can Music Cognition Shed its Cartesian Roots? Paper presented to the Music, Culture, Mind Conference, February 26. Chicago, IL.

Begrich, R. and A. Muehlebach. 1998. *Trancenational Goa: Travelling People, Parties, Images*. Basel: University Basel, audio-visual documentary, 33 min.

Bellah, R. 1979. New Religious Consciousness and the Crisis in Modernity. In *Interpretative Social Science: A Reader* (ed.) P. Rabinow. Berkeley, CA: University California Press.

—— 1985. *Habits of the Heart: Individualism and Commitment in American Life*. Berkeley, CA: University California Press.

Bennett, A. 1999. Subcultures or Neo-Tribes? Rethinking the Relationship between Youth, Style and Musical Taste. *Sociology* 33, 599–617.

—— and K. Kahn-Harris. 2004. *After Subculture*. Basingstoke: Palgrave Macmillan.

Best, B. 1997. Over-the-counter-culture: Retheorizing Resistance in Popular Culture. In *The Clubcultures Reader: Readings in Popular Cultural Studies* (ed.) S. Redehead. Oxford: Blackwell.

Bey, H. 1991. *The Temporary Autonomous Zone: Ontological Anarchy, Poetic Terrorism*. New York: Autonomedia.

Bird, F. and R. Pandya. 1993. Therapeutic Aspects of New Religious Movements. In *The Rajneesh Papers: Studies in a New Religious Movement* (eds) S. Palmer and A. Sharma. Delhi: Motilal Banarsidass.

Blanchard, M. 1998. *Oscar Wilde's America: Counterculture in the Gilded Age*. New Haven, CT: Yale University Press.

Bogue, R. 1996. Gilles Deleuze: The Aesthetics of Force. In *Deleuze: A Critical Reader* (ed.) P. Patton. Cambridge, MA: Blackwell.

Borneman, J. and S. Senders. 2000. Politics Without a Head: Is the 'Love Parade' a New Form of Political Identification? *Cultural Anthropology* 15, 294–317.

Braidotti, R. 1994. *Nomadic Subjects: Embodiment and Sexual Difference in Contemporary Feminist Theory*. New York: Columbia University Press.

British Parliament. 1999. Statement by the Secretary of State for Culture, Media and Sport re-appointing David Quarmby as Chairman of the Board of the British Tourist Authority: Portcullis.

Brooks, D. 2000. *Bobos in Paradise: The New Upper Class and How They Got There*. New York: Touchstone.

Bruford, W.H. 1975. *The German Tradition of Self-Cultivation: 'Bildung' from Humboldt to Thomas Mann*. Cambridge: Cambridge University Press.

Buckland, F. 2002. *Impossible Dance: Club Culture and Queer-World Making*. Middletown, CT: Wesleyan University Press.

Burawoy, M. and Z. Gille. 2000. *Global Ethnography: Forces, Connections, and Imaginations in a Post-Modern World*. Berkeley, CA: University of California Press.

Butts, C. 1997. *Is Harry on the Boat?* London: Orion.

Calhoun, C. 1995. *Critical Social Theory*. Oxford: Blackwell.

Campbell, C. 1989. *The Romantic Ethic and the Spirit of Consumerism*. Oxford: Blackwell.

Carrete, J. and R. King. 2005. *Selling Spirituality: The Silent Takeover of Religion*. London, New York: Routledge.

Carter, L.F. 1990. *Charisma and Control in Rajneeshpuram: The Role of Shared Values in the Creation of Community*. Cambridge: Cambridge University Press.

Castells, M. 1996. *The Rise of Network Society*. Cambridge: Blackwell.

Castles, S. and M. Miller. 2003. *The Age of Migration: International Population Movements in the Modern World*. New York: Guilford.

Cerda-Subirachs, J. and R. Rodriguez-Branchat. 1999. *La Repressio Franquista del Moviment Hippy a Formentera (1968–1970)*. Eivissa: Res Publica.

Clifford, J. 1994. Diasporas. *Cultural Anthropology* 9, 302–38.

—— 1997. *Routes: Travel and Translation in the Late Twentieth Century*. Cambridge, MA: Harvard University Press.

—— 1998. Mixed Feelings. In *Cosmopolitics: Thinking and Feeling Beyond the State* (eds) P. Cheng and B. Robbins. Minneapolis, MN: University Minnesota Press.

Collin, M. 1997. *Altered State: the Story of Ecstasy Culture and Acid House*. London, New York: Serpent's Tail.

Comaroff, J.L. and J. Comaroff. 2000. Millenial Capitalism: First Thoughts on a Second Coming. *Public Culture: Millennial Capitalism and the Culture of Neoliberalism* 12, 291–343.

Corsten, M. 1998a. Ecstasy as 'This-Wordly Path to Salvation': the Techno Youth Scene as a Proto-Religious Collective. In *Alternative Religions among European Youth* (ed.) L. Tomasi. Aldershot: Ashgate.

—— 1998b. Youth Dance Cultures – The Experience of Intramundane Salvation (innerweltliche Erlosung) in the Ritual Dance Practice of the Techno Youth Culture. Paper presented to the International Sociological Association (ISA).

Craik, J. 1997. The Culture of Tourism. In *Touring Cultures: Transformations of Travel and Culture* (eds) C. Rojek and J. Urry. London, New York: Routledge.

Cresswell, T. 1997. Imagining the Nomad: Mobility and the Postmodern Primitive. In *Space and Social Theory: Interpreting Modernity and Postmodernity* (eds) G. Benko and U. Strohmayer. Oxford: Blackwell.

Cribb, R. 1991. *Nomads in Archaeology*. Cambridge: Cambridge University Press.

Curling, C. and M. Llewelyn-Davies. 1974. Masai Women. In *Disappearing World*. UK: Granada Television International.

Damanhur Federation. 2006. www.damanhur.org. Last accessed October 2006.

Dancestar. 2004. Dancestar UK and US Award Winners, Performers and Hosts 2000–2004. www.dancestar.com/usa/2004/downloads/all_ds_winners.pdf. Last accessed on November 12, 2006.

D'Andrea, A. 2000. *O Self Perfeito e a Nova Era: Individualismo e Reflexividade em Religiosidades Pós-Tradicionais*. São Paulo: Ed. Loyola.

—— 2004. Global Nomads: Techno and New Age as Transnational Countercultures in Ibiza and Goa. In *Rave Culture and Religion* (ed.) G. St John. London, New York: Routledge.

—— 2005. Will Work For Party – The Bohemian Worker. *Native-Cultura* Summer, 20–22.

—— 2006. The Spiritual Economy of Nightclubs and Raves: Osho Sannyasins as Party Promoters in Ibiza and Pune-Goa. *Culture and Religion* 7, pp. 61–75.

Dantas, N. (ed.) 1999. *The Transforming of Goa*. Mapusa, Goa: The Other India.

Davis, E. 2004. Hedonic Tantra: Golden Goa's Trance Transmission. In *Rave Culture and Religion* (ed.) G. Saint John. Routledge Advances in Sociology. London/ New York: Routledge.

Davis-Kimball, J. 2003. *Warrior Women: An Archaeologist's Search for History's Hidden Heroines*. New York: Warner Books.

Deleuze, G. 1995. Postscript on Control Societies. In *Negotiations*. New York: Columbia University Press.

—— and F. Guattari. 1980. *A Thousand Plateaus: Capitalism and Schizophrenia* (Volume 2 of *Mille Plateaux*). Minneapolis, MN: University of Minnesota.

Delumeau, J. 1992. *History of Paradise: the Garden of Eden in Myth and Tradition*. New York: Continuum.

deSouza, P. 2000. Pragmatic Politics in Goa, 1987–99. In *Contemporary India – Transitions* (ed.) P. deSouza. New Delhi, London: SAGE.

Devaraj. 1986. *Bhagwan: The Most Godless Yet the Most Godly Man*. Pune: Rebel.

DJ Magazine. 1998. Spirit of Ibiza. 1, 10–14.

Dreyfus, H.L., P. Rabinow and M. Foucault. 1983. *Michel Foucault, Beyond Structuralism and Hermeneutics*. Chicago, IL: University of Chicago Press.

Dumont, L. 1983. *Essais sur l'Individualisme: une perspective anthropologique sur l'idéologie moderne*. (Collection Esprit). Paris: Editions du Seuil.

Durkheim, E. 1995 [1912]. *The Elementary Forms of the Religious Life*. New York: The Free Press.

The Economist. 2004. A Survey of India, February 21–7.

El Temps. 2000. Eivissa, la Discoteca Flotant, August 8–14, 18–27.

Escohotado, A. 1998. *Historia General de Las Drogas*. Madrid: Espasa.

Financial Express. 2003. Goa Gears Up To Partly Use Proposed Intl Airport By 2007. New Delhi, December 25.

Forsyth, A.J.M., M. Barnard and N.P. McKeganey. 1997. Musical Preference as an Indicator of Adolescent Drug Use. *Addiction* 92, Oct, 1317–25.

Fost, J.W. 1999. Neural Rhythmicity, Feature Binding, and Serotonin: A Hypothesis. *Neuroscientist* 5, 79–85.

Foucault, M. 1972. *The Archaeology of Knowledge*. London: Tavistock.

—— 1976. *Histoire de la Sexualité I: la volonté de savoir*. Paris: Gallimard.

—— 1978. *Remarks on Marx*. New York: Semiotext(e).

—— 1984a. À propos de la généalogie de l'éthique: un aperçu du travail en cours (translated from 'On the Genealogy of Ethics: An Overview of Work in Progress,' and reviewed by Foucault). In *Dits et Écrits IV: 1980–1988* (eds) D. Defert and F. Ewald. Paris: Gallimard.

—— 1984b. *Histoire de la Sexualité III: le souci de soi* Collection Tel. Paris: Gallimard.

—— 1984c. The Ethics of the Concern for Self as a Practice of Freedom. In *Foucault Live: Collected Interviews, 1961–1984* (ed.) S. Lotringer. New York: Semiotext(e).

—— 1984d. The Return of Morality. In *Foucault Live: Collected Interviews, 1961–1984* (ed.) S. Lotringer. New York: Semiotext(e).

—— and S. Lotringer. 1989. *Foucault Live: Collected Interviews, 1961–1984*. New York: Semiotext(e).

Fox, J. 2002. *Osho Rajneesh*. Studies in Contemporary Religion series, no. 4.

Frank, T. 1997. *The Conquest of Cool – Business culture, Counterculture, and the Rise of Hip Consumerism*. Chicago: University of Chicago Press.

Fuery, P. 2000. *Cultural Studies and Critical Theory*. Melbourne: Oxford University Press.

Gaillot, M. 1999. *Multiple Meaning: Techno – An Artistic and Political Laboratory of the Present*. Paris: Dis Voir.

Geertz, C. 1973. *The Interpretation of Cultures: Selected Essays*. Basic.

Gellner, E. 1984. Foreword. In *Nomads and the Outside World* (ed.) A. Khazanov. Cambridge: Cambridge University Press.

Gerra, G., A. Zaimovic, D. Franchini *et al*. 1998. Neuroendocrine Responses of Healthy Volunteers to 'Techno-Music': Relationships with Personality Traits and Emotional State. *International Journal of Psychophysiology* 28, 99–111.

Gibson, C. 2001. Appropriating the Means of Production: Dance Music Industries and Contested Digital Spaces. In *FreeNRG: Notes from the Edge of the Dance Floor* (ed.) G. St John. Sydney: Pluto.

Giddens, A. 1989. *The Consequences of Modernity*. Stanford, CA: Stanford University Press.

—— 1991. *Modernity and Self-Identity: Self and Society in the Late Modern Age.* Cambridge: Blackwell.

—— 1992. *The Transformation of Intimacy: Love, Sexuality and Eroticism in Modern Societies.* Oxford, Cambridge: Polity Press in association with Basil Blackwell.

—— 1994. Living in a Post-Traditional Society. In *Reflexive Modernization: Politics, Tradition and Aesthetics in the Modern Social Order* (eds) U. Beck, A. Giddens and S. Lasch. Stanford, CA: Stanford University Press.

Gilbert, J. and E. Pearson. 1999. *Discographies: Dance Music, Culture and the Politics of Sound.* London: Routledge.

Gille, Z. and S. Riain. 2002. Global Ethnography. *Annual Review of Sociology* 28, 271–95.

Ginat, J. and A. Khazanov (eds) 1998. *Changing Nomads in a Changing World.* Portland, OR: Sussex.

Goa Directorate of Planning Statistics and Evaluation. 2000. *Statistical Handbook of Goa.* Panaji: Government of Goa.

—— 2002. *Goa – Economy in Figures – 2002.* Panaji: Goa Goverment.

Goa Gil. n.a. Interview on Radio-V. www.goagil.com. Last accessed October 26, 2004.

Goldman, H. 1988. *Max Weber and Thomas Mann: Calling and the Shaping of the Self.* Berkeley, CA: University California Press.

Goldman, M. 1999. *Passionate Journeys: Why Successful Women Joined a Cult.* Ann Arbor, MI: The University of Michigan Press.

—— 2005. When Leaders Dissolve: Considering Controversy and Stagnation in the Osho Rajneesh Movement. In *Controversial New Religions* (eds) J. Lewis and J. Petersen. New York: Oxford University Press.

Gordon, J.S. 1987. *The Golden Guru: The Strange Journey of Bhagwan Shree Rajneesh.* Lexington, MA: S. Greene Press.

Govern de les Illes Balears – IBAE. 1996. *Padró Municipal d'habitants 1996: Eivissa-Formentera.* Conselleria d'Economia, Hisenda y Innovacio – Institut Balear d'Estadística i Demografia.

—— 2004. *Principales Variables de la Evolución Económica de Baleares (1997–2003).* Conselleria d'Economia, Hisenda y Innovacio – Institut Balear d'Estadística i Demografia.

Govern de les Illes Balears – Conselleria de Turisme. 2002. *Tourist Spending: 2001.*

—— 2003. *Tourism in the Balearic Islands: 2002.*

—— 2006. *El Turisme a les Illes Balears: 2005.*

Govern de les Illes Ballears – Conselleria d'Economia, H.i.I. 2002. *Conjuntura Economica de les Illes Balears.*

Green, M. 1986. *Mountain of Truth: The Counterculture Begins, Ascona, 1900–1920.* Hanover, NH: University Press of New England.

Greer, G.R. and R. Tolbert. 1998. A method of conducting therapeutic sessions with MDMA. *Journal of Psychoactive Drugs* 30, 371–9.

Grossberg, L. 1997. Re-Placing Popular Culture. In *The Clubcultures Reader: Readings in Popular Cultural Studies* (ed.) S. Redhead. Oxford: Blackwell.

The Guardian. 2006. Ibiza rises up against blight of tourism. London, February 26.

Guinness. 2003. *Guinness Book of World Records.* New York: Bantam.

Hacking, I. 1986. Self-Improvement. In *Foucault: a Critical Reader* (ed.) D. Hoy. Oxford: Blackwell.

—— 1998. *Mad Travelers: Reflections on the Reality of Transient Mental Ilnesses*. Charlottesville, VA, London: University Press of Virginia.

Halperin, D.M. 1995. *Saint Foucault: Towards a Gay Hagiography*. New York: Oxford University Press.

Hannerz, U. 1989. Notes on the Global Ecumene. *Public Culture* 1, 65–75.

—— 1996. *Transnational Connections: Culture, People, Places*. London, New York: Routledge.

Hardt, M. and A. Negri. 2000. *Empire*. Cambridge, MA: Harvard University Press.

Hausler, N. 1995. The Snake in 'Paradise'?! – Tourism and Acculturation in Goa. In *Retracing the Track of Tourism: Studies on Travels, Tourists, and Development* (ed.) N. Hausler. Saarbrucken: Entwicklungspolitik.

Hays, J. 2001. Pathologies of Travel (Review). *Bulletin of the History of Medicine* 75, 582–4.

Heelas, P. 1996. *The New Age Movement: the celebration of the self and the sacralization of modernity*. Oxford: Blackwell.

Hemment, D. 1998. E is for Ekstasis. *New Formations* 31, 23–38.

Horkheimer, M. and T. Adorno. 1972. *Dialectic of Enlightenment*. New York: Herder and Herder.

Hutnyk, J. 1999. Magical Mystical Tourism. In *Travel Worlds: Journeys in Contemporary Cultural Politics* (eds) R. Kaur and H. John. London, New York: Zed.

Hutson, S.R. 2000. The Rave: Spiritual Healing in Modern Western Subcultures. *Anthropological Quarterly* 73, 35–49.

Ibiza Now. 1997. What has 'Ibiza Uncovered' to do with Ibiza? September, 3.

Indian Express. 2004. Maroon in the Red? Pune.

Ingham, J., M. Purvis and D. Clarke. 1999. Hearing Places, Making Spaces: Sonorous Geographies, Ephemeral Rhythms, and the Blackburn Warehouse Parties. *Society and Space (Environment and Planning)* 17, 283–305.

Jameson, F. 1991. *Postmodernism, or, The Cultural Logic of Late Capitalism*. Durham, NC: Duke University Press.

Jay, M. 1993. The Limits of Limit-Experience: Bataille and Foucault. Berkeley, CA: Center for German and European Studies, University of California.

Jerusalem Post. 2004. Men in Black. Jerusalem, January 1.

Joan I Mari, B. 1997. *Historia de Ibiza*. Eivissa: Editorial Mediterrania-Eivissa.

Kaplan, C. 1987. Deterritorializations: The Rewriting of Home and Exile in Western Feminist. *Cultural Critique* 6, 187–98.

Kauffman, E. 1995. *History of Ibiza*. Ibiza: Ibiza Now.

Kaur, R. 1999. Parking the Snout in Goa. In *World Travels: Journeys in Contemporary Cultural Politics* (eds) R. Kaur and J. Hutnyk. London, New York: Zed.

Kearney, M. 1995. The Local and the Global: The Anthropology of Globalization and Transnationalism. *Annual Review of Anthropology* 24, 547–65.

Kempster, C. 1996. *History of House*. London: Sanctuary.

Khazanov, A. 1984. *Nomads and the Outside World*. Cambridge: Cambridge University Press.

Kinesis Films. 1990. A Short Film About Chilling. UK: Channel 4 Television Corporation, TV documentary, 40 min.

Krishnananda. 1996. *Face to Face With Fear: A Loving Journey from Co-Dependency to Freedom*. Pune: Koregaon.

—— 1999. *Stepping Out of Fear: Breaking Our Identification with the Emotional Child Inside*. Pune: Koregaon.

—— 2006. Learning Love Seminars. http://learningloveseminars.com. Last accessed September 30, 2006.

Lancaster, W. and F. Lancaster. 1998. Who are these Nomads? What do they do? Continuous Change or Changing Continuities. In *Changing Nomads in a Changing Society* (eds) J. Ginat and A. Khazanov. Portland, OR: Sussex.

Lash, S. 1994. Reflexivity and its Doubles: Structure, Aesthetics, Community. In *Reflexive Modernization: Politics, Tradition and Aesthetics in the Modern Social Order* (eds) U. Beck, A. Giddens and S. Lasch. Stanford, CA: Stanford University.

Levi-Strauss, C. 1962. *The Savage Mind*. Chicago, IL: University of Chicago.

Lloyd, R. 2006. *Neo-Bohemia: Art and Commerce in the Postindustrial City*. New York, London: Routledge.

Luckmann, T. 1991. The New and the Old in Religion. In *Social Theory for a Changing Society* (eds) P. Bourdieu and L. Coleman. San Francisco: Westview.

MacCanell, D. 1989. *The Tourist: a New Theory of the Leisure Class*. Berkeley, CA: University of California Press.

McCraty, R., B. Barrios-Choplin, M. Atkinson and D. Tomasino. 1998. The Effects of Different Types of Music on Mood, Tension, and Mental Clarity. *Alternative Therapies in Health and Medicine* 4, 75–84.

McKay, G. 1996. *Senseless Acts of Beauty: Cultures of Resistance since the Sixties*. London: Verso.

McRobbie, A. 1994a. *Postmodernism and Popular Culture*. London, New York: Routledge.

—— 1994b. Shut Up and Dance: Youth Culture and Changing Modes of Femininity. In *Postmodernism and Popular Culture* (ed.) A. McRobbie. London, New York: Routledge.

Maffesoli, M. 1988. *The Time of Tribes: The Decline of Individualism in Mass Society*. London: SAGE.

Malkki, L. 1992. National Geographic: the Rooting of Peoples and the Territorialization of National Identity Among Scholars and Refugees. *Cultural Anthropology* 7, 24–44.

Maneesha. 1987. *Bhagwan: The Buddha for the Future*. Pune: Rebel.

Manning, S. 1998. Dances of Death: Germany Before Hitler. In *The Routlegde Dance Studies Reader* (ed.) A. Carter. New York, London: Routledge.

Marcus, G.E. 1998. *Ethnography Through Thick and Thin*. Princeton, NJ: Princeton University Press.

Maurel, J.M. 1988. *Geografia de España: Cataluña/Baleares* 9. Barcelona: Planeta.

Mauss, M. 1904. *A General Theory of Magic*. London: Routledge.

Mehta, G. 1990 [1979]. *Karma Cola: Marketing the Mystic East*. India: Penguin Books.

Mercer, K. 1994. Diaspora Culture and Dialogic Imagination: The Aesthetics of Black Independent Film in Britain. In *Welcome to the Jungle: New Positions in Black Cultural Studies*. New York: Routledge, pp. 53–68.

Miller, C. 1993. The Postidentitarian Predicament in the Footnotes of *A Thousand Plateaus*: Nomadology, Anthropology, and Authority. *Diacritics* 23, 6–35.

Mixmag. 1999. The Manumission Story. July, 48–57.

Moraru, C. 2001. The Global Turn in Critical Theory. *Symploke* 9, 74–82.

Muggleton, D. and R. Weinzierl. 2003. *The Post-Subcultures Reader*. Oxford: Berg.

Navhind Times. 2004. Over 3 Lakh Foreign Tourists Visited Goa. Panaji, Goa, July 27.

Nealon, J. and C. Irr (eds) 2002. *Rethinking the Frankfurt School: Alternative Legacies of Cultural Critique.* Albany, NY: State University of New York Press.

Neuenhaus, P. 1993. *Max Weber und Michel Foucault: über Macht und Herrschaft in der Moderne.* (Schnittpunkt Zivilisationsprozess Bd. 14.) Pfaffenweiler: Centaurus-Verlagsgesellschaft.

New York Times. 2004. Aging Hippies Prospering in Lush Bali. New York. March 30.

Newman, R. 2001a. *Of Umbrellas, Goddesses and Dreams: Essays on Goan Culture and Society.* Mapusa, Goa: The Other Indian Press.

—— 2001b. Western Tourists and Goan Pilgrims: a Comparison of Two Ritual Dramas. In *Of Umbrellas, Goddesses, and Dreams: Essays on Goan Culture and Society.* Mapusa, Goa: The Other India Press.

Norris, C. 1994. 'What is Enlightenment?': Kant according to Foucault. In *The Cambridge Companion to Foucault* (ed.) G. Gutting. Cambridge: Cambridge University

Odzer, C. 1995. *Goa Freaks: My Hippie Years in India.* New York: Blue Moon Books.

Ong, A. 1999. *Flexible Citizenship: The Cultural Logics of Transnationality.* Durham, NC and London: Duke University Press.

Osho. 1967. *From Sex to Superconsciousness.* Pune: The Rebel.

—— 1985. *Books I Have Loved.* Pune: Rajneesh Foundation International.

—— 1987. *Zarathustra: A God that Can Dance.* Cologne, Germany: The Rebel Publishing House.

—— 1988. *Meditation: The First and Last Freedom.* Pune: The Rebel.

—— S. Neiman (eds) 2000. *Autobiography of a Spiritually Incorrect Mystic.* Pune: The Rebel.

Osho International Foundation. 2006. www.osho.com. Last accessed September 20, 2006.

Owen, D. 1994. *Maturity and Modernity: Nietzsche, Weber, Foucault, and the Ambivalence of Reason.* London, New York: Routledge.

Palmer, S. 1994. *Moon Sisters, Krishna Mothers, Rajneesh Lovers: Women's Roles in New Religions.* Syracuse, NY: Syracuse University Press.

—— and F. Bird. 1999. Therapy, Charisma and Social Control in the Rajneesh Movement. In *Osho Rajneesh and His Disciples: Some Western Perceptions* (ed.) H. Aveling. Delhi: Motilal Banarsidass.

—— and A. Sharma (eds) 1993. *The Rajneesh Papers: Studies in a New Religious Movement.* Delhi: Motilal Barnasidass.

Parkes, G. 1991. *Nietzsche and Asian Thought.* Chicago, IL: University of Chicago Press.

Paul, E. 1937. *The Life and Death of a Spanish Town.* The Modern Library. New York: Random House.

Pini, M. 1997. Cyborgs, Nomads, and the Raving Feminine. In *Dance in the City,* (ed) H. Thomas. New York: Saint Martin's Press.

—— 2001. *Club Cultures and Female Subjectivity: the Move from Home to House.* Basingstoke, New York: Palgrave.

Planells, M. 1994. *Magic Guide: Through Ibiza and Formentera.* Collecio Gandula. Eivissa: Editorial Mediterranea-Eivissa.

Poster, M. 1989. *Critical Theory and Poststructuralism: in Search of a Context*. Ithaca, NY: Cornell University Press.

Povinelli, E. 2000. Consuming *Geist*: Popontology and the Spirit of Capital in Indigenous Australia. *Public Culture: Millenial Capitalism and the Culture of Neo-liberalism* 12, 501–28.

—— and G. Chauncey. 1999. Thinking Sexuality Transnationally. *GLQ: A Journal of Gay and Lesbian Studies* 5, 1–11.

Pratt, M.L. 1992. *Imperial Eyes: Travel Writing and Transculturation*. London, New York: Routledge.

Quirot, B. 1993. Alienes Migrateurs: Contribuition a une psychopathologie de voyageur, Doctoral thesis, Dept. Medicine Université de Paris.

Ramón-Fajarnés, E. 2000. *Historia del Turismo en Ibiza y Formentera*. Eivissa, Ibiza: Genial.

Rao, A. (ed.) 1987. *The Other Nomads: Peripatetic Minorities in Cross-Cultural Perspective*. Cologne: Bohlau.

Redhead, S. (ed.) 1997. *The Clubcultures Reader*. Oxford: Blackwell.

Reynolds, S. 1998. *Generation Ecstasy: into the World of Techno and Rave Culture*. Boston, MA: Little Brown.

Robbins, B. 1998. Comparative Cosmopolitanisms. In *Cosmopolitics: Thinking and Feeling Beyond the Nation* (eds) P. Cheah and B. Robbins. Minneapolis, MN: Minnesota.

Ronstrom, O. 1999. It Takes Two – or More – to Tango: Researching Traditional Music/Dance Interrelations. In *Dance in the Field* (ed.) T. Buckland. New York: St. Martin.

Roszak, T. 1995. *The Making of a Counterculture: Reflections on the Technocratic Society and its Youthful Opposition* (includes introduction to 1995 edition). Berkeley, CA: University of California.

Routledge, P. 2000. Consuming Goa – Tourist Site as Dispensable Space. *Economic and Political Weekly* 35, 2647–56.

Rozenberg, D. 1990. *Ibiza, una isla para otra vida: inmigrantes utópicos, turismo y cambio cultural*. Colección Monografias; n. 110. Madrid: Centro de Investigaciones Sociológicas: Siglo XXI de España.

Said, E. 1978. *Orientalism*. New York: Vintage.

Saldanha, A. 1999. Goa Trance in Goa: Globalization, Musical Practice and the Politics of Place. Paper presented to the Annual IASPM International Conference, Sydney, 1999.

—— 2004. Goa Trance and Trance in Goa: Smooth Striations. In *Rave Culture and Religion* (ed.) G. Saint John. London, New York: Routledge.

Saunders, N. 1995. *Ecstasy and the Dance Culture*. London: N. Saunders.

Scheurmann, I. and K. Scheurman (eds) 1993. *For Walter Benjamin*. Bonn: AsKI.

Schrift, A.D. 1995. *Nietzsche's French Legacy: a Genealogy of Poststructuralism*. New York: Routledge.

Sen, G. 1999. *Goa Under Siege* (trans.) M.L. Foundation. India.

Sharma, S. 2004. Moolah Rouge: June 29. Discussion List (online). Goanet.

Shunyo, M.P. 1999. *My Diamond Days with Osho*. Delhi: Full Circle.

Sicko, D. 1999. *Techno Rebels: The Renegades of Electronic Funk*. New York: Billboard Books.

Silcott, M. 1999. *Rave America: New School Dancescapes*. Canada: ECW.

Simmel, G. 1971. *On Individuality and Social Forms*. Chicago: University of Chicago Press.

Sky TV. 1998. Ibiza Uncovered. TV series, produced by Natalka Znak.

St John, G. 2003. Post-Rave Technotribalism and the Carnival of Protest. In *The Post-Subcultures Reader* (eds) D. Muggleton and R. Weinzierl. Oxford: Berg.

—— (ed.) 2004. *Rave Culture and Religion*. London, New York: Routledge.

Stabler, M.J. (ed.) 1997. *Tourism and Sustainability: Principles to Practice*. New York, Wallingford: CAB International.

Stalnaker, S. 2002. *Hub Culture: The Next Wave of Urban Consumers*. Singapore: John Wiley and Sons.

Stanley, C. 1997. Not Drowning but Waving: Urban Narratives of Dissent in the Wild Zone. In *The Clubcultures Reader* (ed.) S. Redhead. Oxford: Blackwell.

Stoller, P. 1999. Globalizing Method: The Problem of Doing Ethnography in Transnational Spaces. *Anthropology and Humanism* 22, 81–94.

Stratton, B. 1994. *The Last Boat to Barcelona: The Autobiography of an Expatriate*. Reno, NV: Fourth Dimension Press.

Strauss, S. 1997. Re-Orienting Yoga: Transnational Flows from an Indian Center. PhD Dissertation, Dept. Anthropology, University of Pennsylvania.

Szakolczai, Á. 1998. *Max Weber and Michel Foucault: Parallel Life-Works* (Routledge Studies in Social and Political Thought: 8). New York: Routledge.

Takahashi, M. 2004. The 'Natural High': Altered States, Flashbacks, and Neural Tuning at Raves. In *Rave Culture and Religion* (ed.) G. Saint John. London, New York: Routledge.

Taylor, C. 1990. Lyotard and Weber: Postmodern Rules and Neo-Kantian Values. In *Theories of Modernity and Postmodernity* (ed.) C. Taylor. London: SAGE.

—— 1991. *The Ethics of Authenticity*. Cambridge, MA: Harvard University Press.

Thompson, S.J. 1997. Hashish in Berlin: An Introduction to Walter Benjamin's Uncomplete Work on Hashish. Walter Benjamin Congress, Amsterdam, July.

Thornton, S. 1995. *Club Cultures: Music, Media and Subcultural Capital*. Cambridge: Polity Press/Blackwell.

Times of India. 2004a. Changing Times for a Changing City. Pune, January 1.

—— 2004b. Pune Ranks 8th in 'Rich' Stakes. Pune, March 18.

—— 2004c. Restaurant Owners Protest Foreigners Doing Business, January 1.

—— 2004d. Tourists are Back, but Heading South. New Delhi, January 3.

Torday, L. 1997. *Mounted Archers: the Beginning of Central Asian History*. Edinburgh: Durham Academic Press.

Turnbull, S. 2003. *Mongol Warrior 1200–1350*. Oxford: Osprey.

Turner, B.S. 1994. *Orientalism, Postmodernism, and Globalism*. London, New York: Routledge.

Urban, H. 1996. Zorba, The Buddha: Capitalism, Charisma, and the Cult of Bhagwan Sri Rajneesh. *Religion* 26, 161–82.

Urry, J. 2002. *The Tourist Gaze*. Second edition, Berkley, CA: University of California Press.

—— 2003. *Global Complexity*. Malden, MA: Blackwell.

Van Driel, B. and J. Van Belzen. 1990. The Downfall of Rajneeshpuram in the Print Media: A Cross-National Study. *Journal for the Scientific Study of Religion* 29, 76–90.

Verdoux, H., R. Goumilloux and M. Bourgeois. 1993. Voyages et pathologie psychiatrique: Une Serie de 29 cas. *Annales Medico-Psychologiques* 51, 581–5.

Wallerstein, I. 1989. 1968, Revolution in the World-System: Theses and Queries. *Theory and Society* 18, 431–48.

Watson, S. 1995. *The Birth of the Beat Generation: Visionaries, Rebels and Hipsters, 1944–1960*. New York: Pantheon.

Weber, M. 1913. Religious Groups (The Sociology of Religion). In *Economy and Society* (ed.) G. Roth. Berkeley, CA: University California.

—— 1918. Politics as a Vocation. In *From Max Weber: Essays in Sociology* (ed.) C. Wright Mills. New York: Oxford.

—— 1992 [1905] *The Protestant Ethic and the Spirit of Capitalism*. Introduction by Anthony Giddens. London, New York: Routledge.

Wilson, D. 1997a. Paradoxes of Tourism in Goa. *Annals of Tourism Research* 24, 52–75.

—— 1997b. Strategies for Sustainability: Lessons from Goa and the Seychelles. In *Tourism and Sustainability: Principles to Practice* (ed.) M.J. Stabler. New York,Wallingford: CAB International.

Witte, B. 1991. *Walter Benjamin: an Intellectual Biography*. Detroit, MI: Wayne State University Press.

Wrigley, R. and G. Revill (eds) 2000. *Pathologies of Travel. Clio Medica*. Wellcome Institute Series in the History of Medicine. Amsterdam: Rodopi.

York, M. 1995. *The Emerging Network: A Sociology of the New Age and Neo-Pagan Movements*. Lanham, MD: Rowman and Littlefield.

Zicklin, G. 1983. *Countercultural Communes: a Sociological Perspective*. Westport, CT: Greenwood Press.

Index

subjectivity 25, 32, 34, 77, 133,
165, 167, 173, 190, 207, 208,
209, 229; counterculture 225; crisis
218; globalization 32; *see also*
sexuality
Sufi 21, 142, 152, 231
surveillance 34, 77, 79, 83, 89–90,
178, 209, 215, 223; regulation 63,
79, 128, 223

tai chi 2, 55, 56
Techno 20–1, 39, 41, 176, 188, 209,
213–14, 221; center 170, 177;
counterculture 19, 23, 31, 177;
history 21, 55, 171, 177; political
economies 32; spirituality 178, 205;
studies 22, 176; tribalism 206, 214;
see also clubbers; freak; music;
parties; rave
television 56, 58, 82, 107, 110, 122,
128, 148, 186, 190
terrorism 195
Thailand 53, 118, 191, 192, 220
therapists 26, 29, 36, 50, 52, 55,
58, 62, 67–8, 109, 124, 132,
139, 142–5, 148, 150–3, 160,
161, 164, 165, 169, 170, 173,
192
therapy 38, 52, 68, 119, 133, 136,
142, 160, 173; apartheid 133,
164–5, 169, 172; apprenticeship 55,
57, 67, 142; body 21, 54, 62, 128,
142, 145–6; cathartic 29, 138, 141,
143, 144, 146, 160, 161, 165, 173,
218; certification 229; chromo 52,
70; craniosacral 68; effects 60, 69,
145, 162, 173, 214; massage 67;
screening interviews 143, 147, 165;
sharing 143, 144, 145, 165, 173,
230
tour guides 43, 45, 106, 147, 148
tourism 42, 46, 59, 65, 77, 79, 90,
103–4, 181, 182, 223; anti-
tourism lobby 183; campaign 46,
81, 128; club 46, 106; as context
38, 177; development 90, 223;
gentrification 90, 223; history 83,
109, 116, 215; low-budget 183,
196; mass 42, 59, 78, 82; revenue

45, 95, 104, 182; seasonality 46,
83, 120; spiritual 38, 171, 178;
studies 7, 183, 200
tourists 15, 38, 45, 46, 66, 79, 82, 83,
84, 86, 90, 177, 182, 191, 223;
British 52, 91, 103, 107, 108;
charter 108, 183, 197, 214, 221;
Christian 217; club 89, 105, 108;
German 51; imperialism 194; Indian
196, 220; middle-class 92; typology
51; wealthy 93, 202; working-class
93; young 61, 87, 227
trance music *see* music
trance party *see* party
translator 49, 56, 142, 143, 145, 146,
229
transportation 11, 148, 169, 170, 184,
191, 198; public 57, 65
travel; 4, 6, 9, 15, 33, 49, 54, 57, 60,
118–19, 120, 130, 132, 159, 160,
170, 175–6, 184, 214, 221, 224;
pathogenic 216–17; pathological
216
travelogue 36, 37, 134
tribalism 197, 206, 214
Tribe of Frog 86

UFO 53, 190
underground 39, 75, 99, 115, 185;
see also clubbers
Uruguay 102
US 49, 50, 72, 74, 84, 106, 117, 133,
142, 151, 177, 187, 188
utopia 61, 116, 125–6, 129, 134, 222,
226

Vanuatu 61
village 46, 65, 98, 149, 176, 177,
182, 183, 186, 187, 196, 202, 220,
223; villagers 186, 195, 196, 208,
223
Vilnius 106
violence 8, 29, 109, 140, 144, 212

war 97, 124, 173, 193, 195; Cold 11;
games 232; machine 30–1
We Love Sundays 107, 108, 171
Weber, Max 18, 19, 23, 172, 210,
228

Lightning Source UK Ltd.
Milton Keynes UK
25 November 2009

146625UK00003BA/9/P